praise for *harder to breathe*

"When we first got together and played music, it was one of the best times of my life. In his words, I can practically see and feel those moments again. So, I hope you have fun while reading this—but I also hope you walk away with inspiration from what Ryan has accomplished and achieved."

—Adam Levine

"I didn't know there was so much I didn't know about my friend Ryan. I knew that losing his place in Maroon 5 was a life-changing and extremely difficult experience, but his journey is about so much more than just that. He shares about his pain and discovery with such vulnerability and honesty and wit, and I'm inspired by his transformation. His willingness to invite others towards themselves through his own story, is undoubtedly going to help a lot of people."

—Sara Bareilles

"Ryan captures youth and success in all their contradictions; the delirious joy, the heady sense of discovery, the searing bliss, the heartbreak, the confusion, the pain and disappointment. The real beauty of his story, however, lies in what comes later: finding balance, peace, and meaning as the light and noise of youth and fame dim. His journey to wisdom and grace means a lot to me, having been there for so much of it, but his story resonates with universal truths far deeper than the particulars of his path."

—Mickey Madden

"I'm grateful this document exists to relive these amazing, once in a lifetime events. I often found myself thinking 'how did this actually happen to us??!' But *Harder to Breathe* is not only a detailed chronicle of the early days of the band, but an inspiring story of redemption. Ryan's personal journey is inspiring and will remind those in need of help that change is possible."

—James Valentine

"After everything we had worked for during high school with our first band and all the effort and determination of getting the first Maroon 5 album out into the world, Ryan had to face a devastating loss and step away from the group just as our childhood dreams were coming true. How he navigated his way through such a difficult life experience is admirable and inspiring, and now here is this book for you to read."

—Jesse Carmichael

harder to breathe

harder to breathe

breathe

A Memoir of Making Maroon 5,
Losing It All, and Finding Recovery

ryan dusick

BenBella Books, Inc.
Dallas, TX

BenBella Books, Inc.
10440 N. Central Expressway
Suite 800
Dallas, TX 75231
benbellabooks.com
Send feedback to feedback@benbellabooks.com

BenBella is a federally registered trademark.

Printed in the United States of America
10 9 8 7 6 5 4 3 2 1

Library of Congress Control Number: 2022019358
ISBN 9781637742334 (hardcover)
ISBN 9781637742341 (electronic)

Editing by Stephen S. Power and Scott Calamar
Copyediting by Jennifer Brett Greenstein
Proofreading by Kellie Doherty and Jennifer Canzoneri
Text design and composition by Aaron Edmiston
Cover design by Marc Whitaker, MTWdesign.net
Cover photo by Christopher Wray-McCann, courtesy of Maroon 5
Insert photography by Picture Perfect, Wisconsin Ducks, Inc., and
    ©bobcarmichael.com
Printed by Lake Book Manufacturing

This book is dedicated to the young people (of all ages)
struggling with mental health challenges.

contents

foreword

My friendship with Ryan precedes music.

It was a childhood friendship that started when I was about eleven years old. You'll read about how we met a little later in the book, but here's a teaser because I love telling the story . . .

Essentially, our friendship started when I tried to impress him at the soda dispenser in 7-Eleven. Needless to say, he wasn't impressed!

He was two years my senior, which is an eternity when you're in high school. At the time, I had started what would eventually become Kara's Flowers and later Maroon 5 with Mickey Madden and Jesse Carmichael. To us, Ryan was the unattainable drummer. We were the little freshmen who would've been lucky to have him play with us. We would just watch him beat the shit out of the drums in awe. At the time, we all lived on a steady diet of Pearl Jam, Nirvana, Tool, Alice in Chains, and Ryan's personal favorite, Soundgarden—and he could play all of that. Ryan saw something in me. And it wasn't my charm or good looks, as I was an angsty hormonal teenager with a face full of acne.

Ryan became like a big brother to all of us. His house was sort of our ground zero in those days. School got out at 1:30 PM on Friday. Like clockwork, for three years, we would get in Ryan's Wagoneer and drive east to his garage. We'd play music all day. We did it just for us. Nothing else existed.

All we did was play, laugh, and disappear for those hours. It was the most fun because we had nothing to lose. I was practically failing out of school, yet Ryan was a legitimately good student. I don't know how he found time to do homework, but he was always the adult in the room.

Ryan and I were the most fearless about taking the music in the direction we eventually did. As much as we loved '90s rock 'n' roll, we shared a connection with soul and R&B music too. Ryan helped ignite the flame that became my love affair with Stevie Wonder's music—a love affair that really helped lead us into the sound of what Maroon 5 would become.

Back then, music was much more compartmentalized. Fitting into a scene was part of the way things worked. What we were doing wasn't met with much enthusiasm and often left people confused. We were five white kids in an LA rock band playing soulful R&B pop music. At the time, even some of the other guys in the band thought it was crazy. Once we started writing quality songs, everybody got on board, but it was still super ballsy to make a record like *Songs About Jane*. Nobody knew what the fuck we were. So, we had to believe in each other when nobody else really did. It was a huge risk, but it would pay off.

When we got on the road, Ryan again assumed the role of the adult in the band. He was the parent we needed, in a good way. He made sure we bathed and didn't get in too much trouble.

After Ryan suffered chronic nerve damage, we tried everything we could to make it work. However, and I hate saying it to this day, it wasn't going to—no matter how hard we tried or what we did together. At the time, I had suspected it was something beyond the physical: a mental block of sorts. And I just didn't see a way out that wouldn't potentially derail this momentum that I couldn't let slip away. In this crazy business, you are lucky to get one chance. Telling Ryan he was out of the band is still one of the hardest things I've ever done in my life. We were all kids in our early twenties, and our dreams were coming true. Imagine—he's in the middle of all this success, and he has to get off the train. Everything we had worked for was happening, but he wasn't going to be able to enjoy it. That must've been even more torturous than never making it all. We had spent our whole lives working towards this goal together. Right at the moment it was all happening, he couldn't be a part of it anymore. Even though it was nobody's fault, I can't sympathize enough, because I can't even begin to wrap my head around what he really suffered.

As far as the book goes, there are a lot of great memories I was excited to relive. When we first got together and played music, it was one of the best times of my life. In his words, I can practically see and feel those moments again. So, I hope you have fun while reading this, but I also hope you walk away with inspiration from what Ryan has accomplished and achieved.

What he turned all of this into is nothing short of incredible. When you think about what has gone down in his life, he lost his dream, went through hell, got his life back together, completed school, mastered the things he suffered, and wrote this book you are holding in your hands. That's pretty remarkable. You can't say that for a lot of people in his position. It takes a significant amount of fortitude, a lot of emotional strength, and a ton of courage. I applaud him for it. It's a big deal and something that should be recognized.

I'm completely impressed by it.

Ryan and I may not hang out every day or even see each other for months at a time, but we will be friends forever. We will always be part of each other's lives.

Our friendship will never change. He will always be my brother. Love you, dude. And I'm BEYOND proud.

Adam Levine
June 2022

survivor's note

While my story is unique in some ways, my personal issues with anxiety, depression, perfectionism, obsessive-compulsiveness, and alcoholism are very common. I am one of the very lucky ones, however, because I finally reached out for help, possessed the resources to obtain it, and eventually found the program of recovery I so badly needed. In doing so, I was awakened to a whole new life I could have never imagined possible. Too many others are not so lucky. Whether due to stigma, lack of access to health care, or unawareness of available resources, many of those still struggling with mental health challenges never find the support they need.

When those of us who have overcome obstacles tell our stories of survival, we not only work to reduce the stigma attached to seeking help: we also instill the hope that change is possible, offering solutions that may not have been apparent to those still suffering. The specific realities of how we came to be challenged are often complicated and nuanced, and so can be the recovery process, but by sharing our examples of growth and change, we make recovery that much more viable to those who need it.

So, before I tell my story, let me offer some avenues you can take if you recognize your struggles in mine.

1

The twelve-step community, a tried-and-true form of peer support, is a free asset available to anyone who seeks it. Social programs, free clinics, and nonprofit organizations also offer aid to those who otherwise could not afford it. A few good starting points for finding mental health support are these organizations:

- National Suicide Prevention Lifeline – 1-800-273-TALK— suicidepreventionlifeline.org
- SAMHSA – Substance Abuse and Mental Health Services Administration—samhsa.gov
- NIMH – National Institute of Mental Health—nimh.nih.gov
- NAMI – National Alliance on Mental Illness—nami.org
- AA – Alcoholics Anonymous—aa.org
- NA – Narcotics Anonymous—na.org

prologue

a musician never reveals his secrets

When I arrived at the Houdini Mansion in 2006, to write and record demos for what would be the follow-up to our break-through album *Songs About Jane*, I knew quite well that the moment should have been the culmination of my rock 'n' roll dreams.

Twelve years after Adam, Jesse, Mickey, and I started the band Kara's Flowers in high school, and five years after we added James to become Maroon 5, we had finally climbed to the summit of rock stardom. We had sold over 10 million copies of *Jane*, we had toured the world relentlessly in building an enormous fan base, and the next phase of our skyrocketing career promised a level of success and opportunity far beyond our most grandiose imaginings.

To add to the significance of that moment, we were beginning the next stage at Rick Rubin's legendary residence-style recording studio the Mansion. Previously owned by magician Harry Houdini, the 1918 Laurel Canyon estate had captivated us as teenagers when we first watched the Red Hot

Chili Peppers's film *Funky Monks*, documenting the recording of their classic 1991 album *Blood Sugar Sex Magik*. The funky soulfulness of LA's own band of eclectic misfits, who blended rock, funk, punk, and hip-hop into a timeless recording, all while living in a picturesque, haunted mansion in the Hollywood Hills, seemed to prescribe the perfect formula for all of our musical aspirations.

As I pulled up the long driveway to the glamorous, old-Hollywood manor, I was struck by the grandeur of the sprawling facade of aging stone, the columned stairway leading to the arched entry, and the varied balconies, parapets, and Spanish tiles accenting the sloped roof—together creating the image of a Renaissance chateau. Inside, I was entranced by the foyer's sweeping staircase, which seemed to lead not just to another story of the house but to another place in time. I half expected Gloria Swanson to descend the stairs and greet me with "I'm ready for my close-up, Mr. Dusick."

Then I walked around the place and realized it was a dump.

I had anticipated crystal chandeliers, Persian rugs, fine tapestries, and rare artwork. Instead, I saw worn floorboards, sparse and cheap furniture, and canvas tarps covering the ceilings and walls. The kitchen was long out of date. The supposedly grand hall was scattered with recording equipment and exposed cables running every which way. The entire top floor, including the large master suite and several guest rooms, was carpeted over cheaply and furnished minimally like a fraternity house. Rick Rubin probably figured the place would get trashed by the bands recording there anyway, so investing in a facelift would have been pointless.

In many ways I was similar to that magnificent but decrepit old house. I, too, was a decaying shell of my former self. Despite all the opulence of my extremely successful career and glamorous Hollywood lifestyle, internally I was suffering through overwhelming physical and emotional pain. For two years, I had been barely holding it together as I experienced agonizing joint issues, then confounding discoordination, then a total nervous breakdown. And while I was doing my best to maintain a brave face for my bandmates and the rest of the world, I worried constantly about letting everyone down, embarrassing myself on (literally) the world's biggest stages, and proving myself unworthy of all the adulation. Perhaps it was only my anxiety that kept me going, forcing me to make it through one more song, one more set, one more stand.

Just imagine: You've been working toward something since the age of sixteen, dreaming the biggest dreams you can envision with your high school bandmates, struggling and striving for a decade . . . and you finally reach the mountaintop, where you can see all that work rewarded, but then you teeter on the summit, trying not to fall down the other side of the mountain. I wanted to scream out for help, but I couldn't even verbalize what was wrong with me. It wasn't just the shoulder pain that went back to my pitching days. It wasn't just the fatigue and exhaustion that had built up over a few years of touring. It wasn't just the increasing lack of coordination in my limbs. It wasn't just the overwhelming perfectionism that had led me to hold on too tight, trying to control every outcome. It was something bigger and more to the core of me. I felt that I was defective. That I didn't deserve any of the success. That I was bound to be a failure.

Now I was coming to the moment of truth, preparing to tackle the familiar but daunting set of challenges that would come with another massive album cycle. But I couldn't help but feel that my fate was already sealed. Because I just couldn't figure out how to play the drums anymore. I could barely function as a human being.

As usual, our road crew unloaded our instruments, amps, mics, and other equipment; carried it all into the studio; and set it up immaculately. One of the many perks of success: not having to deal with your own shit. When everything was staged and ready to go in that tarp-covered grand hall—the amps were warmed up, the guitars tuned, and the mics tested—I sat down very hesitantly behind my cherry-stained, custom DW drum kit. I knew full well that the likelihood of my performing to the level that the band hoped and expected of me was very low . . . if not nonexistent. But I wasn't going to give up trying. No matter how pained and discouraged I felt, I would keep playing, perhaps until my arms fell off.

We tried to run through a few of the songs we had begun writing on the road—"Can't Stop," "Makes Me Wonder," and "Won't Go Home Without You"—but the mood in the room was solemn. None of the guys were making eye contact with me; they were looking at the floor or off into the distance, their faces serious. After two years of this kind of disappointment, we were still not talking to one another about the huge elephant in the room. So I just put my head down and struggled to work my way through the songs, losing hope with each passing note.

After only about twenty minutes, we decided to take a "smoke" break (even though most of us didn't smoke). I went outside to pace around the driveway, trying to gather myself, but I was so consumed by my spiraling thoughts that I didn't notice our manager, Jordan Feldstein, approaching.

I had known Jordi since childhood, when we played soccer together in Beverly Hills AYSO (American Youth Soccer Organization). Now he was a robust man of twenty-eight, who was always very direct in his approach to management. He was certainly not one to beat around the bush, so the hesitation in his voice startled me.

"Hey man," he said. "So . . . Adam wants to have a meeting with just the five of you guys right now. Can you go into the dining room with them? It's just the band."

I looked at him for a moment, studying his stoic face. "What is it about?" I asked. "Is it important?" My mind was already spinning, my pulse quickening.

He paused. This was not normal.

"I think you just need to go in there and talk to the guys, okay?" he said.

My heart dropped into my stomach. In that moment, I knew what was coming, even though I had done everything in my power to push it out of my mind. The guys had been walking on eggshells with me for a while, but every time we tried to play together, it became more and more apparent to all of us: this wasn't going to work.

As I walked back into the house, my heart rose up into my throat. Adrenaline pulsed through my body. I watched the guys slowly make their way into the dining room from wherever they had wandered off to around the property. My hands started shaking, as they so often did: my nerve problem still hadn't resolved itself, although the doctors had said it would. Everything felt way too real, yet surreal at the same time, as if I were living in time-lapse and slow-motion sequences simultaneously.

Mickey Madden, the consummate hipster of the band, entered the room first, sporting the unshowered, Keith Richards–circa-1970 style that he and his cool Silver Lake compatriots were wearing at the time. But his demeanor was very different from his usual boisterous attitude. His shoulders were slumped, his face was stern and tight, and he was looking at the floor, as if he were walking into a funeral. James Valentine, on the other hand, showed up like the easygoing, "aw-shucks" jazz geek that he was, with his bright red Nebraska shirt and Levi's. He looked me right in the eye with his wholesome manner and asked, "Hey man, how you doing?" Maybe he was just putting on a cheerful mask as I had been for some time, but his attempt at warmth helped calm me for the moment.

Jesse Carmichael, the searching idealist of the band, who had long since replaced his teenage Malibu surfer vibe with the beard and style of the Band circa *The Last Waltz*, walked in next and looked at me as if I were one of those wounded puppies in an ASPCA commercial. "Aww, there, there, sweetie," his big, green doe eyes seemed to say. "It'll be okay." This didn't calm me. It actually started to make me a little angry.

Adam Levine, who over the course of the previous twelve years had transformed from an insecure, acne-faced, fourteen-year-old with ADD into our cocksure lead singer, front man, and bandleader, strolled into the room last, his face serious but his head held high. A shiny, new, impossibly expensive watch hung casually from his wrist, but the rest of his style was still the vintage-store chic he had been rocking for years. The only difference was that his vintage tees were now collector's items he had purchased at Fred Segal, rather than the bargain-bin fare he had found at a Melrose thrift store. He sat at the head of the table, as he had become accustomed to over the last few years. He seemed to be taking control of the meeting, as a CEO would. But this was a new look for Adam. There was a real confidence in him that I hadn't seen before, as if he had serious business to attend to and he was about to do what needed to be done. I sat down at the opposite end of the table. The others sat awkwardly. They really didn't want to be there, and really didn't want to be doing this but knew they had to.

Adam began slowly but very matter of factly . "Here it is, man. I'm worried . . . I'm really worried. I just don't know what's going on with you and your arm at this point, and I don't think we can wait any longer to see if you can come back from whatever's going on . . . We have an album to make."

Feeling the sting of this first suggestion that they would make an album without me, I initially responded, of course, with defensiveness. "Come on," I fired back at him, "you know how albums are made these days. Everything's looped and pieced together on the grid anyway. We can make it work one way or another."

He replied quickly, a little agitated by my response. "Yeah, but I don't even want to make an album like that at this point. I want to make an album with soul and grit, with real band performances."

I thought that statement seemed a little convenient, given how much he had originally wanted my drums on *Songs About Jane* to be edited and looped in Pro Tools, to achieve the effect of a hip-hop rhythm section. By this point, I knew the standard of perfection to which he held our recordings, so I also knew he was just saying that to shut down any hope of my remaining in the band. My defensiveness turned to desperation.

"You told me in Germany that I would always be a member of this band! That you wouldn't make an album without me—that you couldn't!"

The other guys were getting really uncomfortable. Mickey was fidgeting in his chair, readjusting his position, while looking off into the distance. James was bouncing his knees like he was practicing heavy metal drumming and clearing his throat at regular intervals. And Jesse kept looking at me with what felt like pity. But I couldn't muster much empathy for any of them. I was too busy drowning in my own self-contempt. Deep down, I knew I had done this to myself. But the feeling that came with that thought was just too painful to accept, so I had to keep up my front of anger.

As my voice started to waiver, Adam's own agitation mellowed into calm concern.

"But, Ryan, I'm also worried that, even if you could somehow get through the album, we're gonna have a whole world tour booked after that, and we'll have to cancel it just as it's getting going, when this happens again . . . And by then, Matt will have moved onto another gig, and we won't have him there to replace you."

That one stung even more. It wasn't just that they could no longer place their faith in me and my recovery: they had found a new partner. I had effectively been replaced already.

I pled with him: "Why can't I just transition to a different role but stay a member of the band? I could play pads on a keyboard or strum a rhythm guitar and sing background vocals. I could shake a fucking tambourine for fuck's sake!"

"Yeah! That's a good idea!" Jesse said. God bless his compassion and optimism. "We could probably figure out something like that! You could just move from one thing to another from song to song, like . . ."

"No, no," Adam said. "No, that's ridiculous, come on!" He wanted to shut that idea down very quickly. "What the hell is that? Do you even really want that, Ryan? Come on . . . No . . . No . . . It's time to move on . . . It's over . . . I'm sorry."

I knew the idea was ridiculous. I just couldn't accept the reality of the situation yet. I had failed . . . It was over . . . But that didn't stop me from making one more absurd appeal.

"Then let me produce the album! I can become the producer of the band, and we can work on it together . . . collaboratively . . . the way we always have."

Both Adam and Jesse looked saddened when I said that. Adam hung his head down and put his fingertips together in front of his face. He looked off to the side and just muttered, "No . . . no . . . ," almost smirking in that pained way one does when something feels too tragic to face with seriousness just yet.

Jesse looked up at the ceiling for a moment, and I think that was when he returned from dreamer-Jesse-land to the reality of the situation. "That's a big undertaking, Ryan," he said. "I think we need someone with more experience at producing to be at the helm of this thing. It takes a lot to do that."

Adam just shook his head and grumbled, as if he couldn't believe we were even discussing the idea. He continued to be surprisingly rational about all of it, however, staying relatively levelheaded throughout the conversation. I wouldn't have predicted it a few years before, when he was still an often-distracted and sometimes-irresponsible young man, but in this moment he truly assumed the role of the leader of the band. It was just unfortunate that I was on the receiving end of his managerial decision. He was my brother of more than a decade, my teenage alter ego, my sometime rival, and my musical soul mate, and he was making the critical judgment to end the agony that had been unfolding in our professional relationship for the last two years. Of course, I couldn't understand any of it then, so I held on to my anger toward him and the rest of the band for a while.

I was in a daze as the meeting ended. I felt totally detached from my surroundings. I don't even remember the guys leaving or where they went. I walked sheepishly out of the Mansion's main entry. The shaking in my hands overtook my whole body, and my legs could barely carry me down the grand stairway. I crawled, wobbly, into my brand-new, black Mercedes-Benz (my reward for all our success) and slumped into the driver's seat. My entire body felt weak and frail. My worst nightmare had come to pass. I was a failure.

As I drove slowly back down Laurel Canyon toward Hollywood, the traffic and lights of Sunset Boulevard seemed like chaos to me. The order of the world was lost, and I was grasping for any sense that my life had not just changed forever.

Everything about the future seemed entirely unknowable. And all I could think in that moment was "How has it come to this? How did I go from where I was to where I am now? And where the hell can I possibly go from here?"

My entire identity had been wrapped up in being a member of that band, so I really had no idea who I even was at that point. All I knew was that my physical and psychological issues had finally led to the loss of my performing career, and now my twelve-year partnership with my best friends was over. On top of that, my entire social circle had been wrapped up with the band and its scene, so I now felt entirely alienated and alone. I was crushed. But this was only the beginning of my breakdown.

In the years after I left Maroon 5, the pain of having lost my identity led to a depression unlike anything I had ever felt in my life. The depression led to alcoholism, and the alcoholism led to a pretty severe anxiety disorder. This was not the life that I had thought I would live when we first embarked on our incredible journey as a band. Even worse, I just couldn't imagine how any of this was going to end. I really thought that I had gotten my shot at ultimate happiness, and I had lost it. How the hell could I go on from that?

So, how had it come to this? It took me a very long time to begin to answer that question. When you start recovery, one of the first things some counselors or sponsors will have you do is write an autobiography and then share it with them or the group. So, in the spirit of that process, it's time to go back to the beginning . . .

chapter 1

at the intersection

My brother, Josh, and I grew up at a literal and figurative intersection of Los Angeles in the 1980s. Our humble home was right near Miracle Mile at the corner of Wilshire and San Vicente Boulevards, in a quaint residential area called Carthay Circle. From kindergarten all the way through sixth grade, we walked two blocks down a quiet neighborhood street to our very diverse community school, which stood on the same block that the old Carthay Circle Theatre of golden-era Hollywood once did. The figurative intersection was that of several different worlds overlapping and colliding all around us. Just to our north was West Hollywood: the trendy, up-and-coming area of everything flashy and hip, from Melrose Avenue to the Beverly Center to the "Boystown" of Santa Monica Boulevard. To our west was Beverly Hills: the opulent breeding ground for spoiled rich kids and tacky overindulgence. To our south was the more modest but very warm community of middle-class families that was Carthay Circle. However, to our east were increasingly poor and disenfranchised neighborhoods the farther you went. Hollywood Boulevard in those days had degraded to a state of visible filth, drug addiction, prostitution, and homelessness. The minority communities of South Central and East Los Angeles were suffering through some of the worst epidemics of drugs, poverty, and crime in the country—all while my family was largely insulated in our little cocoon of relative safety and comfort.

I am grateful to have received a balanced perspective on how other families live in Los Angeles, by attending a public school where my circle of friends looked like a United Colors of Benetton ad, representing every ethnic and racial background from Caucasian to African American, Latino to Asian American, and so on. Although some of us were relatively fortunate, living in comfortable, three-bedroom homes and enjoying modest luxuries, my social circle embodied every segment of the city, from inner-city kids who took a bus into our community, to middle-class suburban kids who benefited from greater privilege, to the very wealthy kids I knew from Beverly Hills Little League and AYSO. I like to think that I represent a mix of these varied aspects of the "real" Los Angeles.

I often find it amusing that most of the stereotypical perceptions of LA focus on the Hollywood scene of transplants: people who come from all around the country, clutching desperately to the self-indulgent fantasy of becoming rich and famous. That common tale was not a part of my reality as a born-and-bred Angeleno. I was the child of a Mexican-born mother, whose parents brought her to this country, and a second-generation Jewish American father, whose grandparents came from eastern Europe. To me, nothing could be more LA than that. When I go to Dodger Stadium, I don't know whether to sit in the bleachers or the box seats!

The music that influenced us at an early age was very eclectic as well. Three and a half years older, Josh had very different interests than mine: he was more of a science geek, building rockets and collecting snakes, and I developed passions for writing stories and playing sports. But we always connected about music. Love of music was something that ran through both sides of our family, so I suppose it was in our blood. Although it took some time for us to find our own instruments and styles, we definitely benefited from early exposure to the many musicians and singers in our family.

My mom, Gina (born Maria-Eugena Gonzalez), and her siblings, Gilberto, Beatricia, and Ricardo, had enjoyed hearing their father, Roberto, play the mandolin and the fiddle in their household growing up. Following in his musical footsteps, Gil and Ric picked up the guitar and drums, respectively. And Ric continued to perform around town with his jazz and blues groups throughout our childhood, living the dream in coffee shops and themed restaurants. Josh and I got our first taste of live music watching our uncle Ric and his fellow jazz cats swing.

My dad's father, Jack, had been an amateur songwriter, writing and singing ditties on his upright piano, as my young father, Kenny, and his older sister, Michele, sang harmonies. My aunt Michele grew up to be a Broadway star, and my dad dabbled with a little songwriting himself. Both of their singing voices were very prominent in our young lives. Michele's son, our older cousin David, who had picked up the electric guitar as a teenager, turned us on to rock 'n' roll at a very early age. David was a bit of a rebel at the time, growing up with his two famous actor parents, James Farentino and Michele Lee, and his teenage bedroom was plastered with posters from hard rock bands like AC/DC, Led Zeppelin, and Van Halen. The images of a scowling Angus Young and the occult symbols of Jimmy Page were both scary and intriguing to me as a young boy, but Josh and I became interested in the sounds David was listening to and imitating with his new Fender Stratocaster.

David gifted us with some of our first vinyl LPs, ranging from Pink Floyd to Queen to Van Halen, and by 1984 the sounds of brothers Eddie and Alex's erupting guitar solos and bashing drums were commonly heard echoing through our house. Josh and I used to invite our parents to "concerts" in his bedroom, for which we would draw up little tickets and then take to the theatrical stage of Josh's twin bed, playing air guitars and jumping around like David Lee Roth in the videos for "Jump" and "Panama." I was only about six or seven years old when we were entertaining our audience of two in that way, but I can still remember the thrill of it, feeding off my older brother's burgeoning excitement for the electric guitar and the looks of sheer delight and total joy on our parents' faces.

Adding to our parents' record collection, Josh and I started listening to LPs by artists from the Police to Michael Jackson, Quiet Riot to Run-DMC. We had classic records by the Beatles and Bruce Springsteen and progressive artists like Herbie Hancock and the Art of Noise. In my mom's car, we usually heard either *Rick Dees Weekly Top 40* or the Latin artists representing her roots. And with the advent of MTV, we watched videos by performers from Prince and David Bowie to Ratt and Twisted Sister. Along with every other person in the known world in the 1980s, I became obsessed with Michael Jackson's video for the song "Thriller." We had a VHS tape recording of *The Making of "Thriller,"* which I watched ad infinitum, both terrified of the monsters and in awe of Michael's rhythmic movements and soulful singing.

Without a doubt, the most embarrassing home video from those days is one that my dad took on his brand-new VHS camcorder (think Clark Griswold in *European Vacation*), which featured Josh and me break-dancing to Herbie Hancock's early industrial-techno song "Rocket" in our breakfast room. Having just become obsessed with the movies *Breakin'* and *Breakin' 2: Electric Boogaloo*, Josh had learned a surprising number of the dance moves for a nerdy white kid from the suburbs, but once again, I was just feeding off my older brother's passion, doing my best impression of what I saw. I hadn't learned many of the moves that Josh had, so I just stood in one place and vibrated like a malfunctioning robot. Our parents did their best not to laugh.

Josh and I enjoyed a relatively sheltered existence growing up. Like many who raised the millennial generation after us, our parents were very well-intentioned, extremely loving and supportive, perhaps a bit overprotective, and very focused on boosting our self-esteem. They often told us we were smart, capable, special, kind, and adorable. Following the new trend, we played in soccer and baseball leagues in which all players received a trophy, regardless of how they played or where their teams finished in the standings. And we were insulated by a group of friends mostly put together by parents who were very active in the school community. In general, we enjoyed a sense that the world was made for us and nothing really bad could ever happen to us. This was very comforting to me as a boy, but I sometimes wonder if being coddled to this degree made me ill prepared for hardship, disappointment, and failure.

Our parents might have also been compensating for the sadness and tragedy they had suffered in their own lives. Both of them lost their parents way too young, and both of them have lived with scars as a result. My dad's beloved father, Jack, died from a heart attack when my dad was just twenty-three, and his fragile mother, Sylvia, died of a broken heart just a few years later. As a result, my dad's big heart and fun-loving spirit come along with control issues and a caretaker personality; perhaps he is attempting to make up for the ways he wishes he could have taken care of his parents more. As good intentioned and loving as his impulses always are, they can border on overinvolvement at times.

My mom was forced to move around a lot as a child, due to her father's job as a foreign diplomat. They spent a year living in a war zone in Guatemala when my mom was very young, and she has vivid memories of hiding under the bed when the gunshots and explosions would start. Her mother, Alicia, who was heavily medicated due to the grand mal seizures she suffered, passed away when my mom was just a teenager, and her father, Roberto, died in a car accident a year later. Due to these early traumas, my mom's incredibly sweet and sensitive personality comes along with episodes of anxiety and depression, from which she has suffered greatly at times in her adult life. In a lot of ways, I think my mom's challenges have been the mission for which my dad's caretaking nature was designed. So, as a result, my parents have often played out the roles of dependent and codependent in their relationship.

As a kid, I was more like my mom. I was sensitive and kind, sweet and good-hearted. And my mom and I were very close and affectionate when I was little. I guess you could say I was a bit of a "mama's boy." I wonder now if we acted as each other's security blanket, assuring each other that everything was okay. She had wanted to be a mother all her life, and I was the perfect little angel, in whom she could invest all that maternal love and affection. We were definitely attached to each other, and it was difficult to let go. I was a shy little boy, and I remember clutching her leg when entering an unfamiliar setting or even at family gatherings. I also remember her having a very difficult time letting me go into the classroom on my first day of preschool. It was very emotional for her.

My dad is a much more hyperactive type of person: constantly running around, doing and fixing things. And as a lawyer, he has probably done as much work for his family and friends pro bono as he has for his business. I imagine we would have lived on the other side of that border with Beverly Hills had he not been such a giving person (for which I am grateful). However, my relationship with him growing up was more of a yin-yang type of situation. His energy and charisma were difficult traits with which to compete. His whole side of the family can be a little overwhelming actually. My aunt Michele was a film and TV star by the time I was born, and her personality is even bigger than my dad's. Family events often played out like a big performance, during which it was pretty easy for me to feel invisible.

Most of my dad's best qualities are more aspirational for me than they are things that came naturally to me. I'm much more of an introvert by nature, much more feminine in my sensibilities, and I would get embarrassed when he would invariably strike up conversations with total strangers, trying to make everyone around him happy. Whether it was the corny dad jokes or just his overwhelming sociability, I found myself retreating into an opposite space, more reserved and self-reflective. Imagine a cross between Chevy Chase in the Vacation movies, Steve Martin in *Parenthood*, and just a touch of John Candy in *Planes, Trains, and Automobiles* (engaging you enthusiastically the entire time you sit next to him on a flight), and you've got a pretty good idea of my dad's exuberance—while I was the shy, sensitive boy, observing and internalizing the theatricality of his natural energy.

I have a few distinct memories from my early childhood, and a particular event that stands out in my mind was the one and only time that I got spanked. My parents were certainly not proponents of corporal punishment, but one day as a toddler I ran out into the street in front of our house, and my mom needed to let me know immediately that I absolutely could not do that again. However, what I remember about that incident is not what you might think. Instead of remembering the pain on my backside, the embarrassment for having done something so egregious, or the humiliation of being punished in that way, I distinctly remember being concerned for my mother's emotional well-being. She felt horrible, doing what she was doing. Striking me in any way was the furthest thing from what she would ever want to do, and I could see how upset she was by having to do it. I wonder now if I had become finely tuned to my mother's emotional needs even before I could speak. Perhaps being a perfect little boy was my way of comforting her.

Other than these occasional episodes of emotionality, I didn't think that anything was particularly "wrong" in general. Quite the contrary, to this day I think of my childhood as lovely and perfect. I knew my mom was sensitive, but I actually related to her for that reason. We were a very happy family, blessed with good circumstances in life and an abundance of love and affection. But I've come to understand that even the happiest families, even the people who have everything going for them, still have issues to overcome, and some of those traumas get passed down through the generations.

My dad was an athletic man, always up for any kind of game or sport, and in general, he seemed very self-possessed. He was my coach in soccer and baseball, at night he would play his acoustic guitar and sing songs he had written, and we had frequent wrestling matches in the back hallway of our house on Schumacher Drive. However, it was baseball that became our biggest bond. By the time I was nine years old, it was my greatest passion. My dad had never played it much in his youth, but he was a huge sports fan, so we were able to find mutual inspiration in the Dodgers of the 1980s. I started emulating every batting stance and every pitching mechanic we watched together, and although my dad didn't know the proper mechanics with which to instruct me, our excitement about the sport propelled me to a pretty magical time between ages ten and twelve.

First, we were inspired by the Dodgers' amazing Cinderella season of 1988. Watching a hobbled Kirk Gibson hit that astounding home run to win Game 1 of the World Series, and hearing Vin Scully make his epic pronouncement—"In a year that has been so improbable, the *impossible* has happened!"—really made me feel that anything was possible if I just could dream of it. My personal hero, Orel Hershiser, closed out one of the most remarkable seasons in pitching history in Game 5 to win the championship, and that inspiration projected me forward into a remarkable experience in my last year of Little League.

At age twelve, I was the best pitcher in Beverly Hills Little League. I'm not just saying that—honestly! I threw hard, I had remarkable control for a kid that age, and I had a devastating off-speed pitch that was striking out everybody and winning us complete game shutouts. My team and I only lost one game in which I was on the mound all season, and we went on to win the whole league championship, going on to regional tournaments. Striking out Matt Mesler to win the championship game still stands out as the most epic success of my childhood. We were only up by one run, with two outs and a man on third, in the bottom of the final inning. I had thrown him nothing but fastballs, which he continued to foul off, until we finally reached a full count. I bore down with all my focus and energy, and then I pulled the string. I threw my off-speed pitch perfectly—it sank in just below the strike zone as Matt swung over the top of it, way out in front. All the parents in the stands, the coaches, and my whole team erupted. My catcher ran out and bear-hugged me, and before I knew it, my teammates were carrying me on their shoulders. I can only imagine how proud my doting mom and dad were.

I also have a couple of "only in LA" memories from that time period. The first one involved the famous actor James Caan. His son Scott was on our team when I was eleven, and Jimmy wanted so badly to participate in the practices with us. My dad included as many assistant coaches as he could, but Jimmy was actually in no physical condition to be playing. He'd recently had a spill on his motorcycle, and his shoulder was being held in place by a screw. He would pull up to each practice with his arm in a sling, and then, being the macho, manly guy he was (a real-life Sonny Corleone), he would take the sling off and play catch with the kids, complaining afterward how much it hurt. Caan actually taught me a grip for throwing a curveball unlike anything I was taught before or after, and it was very effective! Maybe it was more of a changeup than a curveball, because it just kind of floated up there and died at the plate, but I always think fondly of Jimmy Caan when I ponder all the success I had with that pitch the following year. At one of the last games of that season, Jimmy rolled up to La Cienega Park (or rather onto La Cienega Park) on his big Harley-Davidson bike, with a beautiful *Playboy* Playmate on the back. They jumped off and joined the rest of the cheering squad of parents, and Jimmy's new girlfriend was sporting a new necklace—the pin from his repaired shoulder hanging from a silver chain. What a baller.

The second "only in LA" story came from another celebrity dad on that same team: superstar Neil Diamond. Neil was very shy most of the two seasons that his son Micah played on the Orioles with us, understandably so. Neil was so famous that he was just trying to avoid getting recognized and cornered by fans. He would sit off to one side of the bleachers at most of the games, with a hat down low and sunglasses covering his face. Usually unshaven and shaggy, he would pop his collar to obscure himself even further. We barely heard a peep out of him for two seasons. Then for some reason, in the last game, when we were playing the Yankees for the league championship, at a very tense moment in the final innings, he jumped up, went right to the front of the bleachers, and started a very enthusiastic chant of "LET'S GO, ORIOLES! LET'S GO, ORIOLES!" Everyone in the area stopped what they were doing and watched Neil Diamond looking about as excited as a teenage cheerleader. It was adorable.

I don't know how or why I was so confident on the pitching mound at that age. I was still a very shy kid, not cocky or overconfident elsewhere in life. I was a good student in school, and I had a close circle of friends, but I was humble and meek in most ways. However, for some reason, on the mound I was a whole other person. I have no memory of having anxiety or self-doubt when I was pitching. I believed that I could do whatever I wanted with a baseball in my hand, and I was going to strike out anyone who faced me. That total lack of self-consciousness or overthinking is baffling to me now. As an adult, I focus very meditatively to try to achieve that kind of commitment to the moment. I have often struggled to keep my mind from interfering in the things that I do. Yet somehow at age twelve, I could just look at the catcher's mitt and perform with total confidence. Maybe I was just emulating my father's self-possession.

So perhaps that was the first time I adopted some of my father's more favorable traits, to go along with the kindness and sensitivity I had gained from my mother's warmth. Sounds like a good combination for a well-adjusted young man, right? Well, adolescence can be rough . . . But by the time I graduated from Carthay at the end of sixth grade, I was a pretty big deal! I was the class president, I had the highest grades, and I was given several honors and awards, so I was actually asked to deliver a speech at our commencement. Talk about an overachiever! However, I had never written or delivered a formal speech, so I had no reference point for what to expect from the experience. As with most things, my dad tried to help me by instructing me on how to do it as well as I possibly could. I don't remember asking him to do that for me, but that's my dad! He's always trying to be helpful (and/or control outcomes). We went over my speech several times, and he gave me notes on how to deliver it with poise and distinction.

"Most importantly, just remember to take your time," said my dad, who has been well known to volunteer to speak at every family occasion you can possibly imagine, from toasts at Thanksgiving, Christmas, Hanukkah, Passover, Yom Kippur, Mother's Day, birthday parties, and so on, to eulogies at the funerals of every family member or family friend who has ever passed away. "Just try to relax and be yourself. You're a smart guy! And everyone likes you. So don't be afraid to just slow down and relax. There's no rush."

When I got up on that stage, however, all of that went out the window. I experienced something for the first time that I think most people go through at some point in their lives, but it was a precursor for some awful things I would experience later in life. As I began my speech, the sheet of paper I held in one hand began to shiver and shake, as my hands succumbed to my nerves. My first thought was "Oh no, I'm not going to be able to read this if my hand keeps shaking!" This one, simple focus on a negative outcome made it much worse. Thinking about how it might go badly for me actually caused it to go badly. My hands started shaking more, and then I really couldn't read the words on the page. I gripped the paper with both hands and somehow got through the speech (probably at lightning speed), so it didn't actually become the disaster that I briefly imagined it would. But I got a serious glimpse into the power of negative thought. This was my first bout with anxiety that manifested itself in physical symptoms, but it wouldn't be my last.

chapter 2

smells like teen spirit

I had been a big fish in a small pond up until middle school, but all of a sudden, I was a guppy in an entirely new pond, populated by a group of bigger fish ... who exhibited a brand of entitlement and cliquishness I had yet to experience. After spending my grade school years in the warm and comfortable community of Carthay, I joined Josh at the very prestigious Brentwood School in the seventh grade, and it was a whole new ball game.

My parents had applied to only the one private prep school for Josh, figuring that if he happened to get admitted, they would just have to figure out how to afford it within their budget. He had been excelling there in math and science by the time I applied, making our family a "legacy," so with my good grades and other achievements, it was a no-brainer that I would go there as well. Neither of us really fit in there socially at all, however.

While being Jewish made me part of the majority of my class, a large portion of my cohort had known each other since preschool, together attending a very exclusive elementary school associated with Stephen Wise Temple, and their social circle was intimidating and alienating to me. They obviously all knew each other very well already, and their ways of talking and interacting were very foreign to a kid from the other side of the tracks. "Valley girls" and "rich snobs" are the best common tropes I can use to describe them. They quite literally would stand in a circle, excluding other kids who were not a part of their clique, and they would gossip about god knows what. I don't know, because I wasn't included! It was also very clear to me that money and status were very important commodities in this scene, and I had neither; at least not at the levels that the "popular" kids did.

Being Mexican made me part of a very small minority as well. Our class had only one other Latino kid, who was often the butt of classist jokes because he dressed in hand-me-down clothes and old shoes and he spoke with a Hispanic accent. Here was a boy who had excelled so much in his own community that Brentwood had given him a full scholarship to attend, and he would travel across the city just for a chance to participate in this opportunity, but that meant nothing to the social scene. He was just another immigrant son to the crowd. For some reason, I was able to "pass" in some ways that seemed more acceptable to this highly insulated community of wealthy kids, however. I remember telling other students that I was Mexican, and the reaction was usually something like "Wait, what? But . . . you're not *that* kind of Mexican." I didn't have to wonder what "that" kind of Mexican was to these children of Brentwood, Santa Monica, the Pacific Palisades, Encino, and Malibu. They were referring to the dark-skinned migrant workers who were familiar to them only as their housekeepers and gardeners. Somehow, because my skin was relatively fair and I didn't speak with an accent, I was different and, dare I say, "better" to them than their usual image of a Mexican American. I don't mean to imply that all these kids were outright racist. It was a distinction probably based on a general lack of experience with minorities, but it was obvious to me, and it didn't help me feel welcome.

Being a shy kid, I found it difficult to acclimate to this new environment. I still did well in school academically, making the dean's list all four semesters of middle school, but I only had a very small circle of friends, mostly centered around baseball. The pitching mound was still the one place where I felt most confident, but that would change in the years to come.

At the age of fourteen, Josh decided to teach himself to play the electric guitar. He had taken some piano lessons at an earlier age, and I had followed suit, but neither of us really took to that instrument. But now, as he was entering high school, Josh found himself being implored by his two childhood best friends, Joel Freidman (who played keyboards and rhythm guitar) and Adam Leibovitz (who played the bass and drums), to learn to play so that they could start a band together. Being the obsessively hardworking overachiever that he was, Josh stayed up all night teaching himself to play Slash's lead part on Guns N' Roses's "Sweet Child O' Mine," simply by looking at guitar magazine tablatures and listening to the album. After one long night and several blisters on his fingers, Josh was off and running with his new passion. Within six weeks, he was the lead guitarist in their band Free Reign, and they began playing gigs around town, covering classic rock songs from the Kinks's "All Day and All of the Night" to Cream's "Sunshine of Your Love." Pretty soon they started composing original songs that featured soaring guitar solos by an increasingly confident shredder of a lead guitarist. Josh took inspiration from the great guitar gods of blues-rock legend—Jimi Hendrix, Eric Clapton, Jeff Beck, and Stevie Ray Vaughan—and by the time the band members were all sixteen, they were booking gigs at famous Sunset Strip nightclubs like the Whisky a Go Go, the Roxy Theatre, and Doug Weston's Troubadour. I had always looked up to my brother growing up, but now I thought he was *cool*.

In the early stages of their band, I watched them perform with awe and longed to be a part of it. No knock on the original drummer, but I remember watching their first show and thinking, "I could do that." He was not the most accomplished musician, and his playing seemed like something I could feasibly learn to do rather easily. I was a pretty coordinated athlete, so I felt confident that I could teach myself to play those basic beats by simply emulating the rock drummers I watched on MTV's *Headbangers Ball*. Around the same time, I began tinkering with the drum set in the middle school music room, first teaching myself to play the beat to Tone Loc's ubiquitous rap song, "Wild Thing." It was a very simple pattern, and I wasn't even playing it right, but it gave me my first taste of creating a rhythm, and I was hooked on it. I begged my parents to buy me a drum kit, and of course they were very hesitant, knowing what a racket the drums can create. My dad tells a story of my begging and pleading with him, "Dad, the drums are inside of me, I can feel it . . . The same way that the guitar was inside of Josh, the drums are inside of me, just waiting to get out." After being told over and over that my parents would not buy me a drum set, I woke up on Christmas morning in 1989 to find a kit set up in our living room. I was more than excited. This was the greatest gift I had ever received in my twelve years, and it took all my energy, focus, and restraint not to start banging on those ratty drums and cymbals before everyone else woke up that morning.

The set was not exactly what I had imagined. It was a rickety, old 1960s jazz kit, with trashy cymbals and rusty hardware, more reminiscent of the kind of drums my uncle Ric played at his jazz and blues gigs. Because I had been watching *Headbangers Ball* every night on MTV, seeing the likes of Guns N' Roses's drummer Steven Adler and Mötley Crüe's Tommy Lee, I had imagined a much more imposing rock drum kit, capable of thumping out hard and heavy beats. These drums looked more like something you would see at a cocktail party or a piano lounge, modestly accenting a quiet background trio of aging jazzers. But it was a start, and I was grateful for it. I began pounding on those little drums every day after school for hours, at first making very little headway in creating a discernible rhythm, but eventually getting down some simple patterns in 4/4 time. Watching those flashy glam rockers of the late 1980s, I think I got my stick twirl down before I got the actual playing part down!

By the eighth grade, I had become a drummer in the same way that Josh had become a guitarist. I taught myself to play simply by emulating my glam-rock heroes. However, my favorite drummer of all time was the Police's Stewart Copeland. He had a very expressive flair behind his drums and cymbals, incorporating influences that were exotic but extremely intriguing to me. Rather than just laying down the typical four-on-the-floor rock beat in every song, he turned the rhythms upside down with accents on the upstrokes, unique cymbal flourishes, and innovative percussion choices. His blend of styles had as much in common with reggae, Latin, and world beat as it did standard rock 'n' roll. Having never been taught the "correct way" to play the drums, I was more inspired by his incredible level of creativity on the instrument than by the standard fare.

The drums represented freedom to me. I saw playing them as an opportunity to express myself, rather than just a way to groove along with the radio. So, very early on, I decided to just do my own thing, without taking lessons or learning the traditional rudiments one usually learns first. My uncle Ric tried to show me a few things, but I was hell-bent on doing it *my way*. I never even learned the proper way to hold and manipulate a drumstick. I just did it by feel, relying on my natural rhythm and athleticism to move my arms and legs around the kit in a coordinated way.

So now I had two distinct passions: baseball and the drums, both of which were providing me a lot of inspiration for the future. Aside from Free Reign, Josh had also started playing with the school pep band, and he eventually invited me to join. I have to say, having heard some horror stories about mean older siblings, I was very blessed to have an older brother who was so encouraging and supportive of me. We had a few little tiffs as young boys, as brothers do, but for the most part we were very close friends who got along very well, especially when we both got into music as teenagers. He told me I was a great drummer even then, as I was first beginning, and he wanted me to be included in the things he was doing as a musician. I love him for that.

The school band wasn't exactly what you would expect from a "pep" band that might normally play cheerleading songs at sporting events. It was more of an opportunity to learn and perform rock songs in front of our peers, thanks to the guidance of our mentor Mr. Castanares. Mr. C., as we called him, was a bit of a hippie musician (as well as an awesome middle school history teacher), and his passion for music, in particular the classic rock of the 1960s to '70s, was infectious to his students. But he also allowed us to explore and experiment with the music of our generation, fostering our development by encouraging us to perform and create like artists. His pep band activity was one of the very few creative outlets available within the very focused, college-prep atmosphere of Brentwood School, and I greatly appreciate him for providing that. I first got to perform with the pep band at the end of the eighth grade, playing the Black Crowes's version of Otis Redding's "Hard to Handle," Cream's "Politician," and AC/DC's "Back in Black" on the field in front of a small crowd of enthusiastic students, faculty, and family. I was now a performing musician, feeling the power of expression that came with being a hard rock drummer, and I wanted to feel that freedom and power as often as possible from that day forward.

High school was the first time that I experienced any real disappointment or failure, and I really wasn't prepared for it. Having been an overachiever who excelled at most things up until that point, I never really had to face any major obstacles in a way that built personal resilience. I had yet to get knocked on my ass and have to get back up. So, when it finally happened, I was stunned, and I couldn't figure out how to move forward with confidence again. The first time was in the ninth grade. Because I had been on the dean's list throughout middle school, at the start of high school I was placed in a bunch of honors classes, one of which was an English class for which I was ill prepared. First off, the teacher gave a summer reading list, and being new to prep school, I took it as a suggestion rather than an assignment, and I did what I had always done: focused on baseball during the summer. When I showed up on the first day of class, the teacher gave us a test on the novel *Cry, the Beloved Country*, and then followed it the next day with another test on the *MLA Handbook* for writing essays. This teacher had no compassion for my misunderstanding whatsoever, and she gave me two failing grades to start off the school year. I would have to work my way back from that all year, just to get a C. It was demoralizing. On top of that, this teacher treated me like I was the class dunce from that day forward. Rather than take me under her wing and help me ascend to the level of study that was required, she took every opportunity to put me down and make me feel like a failure.

It's actually funny looking back now, knowing that I ended up with a degree in English from UCLA years later, because at the time my response was to retreat from that field of study completely. I had enjoyed writing creatively as a kid, but I hadn't yet received any training in formal writing, and this failure was a huge blow to my self-esteem. Rather than bounce back and try harder, I took the defensive stance of "I didn't care about English anyway." But I did care, and it hurt. It would take me an entire year to recover from the disappointment of no longer being academically "perfect," I'm not proud to say. Thankfully, I had another English teacher who helped me get back on the horse the following school year, and by the end of it I had regained some academic confidence, but that freshman experience definitely knocked me on my ass. That youthful feeling that the world was made for me, and that everything would come easily to me, was gone, and I was left with self-doubt and insecurity.

I started having my first difficulties in baseball at Brentwood as well. They began after I broke my hand playing water polo in eighth grade PE class (yep, that's the kind of rich, preppy school Brentwood was: we played water polo in PE). With my excellent throwing arm, I decided it was easier to just hang out around mid-pool and throw long shots at the goal, rather than swim back and forth across the length of the pool for the entire game. This strategy worked for the first half, allowing me to score several goals for our team, but at a certain point a volleyball player with long arms figured out my method and started defending me at mid-pool. As I rose up to throw another long shot across the pool, he rose up as well, swatting at me with his powerful volleyball spike. The palm of his hand hit the top of my fingers as I let go of the ball, compressing my finger into my hand and cracking it at the knuckle. I tried to get through baseball practice after school, but the pain was horrendous, and my hand was blowing up and turning black-and-blue.

I was scheduled to be the starting pitcher for the Brentwood middle school team in the upcoming playoffs, so going down with an injury was devastating. I had to wear a cast for about six weeks, and that was the end of my baseball season. Despite my legitimate injury and inability to throw, one of the "tough guys" on the team bullied me relentlessly, as if I had somehow chosen to break my hand because I was a wimp or a weakling. The asshole varsity coach (who just happened to be my PE coach as well) called me a "pussy" because I didn't demand a soft cast to continue to play first base. Nice guy.

Anxious to get back on the mound, I started throwing at full velocity a little too quickly after getting my cast off that summer. Within a couple of weeks, I was pitching in the Beverly Hills Senior League. At age thirteen, I was playing on a full-size diamond with a sixty-foot pitching mound for the first time, yet somehow I again made the all-star team as the starting pitcher. The first time I felt pain, it was in my elbow, toward the end of one very long game in a second-round tournament. They weren't counting pitches in those days, and I must've thrown like 160 in that one. I remember my dad was furious at the coach, especially because we were winning 13–1, and he still had me in for the last inning. This was also the first time I remember praying to God. Despite having had the obligatory West LA bar mitzvah around that time, I was not a particularly religious person, and I had already decided that I did not believe in God. However, rather than disappoint all my teammates by telling them I was in pain, I just closed my eyes and said to myself, "Please, God, if you help me get through this game, I'll never ask you for anything again."

I did get through the game, but not without the damage having been done. The pain in my elbow lingered, and it eventually made its way into my shoulder the next season, as I tried to pitch through the discomfort on the Brentwood high school team. As a result, I just didn't have the kind of command over a baseball that I once had. All that confidence I used to feel on the mound melted away pretty quickly every time I tried to recover from what turned out to be chronic tendinitis in my rotator cuff. Even though I wasn't always feeling intense pain, having played through it for a while caused me to develop some really bad mechanical habits that I couldn't seem to unlearn, and the ball just didn't come out of my hand right anymore. It was a miserable feeling. Baseball had been my greatest joy and passion up until that point, and it just felt like it was slipping away from me.

This was also the first time I experienced what athletes refer to as "the yips." This unfortunate phenomenon is a form of mental block that happens when trying to execute a relatively simple thing you've done a million times. Whether it was due to the physical issues or the psychological stress of such diminished self-esteem, there were times when I botched very simple things that I had done properly many times in the past, such as throwing a fielded ball to first base, simply because I overthought it. Dodgers second baseman Steve Sax had the same problem in the 1980s when he made thirty throwing errors in one season, because he had become obsessed about not making a throwing error.

I remember the moment that it started for me. The varsity coach decided to put me at third base for some reason, even though I had never played that position before. And sure enough, the first batter hit a hard ground ball right at me. I fielded it with plenty of time to throw him out, but seeing him running toward the bag, I felt a sudden rush of panic come over me, and I felt like I needed to hurry and throw the ball very hard and very accurately to first base. Instead, it went sailing over his head and down the first base line, resulting in a two-base throwing error. I smiled and chuckled a little bit, trying to play it off like it wasn't that big a deal, but the coach yelled loudly at me for everyone on the field to hear, "DO YOU FIND SOMETHING FUNNY ABOUT THAT, DUSICK?" The smile on my face (and my ability to shake off the humiliation) disappeared immediately, and I instantly gained a complex about throwing to first.

It seemed that the harder I would try to do something well, the worse I would do it. There was an inverse relationship between effort and outcome. As most people who suffer from anxiety can attest, we often believe that if we worry about something hard enough, somehow that mental energy will prevent it from happening. But the reality is that the worrying actually makes the negative outcome more likely to manifest. In the same way that positive visualization can help you execute something well, ruminating on the bad result can actually cause you to execute something poorly. This was not a concept I had any great understanding of at the time, but having lived that pattern to its disappointing end several times in my life, I can see it now for what it was—performance anxiety. I guess you could also just call it "psyching myself out."

To make matters worse, I didn't feel at home on the varsity baseball team at all. After being brought up from JV at the end of my freshman year, I was introduced to a much more hard-nosed and unfriendly version of competitive sports, which didn't suit my personality well. The coach was this old-school tough guy, who got the impression that I was soft, so he needed to harden me up by being relentlessly aggressive toward me. And a lot of the older players on the team were these toxically masculine types who bullied me for having long hair and looking like an artist/musician type. When I would take my hat or helmet off, I would receive taunts from my own teammates like "Where's your violin?" and "Put a tent over that circus!" My own catcher would call time-out and come to the mound just to give me shit in the middle of a game. I'm sure these preppie schmucks probably went on to become very successful hedge-fund managers and insider traders, but I recognized pretty quickly that these were not my people. So, as a result, there really was nothing enjoyable about playing baseball for me anymore.

As my adolescence reached full swing, and these few failures and disappointments along with alienation from my peers worked their way into my psyche, my youthful optimism and general good cheer gave way to a much moodier and darker outlook. I suppose the "brooding teenage boy" is not an uncommon trope, but I started to feel that I was different from everyone around me in a way that felt very lonely. My fellow students, the faculty of the school, and even the people I saw on television at night began to seem completely phony to me. I couldn't relate to them, and I felt that they couldn't possibly relate to me. And the things that once had great meaning to me no longer held any meaning at all, which made me start to question the meaning of life in a way I never had in my younger years. I was slipping into a very uncomfortable state of being, which I later came to understand as teenage angst.

Just as I was undergoing this transition in myself and in my view of the world, a major shift in popular music was occurring. The overnight success of Nirvana's 1991 album *Nevermind*, which broke through to the mainstream with its infectious expression of teen confusion in the single "Smells Like Teen Spirit," was followed shortly thereafter by the success of the self-reflective Pearl Jam album *Ten* and the heavy and conflicted blues metal of Soundgarden's *Badmotorfinger*, marking a whole new dimension in my appreciation of music. As the shallow, indulgent era of rock in the late 1980s had transitioned to the more introspective, darker era of alternative rock in the early '90s, the music scene had become a place I felt understood and accepted, at least in my mind. The consciously unselfconscious aesthetic of these dressed-down bands represented to me an uncompromising freedom from societal expectations. Hearing the common theme of alienation from singers like Kurt Cobain, Eddie Vedder, and Chris Cornell was very empowering to my sense of self, and they inspired both a healthy intent to go deeper into my own feelings and a somewhat unhealthy level of self-obsession.

Soundgarden was my favorite of them all: extremely heavy drums and guitars, sludgy musical arrangements and weird time signatures, an overwhelming soundscape of distorted feedback and crashing cymbals—all fronted by an impossibly good-looking, vocally soaring, long-haired god/man . . . obsessed with dogs, snakes, and Jesus. I saw myself in Chris Cornell (or at least what I imagined myself as). He seemed so desperately depressed, judging from the darkness of the songs he wrote, yet he sang with so much power and force that he represented a perfect paradox to me: powerful and fragile at the same time.

Listening to and playing this kind of music started to become a place of refuge for me. But being a grunge kid was not cool at Brentwood. Being in a rock band might make you popular at a lot of high schools, but at Brentwood it was just a sideshow. Most of the preppie kids were more concerned with what kind of car you drove, who your parents were, and how much money you were going to make, so being an artist of any kind made me a bit of an outcast or a loser, especially because I was wearing faded and torn jeans, thrift-store flannel shirts, and well-worn Converse shoes, rather than expensive brands and fashions. But I embraced this new identity as an act of rebellion, and I wore it like a badge of honor. My heroes of defiant individualism were Soundgarden, Pearl Jam, Nirvana, Alice in Chains, Tool, Rage Against the Machine, the Smashing Pumpkins, and the Red Hot Chili Peppers (and on down the list of early '90s alternative rock bands). Their grungy iconoclasm became my aesthetic, and their tormented existential reflection became my ethos. It was an escape for me, and pounding on the drums was as much an act of violent aggression against a world that didn't understand me as it was a musical statement intended to move an audience that did. As I dealt with my growing angst, the drums and heavy music became my mechanisms for coping.

chapter 3

fuck you, i won't do what you tell me

Adam tells a funny story about the time we started our first "band" together, when we were just twelve and thirteen years old. Can you imagine that? We were just babies. I don't remember this particular story happening the way he describes it, but I believe it to be true, because Adam was an impressionable kid a couple of grades younger than me, and it clearly left a dent in his ego. He had just started playing the guitar, and I had been playing the drums for only a year or so, but we had a mutual friend named Adam Salzman who wanted to put together a group. (I know, West LA produced a lot of Jewish kids named Adam, right?) Salzman was a precocious boy of twelve, who had gotten pretty skilled on the guitar by that point, and although Levine and I were less advanced, Salzman recruited us for his band along with a kid named Jesse Nicita, who was to play the bass. I think we had a total of about three or four rehearsals in my parents' garage, which mostly consisted of Levine and Nicita taking turns playing Tommy Lee's drum parts on "Wild Side" on my new drum kit. It was the very early

'90s, but it was still the era of *Headbangers Ball*, and we were a bunch of middle school dorks.

We got as far as naming the band Crush (Salzman's idea, but I couldn't tell you the exact inspiration), but we never booked a show, and I don't think we even finished writing a song. But I do remember taking lots of trips to the corner 7-Eleven for Slurpees, Big Gulps, and nachos. The story Adam remembers is from the first time we walked over to that 7-Eleven, to fill up on tasty crap and waste a bunch of quarters on a video game titled *Bad Dudes*. The barely twelve-year-old Levine, whom I thought of mostly as an annoying little brother at the time, was standing next to the thirteen-year-old me in front of the soda machine with our huge thirty-two-ounce cups in our hands, when he started doing that thing that young boys often do: combining every flavor of soda into one Big Gulp.

"My friend showed me this. It's so much better this way," Adam said proudly, clearly thinking that he was introducing me to something new and wonderful.

I just stood there glaring at him as he added one soda after another, first the Pepsi, then the Dr. Pepper, then the Sprite, and so on down the line, until he finally finished. Then I replied, "I used to do that . . . when I was young and immature."

Adam's face immediately sank. He thought for a second, then he meekly poured his Big Gulp down the drain in shame.

I was actually still a rather innocent and sensitive kid at that age, so that story sounds out of character to me now, but I don't doubt that I wanted to establish myself as dominant in that group of boys. After all, I was the oldest of all of them by a year or two, and as we were entering that very awkward phase of early adolescence, I'm sure that I liked the idea of being the older kid whom they looked up to in some way. Crush was short-lived, because we couldn't get Nicita to show up after the first few rehearsals, so we went our separate ways amicably after a month, and I finished middle school.

Later that year, my family and I attended a family friend's bat mitzvah party on the famous Santa Monica Pier, and I was hanging with Adam

Salzman most of the night, discussing the latest and greatest hard rock bands on *Headbangers Ball*. Toward the end of the night, the DJ organized a lip-sync/air-guitar competition for the kids in attendance. Salzman signed us up, and before I knew it, I was up onstage with him with a plastic balloon shaped like an electric guitar, lip-syncing and rocking out to Metallica's "Enter Sandman." For whatever reason, my adolescent shyness melted away immediately, and I slipped right back into the feeling of being up on my brother's bed, jumping around to Van Halen at age seven. However, this time I was surrounded by a crowd of thirteen-year-old girls, and I was striking a more grown-up and confident rock star pose as I mouthed, "We're off to Never-Neverland!!!!!!"

The feeling was electric. I looked over at Salzman a few times and he seemed to be soaking it up as much as I was, but for the most part I was wholly fixated on just two things: the feeling of rocking out to heavy drums and guitars, and the exhilaration of looking down at a bunch of cute girls screaming for us with their hands in the air, reaching up to touch my leg in adoration. I had never been a real ham before that, never attempted to entertain a real audience as a performer looking for that kind of adulation, but I was reaching an age when female attention was extremely important to me, so I milked that moment for all it was worth. I was terrified of even talking to girls in most settings, but in that fleeting five minutes of headbanging glory, I was a rock god, and nothing else mattered. The rush of it was intoxicating.

After that exhilarating experience, I continued to perform and develop as a drummer, playing with my brother through my freshman year of high school in the Brentwood pep band, where we covered songs across the rock spectrum from Aerosmith's "Walk This Way" to Primus's "Jerry Was a Race Car Driver" (and yes, to Metallica's "Enter Sandman," this time doing my best Lars Ulrich impression). But once that year of exciting rock performances ended, I watched Josh graduate and go off to Cal Berkeley, leaving me and the other musicians we had been playing with behind for the moment. However, after his freshman year, he and his buddies in Free Reign came home for the summer and restarted their band one more time, and that's when I finally got my first opportunity to join a "real" gigging band. I was more than excited. Joel booked us three gigs at the Troubadour, the Whisky, and the Roxy, and at the ripe old age of fifteen I began rehearsing with them for what would be my first performances in Hollywood nightclubs.

Free Reign's revamped lineup excluded their lead singer, so the new sound was not exactly accessible—by that, I mean it featured three guys (plus two of their girlfriends) singing mostly off-key for the entire set list. But it was still a hell of a lot of fun. This was my first real experience in the songwriting process, working on our parts and arrangements from scratch, and it inspired me beyond anything I could have imagined. I was still extremely green, but I had a lot of enthusiasm, and I tried to contribute in any way that I could. My intense drumming style brought a decidedly heavier feel to the songs, and the new material the band was writing was more consistent with the grunge and alternative rock by which we were all being influenced.

The glamour of the Sunset Strip lost some of its luster when I got my first peak behind the curtain that summer, however. Long gone was the heyday of these storied rock venues; instead, it was the era of "pay-to-play," which meant they booked as many as eight bands every night, simply by giving spots to anyone willing to take responsibility for their own ticket sales. There was literally no quality control anymore, nor was there any consistency between the acts and their genre or style. The venues were mostly empty, because these artists had a harder time selling their own tickets than they had imagined. It was a far cry from the Doors, Cream, and the Jimi Hendrix Experience playing these clubs in the 1960s. The dressing rooms were just big, empty spaces, with walls covered in adolescent graffiti and chewing gum. The band members often outnumbered the audience, who must have been wondering what happened to these once-glorious theaters. None of that stopped us from enjoying the experience, however. It was all too exciting to be onstage in these historic rock clubs, playing our songs as loud as our arena-rock heroes.

Grunge and alternative rock were the scene on MTV and radio by that point, but the glam-rock era of the late '80s was still emitting its death rattle on the Sunset Strip. Many of the "adult" bands with which we played still had the big hair and the spandex, but we, the youth of LA, had moved on and fully embraced the flannel, corduroys, Doc Martens, and uncoiffed hair of the early '90s. We rocked all three of those big Hollywood clubs in the summer of 1993, and I knew it was something I definitely wanted to continue doing. Hearing my drums miked up for maximum volume and feeling my kick drum push the subwoofers below the stage made me feel as if I were wielding some serious power with my drum kit. Although I had been shy for the most part up until that age, sitting behind an instrument that could create sonic thunder made me feel strong and confident in a way I hadn't elsewhere in life (except for maybe on the pitching mound at age twelve). It didn't hurt that the clubs were mostly empty, save for our families and close friends, because that comfortable environment helped me avoid any real performance anxiety.

When Josh and his friends went back to college in the fall, I was left with very few desirable options for musicians with whom to continue playing or form a new band. Josh had been the focal point of both Free Reign and the school band, and his guitar was the musical lead that I followed as a learning musician. So, when he and several other mainstays of the pep band left for college, I felt pretty alone at first. Adam Salzman was at Brentwood at that point, and a few other novice musicians remained with whom to jam, but it was becoming time to discover my own place as a performer and to reestablish the school band with some younger blood. I was about to start the eleventh grade, about to turn sixteen years old, when Salzman invited me to come see his new band play at the Troubadour one night . . . and everything changed.

While I had been off playing with Free Reign, Salzman had started his own group with the only other drummer at Brentwood, Richie Rivera. Richie was a good, technical drummer, but he was still stuck in the '80s with his deep affection for bands like Poison and Warrant, embracing all of their glam ridiculousness. Salzman was also still mostly inspired by the extravagant showmen of the guitar shredder era, so he had found in Richie a good match for making some over-the-top cock rock. Being the grunge kid that I was, I scoffed at the stick twirls, brightly colored bandanas, and Ibanez guitars onstage at their performance that night. The band actually sounded pretty tight, but I was looking for any reason to dismiss this rival group. Salzman had turned into quite a ham by then, attempting to channel the flamboyant stage presence of David Lee Roth and coupling it with the indulgent soloing of every Eddie clone to ever plug into a Marshall stack. However . . . standing rather inconspicuously at stage left, dressed in flannel, corduroys, and a backwards baseball cap and meekly strumming his rhythm guitar . . . was Adam Levine, who seemed like a total afterthought in that band.

For the closer, Salzman invited the young Levine to center stage to sing the lead vocal on a cover of Bobby Day's 1950s pop song "Rockin' Robin." It only took a line or two of that song for my entire perspective on the future to change. This was Adam's first-ever performance singing in front of a concert crowd, and although he was unpolished and his manner was timid, his voice was pure and clear. To me, this was a voice that could sing hits someday—and he was only about fourteen years old.

Salzman transferred to another high school that fall (I guess his experience in the prep school environment had been even worse than mine), and apparently he fired Levine from his band when he left. Can you imagine that? His loss was my gain, however, as Adam would start high school at Brentwood that year, providing me with the opportunity to play with him in the pep band and recruit him to form my own group. I was in the eleventh grade by that point, imagining myself as the elder statesman, so I began inviting him over to my house to listen to music and talk about musical inspirations. I had no idea what to do with a "pretty" voice like his, because most of my musical ambitions centered around bands like Soundgarden, Tool, and Rage Against the Machine, but I had been around the music scene just long enough to know that finding a good singer would be the hardest part of starting any band. So I was sure that I had found the centerpiece of whatever was to come.

By the time the school year was in full swing, however, Adam had already started another band with his middle school buddies Mickey Madden and Jesse Carmichael. Mickey had been Adam's first friend in the seventh grade at Brentwood, and after a brief stint playing the drums, he began transitioning to the bass guitar. Mickey grew up in a household with two big music lovers for parents, and his taste in most things artistic was very eclectic and eccentric even then. While most of us were wearing concert tees signifying our love for the well-known rock bands of the time, he mostly wore shirts from obscure indie bands like Tilt, Jawbox, and Superchunk. From the time he was just thirteen years old, he embraced an even more anti-mainstream attitude than the rest of us did.

By the time Adam, Mickey, and Jesse started high school, however, it was Jesse who had become Adam's very best friend; they both stayed up at night dreaming of rock stardom, as they stared at the many magazine photos of Pearl Jam plastered across their teenage bedrooms. And Adam was teaching Jesse to play the guitar, just as Salzman had instructed Adam in the years before. Jesse was another very precocious kid, with a wild-eyed enthusiasm that could be a little overwhelming and even off-putting to me at first. He had an extremely idealistic outlook that was hard to ignore but almost a little too much to deal with. But he was the ambitious one in the trio, taking the initiative to ask me if I would consider playing with the three of them on a cover of Alice in Chains's song "Them Bones" at a pep band show early in the year. I appreciated his gumption, as I was the sought-after, accomplished rock drummer in the school, but I didn't see anything in their playing that inspired me to consider including him and Mickey in my plans for a band. They had barely been playing the guitar and bass for a year, so it was hard to discern if they had any real talent.

After I performed with them for that one Alice in Chains song, Jesse started hounding me daily in PE class, asking if I would consider joining their new group. As much as I admired his tenacity, as he followed me around like a little puppy dog with his tail all aflutter, he struck me as a strange kid. His overt eagerness seemed out of step with the dark, brooding vibe I had adopted, and his manic grandiosity was a little too much for my taste. He also just seemed particularly young to me, despite being precociously smart. As we jogged around the basketball court in our smelly gym clothes one day, he made his full pitch for me to reconsider playing in their new band.

"Our band is awesome. You need to check us out! Adam's almost as good as Salzman on the guitar now, and I'm almost as good as he is already." Jesse's bright eyes were wide with excitement. He smiled broadly. "We're like Stone and Mike," he added, referring to their guitar heroes in Pearl Jam.

"That's cool, man, I don't know . . ." I was playing aloof. "I'm used to playing with more experienced musicians like my brother, so . . . I don't know."

"I know, that's why we want you to play with us! We need your power and speed to be like Pearl Jam. I know you're into Soundgarden and Tool and can play that stuff too. That's what we need!" His already palpable zeal was ramping up to a fever pitch.

I was flattered by his insistence that I was the big missing piece in their extremely inexperienced group, but I just couldn't imagine how guys who had barely learned to play were going to match up to my previous experience.

"We can play together in the pep band some more, and I guess we'll see," I suggested, half humoring him. He just continued on with his sales pitch anyway.

"Oh my god, we learned to play 'Suck My Kiss' recently, and we played it at the homecoming dance, and it sounded almost as good as when you guys did it at that pep rally." He was referring to a time when the previous members of the pep band and I had played the wildly inappropriate Chili Peppers song at a school assembly, for which we later had to apologize to the entire student body and faculty. I guess my rebellious streak was also something these younger kids admired.

"All right, man, we'll see . . ." I tried to close this somewhat overwhelming conversation. "We'll see what happens, bro. Keep practicing, I guess." I can't say he hadn't persuaded me to some degree, but I was still not convinced.

I later had a conversation with Adam in the lobby of the school theater, in which he tried to convert me as well, as I was trying to sway him back to my idea of starting a band separately from these guys.

"I just think it would be awesome if we got a really heavy power trio together, and you could be like Maynard from Tool singing high and melodic on top of our riffs," I explained.

"I can't start a band without Jesse. He's my best friend," Adam asserted, and I could feel the affection in his voice. I respected his loyalty, but I was disappointed by his insistence on this.

"He and I are like musical brothers; I can't really explain it. We talk every night about how we're gonna be like Stone and Mike. I don't even really want to sing that much, I just want to play guitar with Jesse. He hasn't been playing that long, but he's picking it up really fast, and we have the same kind of chemistry together."

This was going off the rails for me a bit. I just wanted Adam to be the singer in my band. I had thought that I would find and enlist a great guitarist and bass player to form a power trio behind him, like Tool, Rage Against the Machine, or the Chili Peppers, but here he was talking about doing something entirely different, and maybe not even singing. I couldn't help but think that his avoidance of embracing a front-man role had a lot to do with the spotlight that would be on him at center stage. Cystic acne had hit him very hard and very suddenly at that age, and the term "pizza face" is not entirely inaccurate to describe what it looked like. It was clearly affecting his self-confidence. This was a fourteen-year-old kid who bragged openly about all the girls he had made out with at summer camp (something I had yet to do even at sixteen), but now he had a hard time even looking people in the eye, let alone singing to a crowd of staring faces.

"Listen, dude, you have a great voice. That's not easy to find for any band. I think you should definitely sing! If you want to play guitar too, that's awesome, but I just don't know if these other guys are good enough yet. And Jesse's a friggin' weirdo!"

"I know Jesse's a weirdo! But that's what's awesome about him too. You don't know him like I do." I could see from his passion that the two of them had formed a real bond and brotherhood. "Trust me, you'll love him if you get to know him. And he's all about the music you're into too, I promise you. With your Stewart Copeland chops, you can play like Dave Abbruzzese . . . me and Jesse can be like Stone and Mike . . . and I guess I can be Eddie too . . . ," he finally admitted somewhat reluctantly. Despite the fact that Adam shared a love for the Police with me, everything was Pearl Jam to these kids. Pearl Jam, Pearl Jam, Pearl Jam. It was all too romantic to say no to outright.

I was still wavering after these conversations, but the two of them had definitely planted the seeds of interest in my mind. However, it took half of that school year for me to finally be convinced. The three of them continued to play and develop in the school band, persistently asking me to accompany them on Pearl Jam songs one pep band show after another. But everything changed one fateful day in the orchestra classroom at school, when Adam, Jesse, Mickey, and I were running through Rage Against the Machine's "Killing in the Name" for a pep rally performance. (Sounds fitting for a prep school assembly, right? "FUCK YOU, I WON'T DO WHAT YOU TELL ME!!!"). Something gelled that day, and it felt like we were becoming a band.

It struck me that it didn't really matter how much experience any of us had. It didn't matter if those guys weren't quite as skilled yet on their instruments: we had a chemistry all of a sudden between the four of us that transcended any other consideration. The force that Jesse's guitar and Mickey's bass made in unison with my drums felt almost as if my internal feelings were exploding out into a symphony of controlled chaos. Even within the incredible inspiration I had felt playing with the older and more accomplished musicians, I had never felt that kind of connection of musical personalities. Our energy and focus were locked in together that day and would be from that day on. We were on the same page about what we were trying to do with the music, and we found a synergy together in which the whole was greater than the sum of the parts. It's not something that I can fully explain, because I hadn't even really hit it off personally with Jesse and Mickey yet, but somehow the force of the four elements in that lineup came together in a way that just felt right. It felt wild but focused . . . it felt adventurous but very simple . . . it felt like it was meant to be.

chapter 4

kara's flowers in bloom

As Adam and I became closer friends, our teenage life became music first, everything else second. We spent every weeknight on the phone, talking about the bands we loved (and the girls we lusted over), and we spent every weekend playing music together. However, despite our newly found connection, Adam and I had a rather dichotomous relationship right from the get-go. I was a more meticulous and overthinking type of guy, always planning and arranging things, while Adam would lose his right arm if it wasn't attached to his body. I had a bit of an obsessive-compulsive personality even then, and Adam was the poster child for attention-deficit disorder. In general, my tendency was to try to control every outcome, and he was more prone to flights of fancy by nature. He was messy and forgetful, with a filthy mouth and an adventurous streak, and I was organized and measured, even anal at times. I was often shocked by the words and phrases that came out of his mouth; his vocabulary for sexual euphemisms was eye-opening. We were like *The Odd Couple*: I was the Felix, and he was the Oscar.

For an image of how this dynamic would play out, picture this common scenario between the two of us: Adam would come over to my house, take a soda can out of the fridge, open it up and take a sip, set it down some-where, go on with the business of playing music, then go back to the fridge a little later and do the same with another can. By the end of our jam ses-sion, there were often five or six soda cans with only one sip out of them scattered around the house. That's how bad his ADD was. And it drove my obsessive-compulsive mind crazy! I would pester him to try to be more mindful and considerate, but it didn't seem to make much of a difference. He just thought I was being an annoying goody-goody, I think. I also had to get used to plans changing at the last minute with regularity, which could be very frustrating for me as well.

So it's not surprising that the band's inception actually began with a change of plans. I don't know if this was by design or if it just happened that way due to Adam's flightiness, but we had planned to get together again this particular weekend, and he threw me a curveball at the last min-ute. As I sat waiting for him, he called to say he didn't have a ride to my house, and I would have to come pick him up somewhere in Santa Mon-ica if I still wanted to hang out. He didn't explain much more than that, but I was really enjoying the bond we were forming as friends and musi-cal compatriots, so I just grumbled at the change in locale, jumped in my hand-me-down 1983 Jeep Wagoneer covered in band stickers, and headed west. I didn't bother to ask why he was stranded somewhere on Wilshire Boulevard; I just went.

When I arrived at the location, I found not just Adam but Jesse as well, standing on the corner of Wilshire and Twenty-Sixth Street. He hadn't mentioned an interloper on the phone. I don't know why I was irritated by this at first. Sure, I thought Jesse was a little weird, but to be honest, I think I just wanted my new friend to myself at that point. I didn't have a ton of friends, and I didn't make new ones all that often, especially ones to whom I felt so connected in respect to music and creativity. The other guys in the band are different from me in that regard; they have always loved making new friends and expanding their circle. Adapting to that sort of lifestyle was a big adjustment for me.

Adam and Jesse jumped into my great white whale of a family wagon, and immediately they had all kinds of ideas for the adventure that would ensue.

"Dude, tonight is gonna be epic!" Adam exclaimed, his enthusiasm clearly ramping up when he was hanging out with his best bro Jesse. "Let's find some chicks and party!"

I had no idea what he had in mind exactly, but partying with chicks sure sounded like fun to me—a little terrifying, but exciting for sure.

"Ryan, can you get us into a club tonight?" Jesse asked. Given that I was only sixteen, had no fake ID, and had never been to a nightclub other than the three where I had performed the previous summer, I had to imagine he was talking about those all-ages clubs to which any of us could just buy a ticket and walk in. But he was so starry-eyed that he seemed to think I somehow had a golden key to the Hollywood nightlife.

Our first stop was a tobacco store. "Dude, let's go in there and get some smokes," Adam said. "Oh my god, have you ever had cloves before, Ryan?"

I had never smoked anything in my life at that point, and I had no idea what he was talking about, but Adam was hell-bent on mixing it up that night. "No, I don't think so . . . ," I said coolly, as if I had tried so many different kinds of tobacco products that I couldn't remember what I had or hadn't tried. This was all just a lot for me already, but I was feeling eager at the same time. I never would have embarked on such a journey for cigarettes and chicks with such gusto if it weren't for these rambunctious partners in crime. "Can you even go into a store like that if you're underage?" I asked, always the sensible one.

"Well, I guess we're gonna find out!" Adam had to pursue every whim. "Oh my god, dude, tonight's gonna be like *Dazed and Confused*! Let's find some weed to roll up in a blunt!"

I had been raised to believe that all drugs were as evil as heroin, but I couldn't stop this train from rolling forward if I tried. The tobacco store was a bust (I'm sure we looked to the shop owner like the teenage idiots we were), so we then went liquor store hopping to try to buy some cigars, Swisher Sweets, or the prized possession: clove cigarettes. Adam was opening my eyes to a lot of new things already with his mischievous spirit. I would hesitate to call him more rebellious than me, because I was certainly a nonconformist in my own way, but I personally tended to reject the typical forms of teenage rebellion like cigarettes, alcohol, or drugs. My rebellion was broader and more based on defying the expectations of our college-prep high school and the world at large that couldn't understand my teenage passions. I related to Holden Caulfield from *The Catcher in the Rye*, thumbing my nose at what I saw as "phony" about the world being laid out before me. But at that point Adam just wanted to have some fun and get in a little trouble.

After we got our hands on some tobacco products of various kinds, we went to the only place we could think of: a rock 'n' roll club. The only problem was that it wasn't even opening time yet. We showed up at the Troubadour as they were doing their last sound check, and we were able to just walk in and sit in the balcony, as if we were with the band. I couldn't tell you the name of the group onstage (or even if they were any good), but it didn't matter. We felt really cool. It was up there, on the long bleachers that sit in the rafters of the Troubadour, that we first discussed forming a new band, as we puffed on a cigar that made me feel nauseated. I didn't know you weren't supposed to inhale.

"Oh my god, dude, Kim M——, I just wanna . . ." Adam clearly thought about this stuff a *lot*. He was like a walking id. I had to hand it to him, though. Even with cystic acne, he did manage to have some very cute freshman girls around him at school. Adam had a way with the girls that I did not. I guess it was just his level of obsession with them that propelled him forward, but he seemed to have a natural knack for flirting that I had not yet developed. But I had developed a crush on one of his friends, Kara, so I was more than intrigued to see where Adam's eagerness for the ladies would take me, if I joined in.

"Yeah, man, Kim's cute . . . Kara's very pretty too . . ."

Jesse changed the subject rather abruptly: "Ryan, the three of us are destined to be a huge band like Pearl Jam or Soundgarden." He still had his eyes on the prize, and he was relentless in his pursuit of his rock 'n' roll dreams. His grand proposal was presented in pure Jesse grandiosity of course, his face lighting up like a Christmas tree.

"That could work . . . you mean like a trio?" I asked.

"Yes! A power trio!" Jesse quickly injected.

"Yeah, I can play the bass I guess," Adam added, again piggybacking on Jesse's level of enthusiasm and focus. "Dude, we could be like the Police! I'll be Sting, you be Stewart, and Jesse can be Andy Summers."

Now they were speaking my language. I started to feel the excitement myself. "I love that! I like the space that I can have in a trio. It gives me so much room to do some cool things. The Police got away with stuff that you couldn't do in a band with a ton of guitars filling up the arrangement. But we could also be like Tool or Rage Against the Machine! We could be like a heavy power trio with your high voice sitting on top of our riffs!"

"Totally! That would be rad!" Malibu surfer-dude Jesse was thrilled that I was finally getting on board with his designs to start a band including him. "I can do so much if I'm the only guitarist too! I can do really outer-spacey stuff like Smashing Pumpkins!"

Although I had been reluctant about Jesse up until that point, I could see his passion, and I could now clearly see that there was a spark in him that really balanced out the personality spectrum between Adam and me. Or better yet, the three of us seemed to make an interesting triangle of creative energy. Adam was a natural savant of musical talent, with a raw sense of melody and harmony, but he was unfocused and a bit scattered with his limited attention span. I was an intense, brooding teenager with a lot of pent-up angst and undirected aggression, just boiling to make a big sound with some fellow disaffected youth, but I could also be obsessive-compulsive and moody. Jesse was more of a freethinker, but at that point it just came out in the form of pure, positive, manic energy. He wanted to change the world with music. He wanted to do things with guitars that nobody had done before (except maybe Billy Corgan). He wanted to incorporate different sounds and instruments, perhaps even industrial music like Nine Inch Nails. There was more complexity in his vision than in mine or Adam's. So, despite my previous hesitation, I just went with it. Change can be uncomfortable for me, but this felt exciting. It felt like we were onto something.

We couldn't wait to get started. After our big powwow at the Troubadour, we headed back to my parents' house and started writing songs. They were terrible, but it was a start. I had one riff that sounded a lot like Rollins Band's "Low Self Opinion," and Jesse had another that sounded like Smashing Pumpkins's "Quiet." They played me a couple of tunes that they had written together for their previous band, and I was impressed by their creativity. In retrospect, the songs were amateurish at best, but at the time they were far beyond anything I could have come up with on my own. Neither of them had studied musical theory or composition at all at that point, but they had incorporated some unique chords that I associated more with jazz in one of their songs titled "Long-Distance Relationship," and I thought it was a really cool thing to do, bringing that into a rock tune. It turns out that Adam had just picked out some major seventh chords solely based on his natural ear for harmony, and that was not something you typically heard in heavy guitar rock, especially not the kind of sludgy garage music we were listening to. Perhaps it was the Police influence that he and I shared.

The sun had gone down as we continued to explore this new musical union, but there was an undeniable feeling between us that this night could not just end unceremoniously. After my parents went to sleep, we stayed up talking and scheming, uninterested in going to sleep. Adam then came up with another one of his big, spontaneous ideas. He remembered that his friend Kara was turning fifteen that morning, and he thought it would be awesome to sneak out and go knock on her window after midnight.

"Dude, this night is *not* over," he insisted. "We can't just go to sleep now. We need to do something *epic*. Kara will be so floored!"

"Oh my god, she'll be so confused!" Jesse added.

"She'll be stoked," Adam corrected.

"You think so?" My attraction to Kara was overcoming my penchant for playing it safe. Again, I had never been likely to partake in this kind of spontaneous mischief before. I was a good kid who followed the rules and never got in trouble growing up. I don't know if it was the spirit of rebellion, the beauty of Kara, or the charisma of Adam Levine, but for some reason this plan started to sound very intriguing to me. Sure, Kara was cute, and I'd had my eye on her from the time I started socializing with Adam, but at that point I was still a very shy guy, who was terrified of girls. I was obsessed with them (as most teenage boys with raging hormones are), but I had no idea what to do about it. I think Adam still looked up to me a little bit, so he just assumed that I had a track record with girls that I definitely did not. I played along with it, though, because I didn't want to disappoint him (or sound like a chump), but at sixteen I was really a virgin who could barely talk to a girl. Though Adam had a way of talking that made anything seem possible.

"Bro, you and I are gonna hook up with Kim and Kara, I promise."

So the initial plan was set: we would sneak out of my parents' house, put the Wagoneer in neutral and quietly move it out onto the street, then head to Kara's house after midnight, to knock on her window and wish her a happy birthday. What a romantic teenage gesture, right? All we needed was a boom box and Peter Gabriel's "In Your Eyes." There was only one problem—Adam had said he knew where Kara lived, but it turns out he only had a vague notion of her living "somewhere in the hills above the Whisky." It wasn't until we had wandered around those winding Hollywood streets in my rickety old Jeep for a half hour that we realized Adam had no idea where we were going.

Fortunately, Brentwood had given us all school rosters with every student's phone number and address, so we actually snuck back into my parents' house to grab mine. This information didn't help us with our quest, however, because none of us knew where Devlin Street was. So we wound up sitting at the Norms restaurant on La Cienega Boulevard, bemoaning our failure over French toast. We were about to give up and just go to bed when we saw a man walking down the street selling flowers at two in the morning. I don't know if this was the sign that we took it to be, but it gave us a reason not to give up on our epic journey into the Hollywood Hills.

Grasping for any reason to continue this adventure, we bought a bouquet from the man and then snuck back into my parents' house a second time to grab a Thomas Guide (for those of you too young to remember, Thomas Guides were street maps like Google Maps, but printed out on this thing called paper). With the school roster in hand, now accompanied with a map and a bouquet of flowers, we finally found Kara's house on Devlin Street around three or four in the morning.

I turned off my headlamps as we quietly pulled into the driveway, realizing that her whole family would obviously be asleep as well. Gently closing the doors to the squeaky Wagoneer, we crept up to the window of Kara's bedroom and pushed the bushes apart to get up close. I, of course, didn't trust that Adam knew this was her bedroom and not her parents', so I let him do the knocking. After a minute or so, the light inside clicked on, and the curtains parted enough to see Kara's pretty face appear, looking confused and rather concerned. The concern quickly melted into a big, blushing smile as she realized that three teenage doofuses were crouched down next to her bedroom window, a bouquet of flowers in tow. She opened the window a crack to greet us.

"What the fuck?" she whispered, chuckling. "What are you doing here?"

I was silent as usual, inarticulate in the face of beauty. Adam didn't miss a beat, though. "It's your birthday! We had to bring you flowers to commemorate the occasion, because we just started the greatest band in history, and you were the first thing on our mind." She blushed even harder.

"You guys are crazy. I love it." She was laughing, clearly flattered by the gesture though she still seemed rather confused. "Oh my god, you guys are so funny. Thank you, I guess. This is so random!" Adam was right. She was floored . . . and stoked.

Having finally enjoyed the cinematic ending to our romantic teenage adventure, we convened back in my bedroom as the sun was about to come up, and we decided to mark this momentous occasion by naming our new band Kara's Flowers and calling our first song "Devlin" (featuring my riff that sounded like Rollins Band). We were a trio of hopelessly idealistic adolescents, dreaming of being the next Pearl Jam, and once again, the world felt like it was made for me and my friends, just like it had before the disillusionment of my early adolescence. The three of us had no idea what we were doing or how we would achieve those dreams, but we were just so exhilarated by the splendor of the moment. The initial plan was for Adam to sing and play the bass, leaving the guitar duties to Jesse (even though Adam was a little more established as a guitar player by that point), but we realized the very next day that this arrangement was not ideal.

"Mickey, we started a band this weekend, and we want you to join it too," Jesse stated emphatically, always the one to ambitiously vocalize the band's whims. "We need two guitars to make the amount of noise we want to make, and we need a dedicated bass player to hold down the fort."

Mickey seemed a little bummed that he hadn't been there for the initial formation, but he was still very pleased to be included, so his disappointment disappeared quickly and turned to anticipation. "Oh man! This is going to be so badass!"

Mickey's indie-rock/punk-minded approach and style added yet another element to what the other three of us were bringing to the table. He was a big personality as well, stubborn and opinionated about music and everything else, so we now had four musical alphas battling and loving one another with gusto. The original lineup was complete . . . and we were now on a mission to conquer the world.

chapter 5

just like suicide

sometimes wonder if I would have been such a moody teenager had I just gotten more sleep. Carpooling from Carthay Circle to Brentwood every morning at 6 AM, coming home from baseball practice around 7 PM, attempting to keep up with the overwhelming load of schoolwork, and then also wanting to play the drums, talk to my friends on the phone, and do whatever else a hormonal teenage boy does, I rarely got more than five or six hours of rest each night during the week. Getting straight As in my classes seemed next to impossible with everything else on my plate, so I decided to just make Kara's Flowers and the school newspaper my number one and number two priorities, respectively.

I began as a freshman on the *Brentwood Flyer* staff, simply because I enjoyed writing as a kid, but as my understanding of journalism developed, I worked my way up the editorial board to editor in chief, gaining more confidence as I took on more responsibility and authority. I also saw journalism as another subversive way to question authority, as evidenced from the columns I ended up writing. I recently read some of the stuff I wrote back then, and boy, was I a pissy little shit! I criticized everything and everyone from the school librarian to my own parents (who didn't deserve it, by the way).

I also often wrote in a way that was intentionally obscure, attempting to sound more poetic or even just "random" at times, in order to throw even the expectations of journalism under the bus. I got reprimanded by our very patient teacher, Ms. Turner-Jones, a few times when, right before the final edit went to press, I slipped some bizarre lines like "Car in the wind; find a lucky tavern" and "This is a pancake, said Beatrice" into my column, just because I thought it would be funny. Another time, I blew off a whole Saturday night and Sunday morning of a production weekend to help throw a party at Adam's parentless condo. I don't know why I was pushing back against even Ms. Turner-Jones; she was one of the few authority figures who really cared and took the time to foster my talents. But that's just where I was as a teenager: I was testing every boundary and questioning every expectation of me.

I even managed to antagonize our caring, sensitive, and inspiringly passionate pep band leader, Mr. Castanares, with one of my articles, in which I criticized the school for not providing more artistic outlets. Quite honestly, my intention was not to impugn Mr. C. when I suggested that the school give the pep band a regular daily class, rather than a once-a-week "activities" period, so that we could receive more teaching and instruction. However, I can fully understand why Mr. C. took my words to imply that he was not teaching us enough. Perhaps it was just my poor syntax, or maybe it was the aggressive tone of my writing style, but he was definitely not pleased with my editorial. I did apologize and express my regret, but I wish now that I had told him how much I actually did appreciate him and everything that he did for us. I just didn't have that kind of maturity at that age.

I was also in a phase in which I would barely speak to my parents at all when I got home from school. Most days I would either go straight to the garage to play the drums or straight into my bedroom and lock the door. Adam and I had gone down to Venice Beach one day and bought some incense, which I was burning in my bedroom most nights, so my parents started suspecting that I was doing drugs. I don't blame them—I was moody, detached, and losing interest in the things I used to enjoy—and now odd, smoky scents were wafting from my bedroom. I actually only tried alcohol maybe three or four times as a teenager, and I never tried pot (even adopting a "straight-edge" mentality at one point), but my parents wouldn't have known that, because I had stopped talking to them almost entirely. They actually sent me to a therapist once, but it was entirely unproductive—because I refused to talk to him either!

In the eleventh grade, my sleep deprivation got so bad that I would sometimes ditch class to take a nap in my car or on one of the couches in the lobby of the school theater. I remember falling asleep sitting at a stoplight on the way home from school more than once. So it's no mystery that I was a grumpy, angst-filled grunge kid. I didn't understand my issue to be anxiety or depression in those days, but I often felt self-consciously detached from my surroundings. It was as if I was walking through my day in a dream, not actually present with the reality of what was going on around me. I would sometimes focus all my attention on my throat and my breathing for some reason, and this would cause me to hyperventilate and get light-headed. It would start with a feeling of a lump in my throat, and I would become very self-conscious of the feeling, thinking there was something wrong or there was something in my throat, blocking it or constricting it. I often felt as if there were a swelling or an inflammation in there that made it harder to breathe. Becoming intent on breathing properly, I would lose my attention to the world around me, focusing it solely on the sensation of my throat and my breathing, which would give me a head rush and a feeling of dissociation. It wasn't what I would describe as a full-on panic attack, because I didn't feel like I was dying, but I began to develop an obsession with this sensation, and the more I would fixate on it, the more it would bother me.

To make matters worse, I got caught ditching Spanish class to sleep in my car several times, and the dean of students sentenced me to "indefinite early-morning detention." When my parents found out about this and the production weekend debacle, they finally read me the riot act and grounded me for a whole month.

"They will kick you out of that school, Ryan! What the hell are you thinking?" my dad asked, looking both angry and forlorn. My parents' previous concern about declining grades and possible drug use had escalated to downright exasperation. I still wasn't really communicating with them very much after that, so my dad finally took some drastic action to try to get me to change my behavior. One weekend, he demanded I get in the car with him, saying only that we would be going for a drive to an undisclosed location in the San Fernando Valley. I sat quietly in the passenger seat of his Ford Explorer as we rode out over the Sepulveda Pass, not knowing how long this trip would be or what it would entail. We finally pulled up to a Jewish cemetery, where we stopped and parked in the driveway for the moment.

"My parents are buried in there," my dad said, with a heavier tone than I had ever heard from him. "After my father died, I had a lot of regrets, wishing that my relationship with him had been more complete. But there just wasn't enough time. I wondered if he knew that I loved him and that I appreciated everything he was to me."

I sat there silently, staring forward into the graveyard, feeling my muscles tense up until I was stiff as a board. This was already more than I had anticipated, but it got even heavier.

". . . But my mom took it worse. She fell into a deep depression that she just couldn't get out of . . . and she eventually took her own life." His voice warbled as he shared this information with me for the first time. ". . . and that is the biggest regret I've had in my life . . . not being able to do more for her . . . It's something I carry with me to this day."

I wanted to cry, but I felt stuck like a statue. As intense and brooding as I was in my adolescent passions, I was still pretty detached from my emotions and uncomfortable with the idea of allowing myself to feel them fully.

"You think your parents are going to be around forever, and then they're just gone . . . and there's nothing you can do about it. You just have to live with how you left things with them forever . . . and you wish you could just have one more day with them, to tell them you love them or to do something more for them . . ."

"Don't worry, Mom and I are fine," he clarified. "I'm not trying to scare you . . . We'll most likely be around for a very long time . . . but I just don't want you to have to go through what I've had to go through, feeling incomplete in my relationship with my parents. I know you're a teenager, and your parents just seem nagging and annoying to you right now . . . I get that . . . But don't let it go on too long. You only get one family, and we love you no matter what. Don't forget that."

This conversation had a profound effect on me. I didn't change my selfish ways immediately, because I was still a sixteen-year-old boy, stuck in that phase of self-obsession, but it did allow me to take stock of my life to a certain degree and to begin to rethink my value system. I think the effect it had on me would take more shape later in my life, though.

Music continued to be my one great escape from the discomfort of adolescence. None of my anxieties, insecurities, or restlessness bothered me when I was playing the drums in my new band. I felt powerful behind my drum set, writing and rehearsing songs in my parents' garage every weekend with Kara's Flowers. Pounding the fuck out of those drums and cymbals to the searing sounds of heavily distorted guitars was a physical catharsis as much as it was an artistic endeavor, and I had found the perfect mates to join me in this visceral and creative experience. I wasn't even sure what I wanted to say as an artist exactly, but I knew I wanted to say it loud, and I wanted people to have the same physical reaction that I had when I listened to my favorite bands: moved by the sound from head to toe, feeling goose bumps all over from the wave of vibrations.

I wrote a good chunk of the material in those early days, mostly starting with bass lines and heavy riffs I came up with on my Yamaha P-Bass knockoff, which my parents had bought me for Christmas that year. I even wrote some of the melodies and lyrics, mostly trying to channel the dark and ruminating soul of Chris Cornell. Mickey also turned me on to the legendary indie-rock band Fugazi, who became another big influence on a lot of what we were doing both musically and personally (hence the "straight-edge" thing Mickey and I adopted). As an example, the following are the lyrics to a song I wrote called "Miner." If you're as big a Fugazi fan as I am, just try to imagine a pulsing Joe Lally bass line, the churning drums of Brendan Canty, and the dissonant yet musical guitars of Ian MacKaye and Guy Picciotto . . . but then add Adam's rather sweet, boyish voice singing the melody atop these sounds.

> *Choose my direction, make me stir,*
> *Which way do other miners go?*
> *That's your injection, strip my fur,*
> *Will someone teach me why it's so?*
> *Where is my lesson? Give me faith,*
> *When will I really have a chance?*
> *You'll choose the tension, yet it's mine,*
> *Give me the time to form a stance.*
> *Choose my direction, make me stir,*
> *Which way do other miners go?*

Profound, right? I'm surprised we didn't win a Grammy for that one.

Adam and Jesse started writing a lot of the band's music as well, more based on actual progressions, with Jesse's creative guitar embellishments and lyrics that Adam scribbled in his composition notebook. He would often change the lyrics when he sang them, though, even while performing onstage, and he sometimes mumbled complete nonsense in the process. I don't know if this was done in the spirit of improvisation, or if he just couldn't remember them (or didn't care to). Adam was a diamond in the rough in those days, but even then, he had a certain knack for melody, harmony, and picking words that sounded good together (even though they were almost entirely meaningless). Jesse has pretty accurately described our early sound as "Fugazi meets *Sesame Street*," in that the arrangements were very noisy and dissonant, with cool riffs and frenetic drums underneath the chaos, and were topped with almost entirely unintelligible and juvenile words. Of course, those lyrics were being sung by a squawking fifteen-year-old boy, who was trying to imitate heavy rock singers whose voices were essentially very different from his.

The process of arranging the material was almost entirely collaborative. All four of us would jump into my Wagoneer every Friday when school ended, and we would head across town to my parents' house, where we would spend the whole weekend jamming and arranging songs from scratch. Everybody had a say in the final product, and every choice we made was entirely democratic. We decided early on that we wouldn't do anything as a band that we hadn't all happily endorsed. This wasn't too much of a problem in those days, because we were all just so excited about everything we were doing. And everything that I would write, Adam and Jesse were free to embellish upon, and everything they would write, Mickey and I could put our stamp on as a rhythm section. We were entirely supportive of one another in that way.

This inspiring, new musical union was also exciting for me in that I now had some cute girls around me a lot of the time. It wasn't long before four or five of my bandmates' freshman friends were following along on our adventures, and we began to have an all-female entourage of sorts. Pretty soon, Mickey was dating a girl in his class named Nicole, and Adam and I were working on courting Kim and Kara, respectively. The three girls and their friends Leslie and Adele would sometimes make the jaunt across town to my parents' garage, to watch us jam or just to come hang out as a big group. We started taking trips to Melrose to shop together and to the Third Street Promenade for movies, and we even went to Anaheim for a day at Disneyland. Soon, I finally had my chance to make out with Kara, in the front seat of my great white whale of a car, while Adam made out with Kim in the back . . . to the romantic sounds of Rage Against the Machine's first album pumping from the tape deck ("FUCK YOU, I WON'T DO WHAT YOU TELL ME!!!!!!!"). What little Casanovas we were, right? Having my first real make-out session was almost entirely awkward, because I had no idea what I was doing. And I left hickeys all over her neck, because I thought that's what you were supposed to do! I think she thought I was a total weirdo after that, but it didn't bother me too much. We were all just having too much fun. The group became a little incestuous, though, as each of the guys made out with each of the girls at one point or another, but it was all pretty innocent overall.

Our first real show was at a dive called the Natural Fudge Co. in a very seedy part of East Hollywood. When I first showed up at the place, I immediately felt bad that we had invited a bunch of fourteen- and fifteen-year-old kids to this dangerous neighborhood and shady, run-down venue. After our relatively conservative families and the sheltered children of Brentwood School filed into this dingy little nightclub, they were greeted by an opening comedic set performed by a middle-aged man who had just gotten out of prison and whose set consisted mostly of anal-rape jokes. Many of the parents in attendance were laughing uncomfortably while clutching their pearls, so to speak.

Our set went over well, however, as we pummeled through an unrelenting half hour of heavy guitar riffs and bashing drums, impressing our mild-mannered family and friends (who were plugging their ears to fend off the sonic onslaught). My hard rock music–loving cousin David was particularly impressed, because this was the first time he had seen me "rock out" to this degree.

"That was awesome, cuz! Man, you play hard!" he complimented.

Knowing his taste for vintage classic rock, I was gratified by his happy response. David's best friend, Jordan (who is like another cousin to me and a great keyboardist in his own right), seemed a little stunned by the volume and intensity of our teenage band, and he seemed rather impressed as well. He had a big smile on his face.

"That was really good! You play behind the beat really well. It sounded really heavy."

I think that might have been the first time I had heard that phrase used, but "playing behind the beat" refers to a style in which a drummer hits the backbeat on the snare slightly late in the pattern, giving the overall groove a heavier feel. Knowing David's teenage love of Led Zeppelin and AC/DC, and having enjoyed the soulful style of Jordan's music many times, I took this statement as a big compliment. Led Zeppelin's John Bonham and AC/

DC's Phil Rudd were best known for that kind of weighty groove, and that was good company to consider myself in. Playing behind the beat wasn't something I did on purpose, though. I guess it had just developed as I emulated some of the heavy drummers I loved.

"There's only one thing I would recommend: you can play with a little softer feel in the verses and breakdowns, so that there's more dynamic within a song," Jordan suggested. I had seen his band play around town enough to know that he knew what he was talking about. "I just watched Chad Smith play a whole set at the Viper Room the other night, and he's actually got a really subtle feel a lot of the time. He's known for being this big, badass drummer, but he actually reins it in when you need to hear the song. And then the song just explodes when he hits the chorus."

The rebellious and hard-rocking teenager that I was wanted to reject that notion outright when I first heard it, but the proposition of playing more like Chad Smith sounded very tempting to me, causing me to reconsider my initial defensiveness. The idea of playing softer and more subtly was hard for me to wrap my head around at first, because I loved the sound of a booming kick, a loud cracking snare, and constant crashing cymbals, but in time I would come to embrace this more "musical" approach to drumming.

I took the ball and ran with it after that, booking us at every venue around town that I could find, from the Whisky, Roxy, and Troubadour to any other club that would have us. I sort of stepped into the role of the band's manager and agent in those early days, looking for all the possible venues to play, negotiating the terms of our bookings, collecting and maintaining a mailing list, selling the tickets, organizing the guest lists, and drawing up the set lists. We had begun recording demos on my brother's four-track cassette recorder in my parents' garage, so we now had a brand-new, four-song demo to help promote us in booking these venues. I haven't listened to those recordings in a long time, but I remember them sounding pretty good for having been recorded with only one room mic on the whole rhythm section, with the vocals then overdubbed. My brother ended up taking that four-track recorder back up to Berkeley when he started another school year, so eventually Jesse and I got our own four-tracks, and we started doing a lot more recording pretty soon thereafter.

Despite my anxiety elsewhere in life, I felt very comfortable onstage performing with Kara's Flowers. It was like that feeling I had on the pitching mound when I was twelve, just reaching back and letting the ball fly with total confidence. This time, I was just letting the sticks fly, flailing around my drum set with power and control, at breakneck speed. I didn't need to think when I was playing our music. I just needed to pound the hell out of those drums and blow the roof off the place! After the band's first show at the Whisky, Jordan's mother, Suzie (who is like another aunt to me), dubbed me "the Drum God." Apparently, this moniker came to her because the Whisky had a very high drum riser, with spotlights streaming down from above, and I played with such ferocity that it was like thunder and lightning coming down off a mountaintop. Man, that felt powerful! I embraced the image of that fully, and I began to revel in the feeling of dominance and power that came from being up on that riser, reigning down on the audience. I almost went to the DMV to demand a vanity license plate with "DRUM GOD" inscribed on it.

It's kind of funny thinking about the fact that my high school baseball coach and teammates labeled me as soft, when I consider how strong and powerful I was as a drummer. Many of those who watched me noticed a discernible grimace I would get on my face when I played, as if I was angry at the drums and I was taking out my pent-up aggression on them.

As intense as we were about our music and performing it, the four of us in the band didn't take ourselves too seriously when we were together socially. Quite the contrary, we were a really silly group of weirdos in those days. The best way to describe our sense of humor (just like my early writing style) was *random*. We would say and do the most bizarre and irreverent things just to make each other laugh. Sure, a lot of it was typical, teenage-boy dick jokes and toilet humor, but the presentation was much more ironic and intentionally weird than your average silliness.

Adam used to do this thing that would have my sides hurting from laughing so hard. He would rap in Spanish—only he didn't speak Spanish.

Somehow, he had this ability to cobble together the few words and phrases he knew, and then fill in the blanks with totally made-up words that sounded like they could be Spanish, and pack it all into a rhyme and a rhythm. He would rap so confidently and emphatically in this faux language, with what sounded like perfect pronunciation, that he sounded almost exactly like Gerardo in "Rico Suave" (remember that song?). It was both impressive and hysterical. Adam also had a knack for making intentional spoonerisms, in which he would rearrange the first consonants of words in a phrase, creating funny-sounding new phrases like "Pashing Smumkins."

Of course, consistent with our "randomness," we would give some of our songs strange names that had no relation to the content of the lyrics. Jesse was prone to creating new words by accident, by combining two words or poorly conjugating a verb, which produced song titles that made us laugh, like "Clomb" and "Overneath." And we even started giving our demos bizarre, meaningless "album titles" like *Throbido's Knife* and *Szechuan Children*.

I never considered myself a natural comic, but this quartet of witty alternative kids inspired some newly found ridiculousness in me. For the first time, I started taking pride in doing or saying things that would have my buddies in stitches. It was like a little game we played with each other. I'm sure to everyone else we just seemed like a bunch of very strange teenage boys, but we felt like we were the funniest group of friends in the world, uninterested in what "normal people" thought was funny or acceptable behavior.

Our first summer as a band, Mickey's friend Noah, who had a half-inch reel-to-reel recording system in his garage, offered to record a bunch of our songs to release as a CD at our shows. We spent a couple of weeks tracking eleven songs, and we had our first "album" in the can. It sounded terrible, but it was an enlightening experience for us, taking our garage productions to another level of ambition. The best part of it was seeing the five hundred printed CD labels with our band's name on them, along with the title "...*we like digging?*" The inspiration for the name was, again, just our desire progression for me. By the time I heard the whole medley on the B side of *Abbey Road*, I was absolutely hooked, and I became a hard-core fan, collecting every recording they ever released and watching the new Beatles *Anthology* videos front to back several times over. Jesse and Mickey were doing the same thing, and we were all soon transfixed in full Beatlemania, learning and emulating every detail of the band's musical journey.

By the mid-'90s, bands like Weezer and Green Day had supplanted the grunge scene on the radio and MTV, and we followed that transition pretty smoothly as well. As a result, our song structures became simpler, our arrangements more streamlined, and our rhythms more linear. I did my best to maintain some of my own unique flair through that stylistic change, as a lot of the drummers in that genre felt a little boring and predictable to me. I had always appreciated more progressive players, who were more adventurous than the average punk drummer. So remnants of the Stewart Copeland, Dave Abbruzzese, and Chad Smith influences were still evident in my playing style, as well as a new appreciation for the solid grooves and eccentricities of Ringo Starr (the most underrated drummer of all time). We were also still very collaborative in our creative process, but having discovered this newly found natural talent for writing catchy melodies, Adam and Jesse started composing pop-rock songs together that totally reinvented our sound and style. And we all cleaned up nicely when we cut off the long hair and traded in our flannel for full mod regalia, inspired by Mickey's and Jesse's obsession with all things British and the 1960s.

The dynamics of the band and our relationship changed a bit at that time as well. In the first incarnation of Kara's Flowers, I was writing a lot of the music, and in some ways I was the "leader" of the band. I had kind of organized the whole thing and booked all our early shows, and despite Adam and Jesse's substantial contributions on their guitars, it was all still within the realm of what I had imagined for us. However, Mickey's punk-istic influence started to come into the fold more as the pop/punk era of modern rock ensued. He had been a big proponent of indie-label bands like Green Day (before they made the jump to Reprise/Warner), Jawbreaker, and Rancid, and his emphasis on creating a simpler, more streamlined

to be totally random and weird. We had pulled the phrase from a line in a children's book by, you guessed it, *Sesame Street*.

Amid all of the innocent fun, ambitious endeavor, and irreverent humor of this auspicious beginning to the band's career, we were struck with a sad reality about the gravity beneath the heavy music and the torment of the artists we loved so much, with the suicide of one of our heroes, Kurt Cobain. As much as I had felt that Nirvana and their alternative rock brethren were speaking for me with their music, I still had thought the weighty subject matter to be more of an artistic choice than a realistic statement of extreme depression, drug addiction, and suicidality. As disillusioned as I had been in my adolescence, I was still a pretty innocent kid, who hadn't come to terms with the more devastating side of these realities. When we learned of Cobain's death, we were overcome with grief. He had been the first and most prominent icon of our early '90s Generation X culture, and it was hard to accept that he was just gone forever. When I stop to think that every sad lyric he wrote, every defiant thing he did, and every self-destructive tendency he displayed were as much a product of his crippling insecurity as they were an expression of his artistic talent, it makes me very sad, both as a fan and just as a human being. I think we all started to rethink the extent to which we were posturing that level of gloom in our music, realizing that this stuff was no joke, and it was not just a "pop-culture trend." It was a mental health tragedy unfolding before our very eyes.

chapter 6

the times they
are a-changin'

I finally had my first real girlfriend in my senior year of high school. My yenta father actually introduced her to me, after meeting her and her family out at dinner one night and showing them a photo of me (palm to face, Dad!). But I guess the fact that I took him up on the offer demonstrates that I was beginning to soften in my teenage rejection of my parents' involvement in my life.

She was a very attractive girl with pretty blue eyes, but she was complicated emotionally, with frequent mood swings and an intense fear of abandonment. However, to me, our relationship felt just like what I imagined a grown-up relationship to be, based on what I saw in the movies and on TV—by that, I mean it was constant drama. One moment we would be on cloud nine, feeling romantically attached to each other in the most idealized ways, and the next moment she would be crying hysterically, proclaiming that I was going to leave her and break her heart. As frustrating as this pattern could be, it filled a particular void in my life at first, making me

feel needed and loved. I served a purpose by consoling her. I would later come to feel that I was being manipulated by her emotional swings, but for the time it felt like love to me.

On the band front, the garage-rock era of Kara's Flowers seemed like a lifetime unto itself when we were in it, but it was actually pretty short-lived. The sludgy grunge we were playing in 1994 was almost entirely replaced by a more musical sound by the end of '95. The eccentric alternative kids we had been in those formative days transitioned to a more polished and melodic sensibility, mostly influenced by our love affair with the Beatles. The greasy hair and flannel shirts of the early shows, with their mosh pits and slam dancing, were replaced by coiffed hair, mod suits, and skinny ties by '96.

The Beatles influence was earth moving for us. Their combination of youthful energy, harmonic complexity, and studio wizardry was aspirational for our band, as we began to set our sights beyond the musical trends of the moment. It wasn't something that happened overnight, because most of us grew up with some exposure to the mop tops, but Adam's sensibilities as musician, singer, and songwriter took a dramatic shift when he embrace his childhood roots, emulating the great singer-songwriters of the 19 and '70s, whom his mother had played for him when he was growin He discovered in due time that he could sing in a sweeter tone and a register like Paul McCartney or Paul Simon, and even as high as Sting began to embrace our Police roots as well. It was also just a matter before Adam's innate talent for melody and harmony transcende rock and started to manifest in prettier compositions.

The connection with the Beatles for me happened the first tened to *Abbey Road* all the way through. Of course, I had hea "Come Together," "Something," and "Here Comes the Sun" the darker and moodier tracks such as "I Want You (She's S "Because" were more of a direct link to my favorite band whose biggest hit was the largely Beatles-influenced song " The album *Superunknown* featured several other tracks of John Lennon compositions, making the leap to the B

approach to punk-minded melodic rock was now consistent with what was happening on the radio and MTV in the mid-'90s. So we just decided to combine that influence with the harmonic stylings of the music that Adam and Jesse were bringing in as songwriters. It also became clear that the two of them had a growing creative chemistry together, and it was evolving beyond what I could bring to the table in that regard. I wasn't thrilled about losing some of the creative control at that point, but I was too excited about the level of talent the band was showing to question it. That natural synergy that had sparked the band was now flourishing to a point of real artistry.

It didn't take long for the record industry to take notice of what we were doing in our transition to more tuneful pop. Our first break came in 1995, right after we recorded our first proper demo, in a small studio on Hollywood Boulevard called Room 222. The three-song demo we recorded on New Year's Day featured our first versions of the songs "Future Kid," "Loving the Small Time," and "Pantry Queen," which would later show up on our first real album.

After we wrapped that recording session, we drove all the way across town to play a party in Malibu that night, where a musician named Tommy Allen came walking along the beach and heard the commotion inside. Tommy's partner John DeNicola had had success cowriting the massive hit songs "(I've Had) the Time of My Life" and "Hungry Eyes" for the movie *Dirty Dancing*, and together they were starting an independent label called Omad Records, to which they would sign new talent. I don't know what Tommy heard in that very loose jam that night, but he came right in and introduced himself to us. Before we knew it, my dad was negotiating a record contract with Tommy and John, and we were working on a full-length album for Omad, just as I was about to finish high school.

This experience was the absolute "time of our lives." We were recording at the world-famous Sound City Studios (where Nirvana and Rage Against the Machine had recorded) and the equally prestigious Rumbo Recorders (where Guns N' Roses made *Appetite for Destruction*), and we were making sounds of a quality we couldn't have imagined coming from a garage band like us. Tommy and John were just a great couple of guys, who really took us under their wing, teaching us the ropes of how to craft a solid musical production on tape. The two of them wanted to be a part of something new and exciting as much as we did, and their enthusiasm gave us a lot of encouragement. They also suggested we simplify the parts we were playing, providing us valuable lessons on how to arrange the tracks with more of an ear toward the song first and the individual performances second.

We were on a sugar high the entire time we were in the studio with Tommy and John. After we laid down a basic track, we would all congregate in the control room and rock out to the performance we had just recorded, headbanging and playing air guitar like we were listening to one of our favorite rock records. We would look around at each other with such delight and joy that the sheer excitement was palpable for everyone in the room, including the second engineer and the food runner. I can still hear Tommy's catch phrase "One-Take Jimmy" echoing in my ears when I think about that session. To commemorate a good performance by one or all of us, he would exclaim, "You guys are a bunch of One-Take Jimmies!" or "One-Take Jimmy and his brother Sam!"

The thirteen songs we recorded with Omad in the spring of 1995 were the sonic bridge between that early heavier version of Kara's Flowers and the "power-pop" version that was to come. However, I don't think any of us could have expected that those recordings would end up becoming lightning in a bottle. There was so much interest in the band as a result of that recording that Tommy and John decided to forego releasing it on their own label. Instead, we began a process of shopping the record to major labels like Epic, Sony, and Atlantic. Tommy and John just wanted a chance see the album released on a bigger scale (with more money to promote it), but we started getting stars in our eyes. We were still high-school kids, but now we were taking meetings with the biggest record executives in the industry, who were telling us we were going to be rock stars, over lunch at the Beverly Hills Hotel or the Ivy at the Shore.

Unfortunately, neither Epic nor Sony offered us a deal, but the disappointment of that rejection was brief, because we came very close to signing with Tim Sommer at Atlantic Records shortly thereafter. However, it was when we were introduced to Rob Cavallo at Reprise/Warner Bros. that things got away from Tommy and John. We were enamored with Rob. He had produced Green Day's hit album *Dookie* and Jawbreaker's *Dear You* (as well as a number of other hit records that would come out that year). He was a charming young man of around thirty-three at the time, reminding us of a mix between Tim Robbins and Quentin Tarantino, and his father, Bob Cavallo Sr., owned a major management company, which also wanted to take us on. Bob began referring to Tommy and John as "these characters" in our presence, insinuating that they were disreputable or in over their heads, and messing with our perception of them as really sweet guys who had nourished our early talent. But as much as we loved Tommy and John and everything they had done for us, the Cavallos were just too big-time to pass up. Warner Bros. ended up buying Omad out of its contract, leaving Tommy and John in the dust, and we went full steam ahead with the Cavallo family at the helm. I didn't, and I don't, feel good about how we left Tommy and John behind, but it was the nature of the beast at that point. We were young and impressionable, and we thought that signing with a major label meant surefire success on the level of Pearl Jam—or even the Beatles—which is what these bigwigs were promising us.

I had graduated from Brentwood in the spring and enrolled at UCLA in the fall of 1995, but I had no intention of ever graduating. I was convinced that we were going to make an album, go on tour, and become big rock stars before I would have the chance. A year or two of college was just something to pass the time and keep my parents off my back until our career really took off. My parents were actually very supportive of the band by this point (as were the parents of the other band members), but I was eighteen years old, and I just wanted to get out of the house and go live in the dorms while we were embarking on our musical career. I didn't even declare a major, though, because most of my attention was focused on the album we were making with Rob.

During my first two years at UCLA, when we were working on the record deal and then recording the album that it spawned, I started to feel a little disconnected from the other guys in the band. They were still in high school, just hitting the peak of that experience, and between the nature of their infectious personalities and the glamour of signing a major recording contract, they seemed to be living largely with an ever-expanding group of friends and the party lifestyle that went along with it. Adam had become quite the ladies' man during that time, hooking up with more girls than I could count ("hooking up" just meant making out in those days, as opposed to sex, although I imagine he was having more sex as well). And I was living a slightly quieter life in my dorm, spending the weekends with my girlfriend mostly. That seems a little backwards I suppose, because college is the time when most people live it up, but I was a little melancholy, longing for the days when the four of us would spend most of our time together as a tight unit, rather than running around town with a hundred new friends.

To fill the void, I started spending a lot of time in the dorms with a couple of very funny guys named Brad Delson and Dave Farrell, who would later become the guitarist and bassist of the band Linkin Park. Brad had dated a friend of mine in high school, at which time I had seen his band perform at the Whisky once. They were a bit of a Rage Against the Machine knockoff, but I enjoyed their energy. He was between bands as we started at UCLA together, and because Adam and Jesse were writing most of the songs for Kara's Flowers by that time, I decided to play for Brad and Dave some of the material I was writing on my own. They were so delighted by my tunes that they actually wanted to start another project with me as their singer-songwriter! This didn't seem like a feasible situation for me with everything going on for Kara's Flowers, but I was flattered by their interest, so we spent some time jamming and working out arrangements.

I had a great time hanging out and writing music with Brad and Dave. It was more silly fun than inspired musicianship, but it filled a space inside of me for sure. The control I had been losing in my band was temporarily replaced by this creative outlet, in which these two musicians were deferring to me as the guy with more experience writing songs. Brad was the kind of guy who liked to push your buttons just to get a rise out of you, though it took me a while to realize that was what he was doing. At first, I just thought he could be kind of annoying at times, but then I realized he was actually really funny.

"I like the Deftones more than the Beatles," he once said, making my brain explode.

"Uh, whaaaaa? You're joking, right?"

"The Deftones make music that's, like, really moving and emotional to me. The Beatles were great and everything, but I'm more moved by the Deftones," Brad claimed, a snide grin on his face, which made it hard for me to tell if he was being serious or not.

"Dude, the Beatles are the greatest band in the history of music! You can't say that!"

"They're all right, I guess. I think they're kind of overrated."

I didn't know what to do with myself. This was just an injustice to all of humanity as far as I was concerned. I made it my mission to convert him and Dave after that, beseeching them to watch the Beatles *Anthology* with me and imploring them to consider their influence on the history of popular music. Dave actually admitted after watching him that Paul was a badass on the bass guitar, but Brad always had that sarcastic smile on his face whenever we would talk about this stuff. I think he just thought it was hilarious to see me get all riled up about it.

Brad also once made the ridiculous claim that "311 is a better band than Queen." I just stopped in my tracks with my jaw hanging open after that one. I think he might have actually believed some of these things when he said them, but he also knew that they would infuriate me, so he would just drop those doozies into a conversation and wait to see steam come out of my ears. I don't know why I fell for it every time.

When I finally did end things with my girlfriend around that time, Brad also liked to tease me about how uncomfortable being single seemed to be for me.

"You, like, can't be alone, bro," he told me. "It's really cute."

"What are you talking about?" I was getting defensive already.

"Everywhere we go, you're, like, always on the prowl for a new girl-friend. It's really kind of funny."

"Aren't all guys our age on the prowl for girls?" I asked, not under-standing why he was implying that this was a bad thing.

"Most guys are on the prowl to get laid! You're on the prowl to find a girlfriend like ASAP! You can't be alone, dude! You need to learn to chill!"

I didn't think this was necessarily the case. At least, I didn't think I was doing that consciously, but perhaps I wasn't quite as self-aware as I thought.

Needing to "learn to chill" was also another thing that Brad and Dave used to tease me about constantly, because I would put on slacks and dress shoes and style my hair just to go to class or hang out on campus. I had become what we used to call "metrosexual," which they also found to be hilarious. I don't know, I just liked to look my best . . . and maybe I was a little obsessive-compulsive about grooming as well. I didn't think of it as vanity; I just wanted everything to be "perfect" all the time.

At one point in that year, the singer in Brad's old band asked Brad if he would put together a new band, to join him and his new partner, Mike Shinoda, for some showcases of material they had demoed. Brad asked if I would consider playing the drums for these showcases, and I politely declined, being committed to my own band already. I did support my new friends by showing up and cheering them on at every show they did, but I honestly didn't see much of a future for them. They were a little unpol-ished at the time. Who knows? Maybe I could have been the drummer in Linkin Park too!

One day when I was driving out to the valley to join the rest of the band at the studio, my Jeep Wagoneer finally broke down as I pulled off the 101 freeway in Canoga Park. The great white whale had served me and the band well since I was sixteen, but it was finally completely dead and gone. I got Adam to come pick me up and drive me the rest of the way to the studio, but I had no way to get home at the end of the workday. Adam suggested I tag along with him to Jonah Feldstein's bar mitzvah that night (you may know Jonah Feldstein now as the hilarious and multitalented actor Jonah Hill). I felt weird going to the Feldstein family's big event without having been invited, but again, I had nowhere else to go, and Adam assured me it would be fine, and it might actually be fun.

As fate would have it, we were seated at a table with a couple of very cute blonde girls, and I hit it off with the one named Taryn immediately. We spent the rest of the night talking and dancing together, and by the end of the night we were exchanging numbers and making plans to see each other again. I called and invited her to come to the studio the next week, to show off how much of a rock star in the making I was. After picking her up in my parents' Ford Explorer, I called ahead to the studio, asking the runner to bring in food from the Cheesecake Factory. She was very impressed.

Taryn was much less complicated than my first girlfriend. She was adorable and sweet, and she just seemed to think that everything I did was amazing, which of course felt very validating. We fell in love very quickly, and this time it was much more of a real puppy-love type of infatuation. There was almost no drama between us, and I can't even really remember ever arguing at all. I don't know if that's a good thing necessarily. But for the time, it felt very kind and loving, and I felt much more comfortable knowing that I had a stable relationship with someone who really appreciated me in a genuine way.

However, I couldn't help but feel that Taryn didn't know all of me. The dark side of me that had been somewhat subdued by the excitement of the band and the delights of young love was still there under the surface; it was just lying dormant for the time being. I don't think Taryn got a glimpse of my melancholy side more than once or twice, and when she did, she seemed very confused by it. So I just made a point of not letting that part of me out around her. It wasn't too hard to do, because we were just so sweet and affectionate with each other most of the time, but I couldn't help but feel that she wouldn't really like the other sides of me if I let them come to the surface.

I remember trying to talk to Taryn once about some of the concerns I was having about going on tour for the first time. I was worried that it wouldn't be the kind of life I wanted to live: that it would be too much change all the time, that my personality was too different from the other guys' personalities, and that I might lose my mind and go to a dark place. She seemed confused, as she didn't understand how I could be in fear of my biggest dreams coming true, and she was frightened by the fact that my mood was heavier than she had ever seen. So I pulled myself together quickly, realizing she was not comfortable with this darker side of me. I told her not to worry, that I would be okay.

But I wasn't so sure.

chapter 7

breaking the fourth world

We learned a lot from the experience of making the Reprise/Warner album, but the mood and the vibe in the studio were very different from the loose and jovial tone of the sessions with Tommy and John. Recording most of the same songs again, this time at the ultra-high-end Conway Recording Studios, we sensed a feeling in the air that we had reached the big time, and I for one felt the pressure to churn out radio-ready tracks with every take we laid down.

Warner Bros. threw a ton of money at the project, and we spent over a year making it, working nights and weekends while the guys finished their senior year of high school. These were the old days of the record business, when major labels would sign ten acts a year, spend a million dollars on each of them, then make all their money on the one or two that hit it big. Of course, they would then drop the rest of the bands from their label when they inevitably failed. It was a "sink-or-swim" kind of proposition, but we didn't know any of that going into it—we just wanted so badly to believe the hype that we were going to be the next big thing! And spending all that cash on the album and video was "chump change," as Bob Cavallo Sr. put it. We even got to put a full-scale orchestra on some of the tracks, conducted by the top-flight string arranger David Campbell (father of singer-songwriter Beck). But we hadn't really earned any of it at that point. Who the hell were we to have all that decadent luxury draped across us?

Because the sessions stretched out over the course of a year, and because we were spending so much time looking at everything under a microscope, I felt that the album lost some of the energy and fire that Tommy and John's recordings had captured. Their version of the album had a certain youthful zeal that was somewhat diminished on the Reprise/Warner version. Also, I was simplifying my drum parts even more, in our attempt to streamline the sound for radio, and the end result was a bit more generic, lacking some of the Stewart Copeland flourishes and Dave Abbruzzese intensity that had been my calling cards. I don't know if anyone else would be able to hear these subtle changes from the former version, because the resulting album was a very polished and well-produced recording that Rob and engineer/mixer Jerry Finn constructed using their many talents, but I can't help but feel that we lost a little bit of the chemistry that made us great as a result of the long, drawn-out, and meticulous process.

Rob was certainly not to blame for any of this. He was a very accomplished producer, working simultaneously on Fleetwood Mac's reunion album (Lindsey Buckingham even came down to one of our sessions to say hi) and Green Day's follow-up album (Mike Dirnt and Tré Cool came down to check us out as well), but we were just very inexperienced musicians, not ready to deliver the kind of work that could connect to a larger audience. As very young artists, we had often made up for our lack of maturity and experience with sheer intensity and reckless abandon, but without that, we were just precocious kids, presenting ourselves as the underdeveloped, not-ready-for-prime-time players that we were.

When I think about those sessions, a few things leap to mind: First, I remember doing a ton of takes, then intensely listening and comparing, slaving over every performance in trying to achieve "perfection." Second, I remember a lot more arguments between the four of us, as we picked apart every detail and sometimes became a little too idealistic in our vision. I remember Rob getting frustrated with us more than once and having to walk out of the control room and into the tracking room to try to get us to resolve our dispute and get back to recording. The arguments were never personal, and never disrespectful, but they were pretty intense debates over anything and everything, small or large.

Third, there was at times a level of decadence that we hadn't experienced before. Rob was a man with a big appetite, literally and figuratively. I remember watching him eat a caloric monster of a Monte Cristo sandwich from Jerry's Famous Deli, then order a runner to go fetch him a Double-Double from In-N-Out, because the Monte Cristo hadn't fully satiated him. Another time, he ordered a "4 × 4" (four patties, four slices of cheese) plus a Double-Double at once, for a total of six patties and six slices of cheese, then ate all of that in one sitting. And then there were the obligatory nights of rock 'n' roll debauchery that ensued, in an attempt to blow off some steam from the intensity of the recording sessions, although I certainly don't hold that against him at all. I was still a teetotaler in those days, but I enjoyed living it up with the guys.

Lastly, I remember the quality of the lyrics becoming an issue for the first time. Our managers complained that some of the songs sounded meaningless and juvenile, but Adam just hadn't progressed beyond that level of his development yet. The music had risen to a higher point of composition, but most of the lyrics were still a product of just stringing words and phrases together to sound as if they meant something. Bob also insisted we drop one of the songs we loved most, called "It's Not So Bad," because it sounded entirely spoiled and tone-deaf for a bunch of privileged white kids from Brentwood School to be lecturing their generation not to take their troubles so seriously. In our attempt to swing back away from the doom and gloom of the grunge era, we had definitely overcompensated, trying to be more upbeat and positive in our imagery. There was also no irony in our songs—this was out of step with the style of mid-to-late-'90s pop culture.

We went out on tour for the first time in the summer of 1997, just as we were releasing our first single, "Soap Disco," and the album we had decided to name *The Fourth World.* Mickey and Jesse had pulled that title from a Peter Jackson movie called *Heavenly Creatures,* but Adam and I didn't really know what it meant. It just seemed like a phrase that could have multiple meanings, and being a bit obscure was still a part of our lyrical vibe, so it seemed to fit. We set out to drive ourselves around the country in a standard passenger van, with just a tour manager/soundman named Ricki, who shared the driving time with us and dealt with the club managers.

We would pull into each town we were playing, pull all of our equipment out of the back of the van and set it up onstage ourselves (from drum hardware to amps, cables, and guitars), play the gig, then pack it all up ourselves again and head to the next town. Sometimes we would sleep in a couple of hotel rooms until sunrise and then hit the road; sometimes we would drive through the night. I was exhausted the first few weeks of touring, until I figured out how to sleep in the van. We picked up a second crew guy named Pete at one point, and he and Ricki would share the driving after that, but Jesse and I did a lot of the driving at first. Adam either "didn't feel like it" or was too scared to drive a big van with a U-Haul trailing behind. And none of us wanted Mickey to drive . . .

Although we saw ourselves as the next Beatles, but played in the power-pop style of Weezer, the only headlining acts we could get to take us on tour were third-wave ska bands like Reel Big Fish, Save Ferris, and Goldfinger, so it wasn't exactly a perfect fit in terms of album promotion. The consistent comments we received from fans at the merch table were things like "Have you thought about playing your guitars on the upstroke?" as if ska music was the only music with which they were familiar. And of course, there was the classic "You guys would be better if you had horns." We knew that they meant a horn section, but we thought it was hilarious to imagine that they meant horns growing out of our heads.

Our random teenage sense of humor had evolved to a greater place of wit by the time we were driving around the country in 1997, but we were still pretty silly and ridiculous. We would get into arguments about the stupidest things just to keep ourselves entertained on long drives, but we knew it was all in good fun. One day, somewhere at a U-Haul station in middle America, this doozy of an argument broke out.

"Jesse, a velociraptor could not get into this store! We would be safe in here!" Mickey said, incensed by Jesse's insistence that velociraptors knew no bounds.

"No, dude, they would just rear up and knock those big windows out, and then they could jump up and over the wall into the store! We'd be dead!" Jesse said.

"That's ridiculous, Jesse! You're just saying that to argue with me. *Jurassic Park* was not realistic! This is a modern building, built in a way that a prehistoric animal could not break into. There's no way that they could get in here!"

"No, Mickey, you're being ridiculous! They're clever girls! They would find a way! Nature finds a way!" Jesse said.

"You're both being ridiculous," Adam said.

This went on for about an hour, while we waited for Ricki to shore up the business with the U-Haul people.

Traveling the country in a van, and playing in front of crowds of hundreds or sometimes thousands, was a very exciting prospect for all of us, but I wasn't really prepared for it in a lot of ways. I tend to be uncomfortable with change in general, but this was an entirely different lifestyle than anything I had experienced before. Sure, I had moved out of my parents' house and into the dorms at UCLA, but now we were driving hundreds of miles a day in a van with all our musical equipment in tow, sleeping in motel rooms most nights (except for the nights when we slept in the van), and having to get up with the sunrise to make it to the next city in time for sound check. And I was doing all of it without enough sleep much of the time.

I was homesick a lot too. I loved being with my friends, seeing the country, and playing music with them every day, but I also missed Taryn back home, and I longed to see her most of the time. I'm more of a home-body than the other guys, and the constant motion and change was hard on me. Also, being more of an introvert by nature, I was frustrated by how little time alone I had in that lifestyle. We were together constantly. And this was also still in the era before cell phones, so to even talk to my girlfriend or family back home often meant trying to find a pay phone in the back of a noisy nightclub. It's also worth noting that Mickey and I were both still "straight edge" in those days, so there was no real partying going on. After trying drunkenness a few times as a teenager, I had ultimately decided that keeping my wits about me was much more "badass" than being a rock 'n' roll cliché. I'm pretty sure Adam and Jesse thought I had a stick up my butt, because I was so against partying.

It's also worth mentioning that there were times on tour when I felt a little alienated from the other three guys in the band, although we were all good friends. Perhaps it was just my self-conscious and overthinking mind, but there were times when I thought the three of them were closer with each other than with me. I had always been closest with Adam, but there were moments, even as simple as just walking down the street in a new city, when I physically felt the three of them huddling together to talk, and I was having a difficult time getting my head into their little discussion triangle. I would sometimes just lag behind them, having felt somewhat ousted from the fellowship. This was not a pleasant feeling, and I did my best not to get too resentful, but I couldn't help but feel that they were either consciously or unconsciously snubbing me.

I watched an interview with Ringo Starr once, in which he described a time when he almost left the Beatles, and he went to John Lennon's house to tell him he felt like an outsider, thinking that the other three were really close, to which John said, "I thought it was you three!" Then Ringo went to Paul McCartney's house, and Paul said, "I thought it was you three!" And then Ringo went to George Harrison's house, and George said, "I thought it was you three!" So I don't know if that's just something that happens in bands. I always felt that being in a band was like being married to three people. Imagine trying to make that work!

I probably could have dealt with all the strain of touring better, though, if I hadn't started experiencing symptoms of anxiety for the first time in conjunction with performing. Most bands come home from touring after a few months and they sound a lot tighter than they did before they started, playing with an ease and comfort that grows from performing together every night. We definitely did sound more polished as a group, but I also felt that performing was becoming more stressful for me. Instead of thinking first and foremost about the energy and vibe of the concerts, I was most consumed with whether or not I did everything exactly the way I imagined doing it, from the opening count-in to the very last beat of the set. In my visualizations of it before the show, I could see myself striking every drum and every cymbal hit cleanly and perfectly for every beat and sub-beat of the entire show, without any mistakes or flubs, feeling total control over my instrument. This perfectionistic attitude often limited my ability to even enjoy the show, because I was so concerned with how well I was doing individually.

There were many times when we would walk offstage and Adam would be raving about how great the energy was, but I would be complaining about how I dropped or broke a stick in song four, or I had flubbed a fill in song six. Conversely, there were times when I was elated that I had played the whole set perfectly, and then Adam would comment that the energy and vibe was totally dead. He was more tuned in to the feeling he was getting from the crowd and the performance as a whole, while I was clearly wrapped up in my own obsessive thoughts of perfection.

As a result, I often felt like I was just holding on for dear life when I was playing. I started guiding and overcontrolling the sticks more, trying to make sure I struck everything precisely and evenly and never made a mistake. Gone were the days of just letting the sticks fly around the drum kit like I let the baseball fly out of my hand as a confident twelve-year-old pitcher. My experience when playing was now more similar to that feeling of "the yips" from my high school baseball days: I felt an overwhelming need to control the outcome by bearing down and trying harder, but there was often an inverse relationship between effort and outcome. I had no training to fall back on in terms of mechanics or a balanced approach to drumming, so I was subject to the whims of my overthinking mind. I often had waking nightmares about the ultimate embarrassment of ruining a performance in front of thousands of people or, worse yet, in front of millions on live TV. The idea of this happening to me was absolutely terrifying.

My anxieties also started to express themselves in obsessive-compulsiveness about the drums themselves. I would spend a lot of time in sound check, tuning and positioning my drums, somehow convincing myself that if I got my drums set up just right, I could avoid disaster. Sure, this was also just a part of my tendency to be meticulously neat and organized, but it was also another control mechanism, an attempt to regulate the perfection that was slipping from my grasp. I actually didn't even really know how to properly tune a drum kit back in those days, but I would spend hours trying to make it perfect anyway. I would twist the screws over and over until they were stripped, often causing hardware to break down. So I was actually causing more problems than I was solving, not to mention the fact that the behavior itself was probably only exacerbating my anxiety. And I would often just get angry at the drums themselves in the middle of the set, as if it were their fault. I remember one very small and inconsequential show on South Street in Philadelphia, attended only by my aunt Bea, my uncle Carlos, their son Carlos Jr., and his wife, Grace, at which my drum hardware was angering me so much that I pushed over a cymbal stand and stormed off the stage to end the set, like a petulant child.

Underneath these perfectionistic thoughts was a powerful case of impostor syndrome. Because I had never studied and practiced the rudiments of drumming (or been taught proper technique by a professional instructor), I often felt that I was just faking it, and that I was a fraud who would be exposed sooner or later. One of the bands with whom we toured for a while, a cartoonish ska band called the Aquabats, featured an impressive young drummer named Travis Barker, whom we would watch from the side of the stage most nights. Travis came from a marching band background, and his technique and skill were leagues beyond mine or those of anyone else we watched play, which made me feel even more self-conscious about my own playing. He was so dedicated to his craft that he had a drum pad strapped to his knee most of the day, and he would practice his paradiddles while the rest of us were just hanging out backstage. I didn't even know what a paradiddle was, let alone how to play one as fast as he did with his perfect sticking technique. As result of this kind of training, he could play with greater speed and precision than I had thought was possible. In my state of self-doubt, I would watch him play with envy, knowing that I was not in the same ballpark in terms of drumming skill. Every other band we toured with was trying desperately to steal him from the Aquabats, and Blink-182 eventually did.

I do believe that teaching myself to play gave me a uniquely expressive style, which provided the band with some soul and flair that another drummer with "proper" mechanics may not have had, but that didn't help my confidence as a performer at the time. It didn't matter that other musicians (including Travis Barker) would praise me for my style and for our chemistry as a band, that the guys in my band still thought I was great and would cheer me on to do drum solos during sound check, or that the other bands with which we toured would watch me play and give me compliments. My inner critic was much louder than any of them. As a result, I often felt that drumming became harder and harder for me the longer a tour stretched on. Whereas playing our set felt easy and free after a short break, playing for the thirtieth day in a row felt like I was trudging through snow uphill. I didn't understand it at the time. I suppose I had a vague notion that this feeling was being caused by my own psychology, because I could feel the obsession about it growing within my mind, but if anything, that idea made me feel even more flawed. What was wrong with me, that I would make it all so much harder on myself than it needed to be? Why couldn't I just play my instrument with swagger and confidence like the other guys did? The only answer my brain could come up with was that I was defective in some way.

My anxiety (which I still didn't understand as anxiety) also began to manifest in more physical ways. I started to have stomach issues as well as that lingering feeling of a lump in my throat. My stomach just felt uneasy a lot of the time, and I often lost my appetite. Eating breakfast would make me feel nauseated, so I skipped it most days. I didn't like the feeling of being full or having indigestion onstage, so I would often wait until after the show to go find some greasy, disgusting chicken fingers or something like that to finally satiate myself. I got really skinny on the road, as most days I ate only two meals and sweated out a ton of calories, and I was always very conscious about not feeling "bloated" for performances.

To add insult to injury, I got salmonella food poisoning at one point as well, but I didn't even realize that's what it was at first, because it just seemed so much in line with what I felt most of the time, only worse. Funny enough, though, it happened on the set of *Beverly Hills, 90210*, which had booked our band for an appearance on the show. The teenage drama had been a huge obsession for the girls at our high school, so we just couldn't turn down the opportunity to play at the show's Peach Pit After Dark when they offered it to us. It was a surreal experience, but particularly because I got very ill for the second half of the day, right when we were finally going to shoot our scene. You would never guess from the finished product, because as usual I put on a brave face for the performance, but I was nauseated and miserable on the inside. We ended up performing at the Hollywood Palladium for the first time that weekend, and I have very little memory of it because I was so sick.

It never came down to playing on live TV in front of millions of people in 1997. After one decent week of radio-adds for "Soap Disco" ("radio-adds" is industry jargon for the number of stations that add your song into their rotation that week) and a couple of spins of the video on the late-night MTV show *120 Minutes*, the album never took off as everyone had expected, and our campaign for world domination ended unceremoniously around the end of that year. After we came home for the holidays, we were informed that the label was pulling the plug and there would be no more touring in promotion of *The Fourth World*. We had thought that the second single, "Myself," could be a big hit, but we never even got the chance to make a video or promote it to radio. It was just over, and we had to accept it, as painful as it was. So we now had a failed album on our résumé, and we were forced to try to pick up the pieces and move on as just another sad casualty of the sink-or-swim record industry model.

chapter 8

searching for the ground, with my good eye closed

The year 1998 was a weird one for Kara's Flowers. After the failure of *The Fourth World*, we experienced a collective identity crisis. None of us really expressed our emotions out loud to one another (because what nineteen-year-old boys do?), but I know that Adam was very affected by the disappointment, judging from his behavior. First off, he immediately rejected any value in our previous music, calling it "stupid" and "pointless." Even though we still had a good fan base in LA and could sell out a club like the Roxy, he no longer wanted to play any of the songs from the album. He was hell-bent on establishing a new identity that was a complete rejection of the previous form. In the same way that the gloss and optimism of *The Fourth World* had probably been an overreaction to the sludge and darkness of our early stuff, Adam wanted to throw out the baby with the bathwater again and move on completely.

The first few shows back in LA featured new material that was very different and strongly influenced by the British alt-rock bands of the time.

Jesse and Mickey were inspired by groups like Radiohead and Blur, and Adam was so obsessed with Oasis that he started wearing sunglasses onstage and tilting the microphone down at himself like he was Liam Gallagher. That phase ended quickly, though, as we received a rather cool reaction from our fans expecting to hear "Soap Disco" and "Myself." The LA crowd couldn't care less about the whole Oasis/Blur British obsession. So Adam did another about-face, making a sudden proclamation that his new vibe was going to be much more granola. He put down his electric guitar for an acoustic, grew a chin beard, and started wearing Birkenstocks and baggy corduroys.

"You guys, I've realized that I'm really just a hippie at heart," he announced very earnestly at band rehearsal one day. "I just think I can be more myself if I'm in cords and Birks and I play acoustic from now on. I can't really deny it anymore. I'm a chill dude! I just want to play mellow music, smoke pot, and have good vibes. You guys are going to have to get used to it, I think. I've been pretending to be something else for too long."

Mickey's scoff and grumble indicated that he was just as annoyed by this as I was. He and I were definitely on the other side of the fence from Adam and Jesse on this one. If I didn't know Adam better, I would have thought this was a real "come-to-Jesus" moment for him (and a colossal disaster for the band), but I was sure that this was just another one of his flights of fancy.

"Adam, this is a phase . . . like Pearl Jam was a phase, and Green Day was a phase, and Oasis was a phase . . . next month it'll be something else," I said rather dismissively. "I like Dave Matthews Band as much as the next guy, dude. But come on! This isn't your one true self . . . it's your true self this week."

"No, dude, I swear to you," Adam protested, "I've been into this vibe for a long time. Ever since French Woods," a performing arts camp that he and Jesse attended. "I just hadn't fully embraced it until now. This isn't going to change, guys! This *is* my true self."

I had to just roll my eyes and go along with it, humoring him for the moment with my terrible impression of a Carter Beauford drum part to accompany the sappy love long, "Angel in Blue Jeans," he had just written (about some girl named Jane he had just met).

Jesse was still more in lockstep with Adam. He loved the idea of jamming more freely and embracing the "positive vibes" with our music and style. Having established their love affair with *Dazed and Confused* in the ninth grade, and then spending a summer together at that camp they spoke of so fondly as some kind of Bohemian paradise for dreamers and lovers, the two of them shared this hippie ideal for the moment, enjoying marathon jam sessions in which they did their best Phish impressions. The resultant music they wrote was still very influenced by Adam's early singer-songwriter inspirations like Paul Simon, Paul McCartney, and Billy Joel, but their aesthetic and style were heading more in the direction of the Grateful Dead. Mickey and I complained to each other privately and only half-heartedly continued to follow their creative lead.

Things were not much better on the business front. As we searched for our new sound, we were just assuming that Reprise would honor their commitment to making a second LP, according to the terms of our contract. However, the management at Warner Bros. had been replaced during the time we were on the road, and all that the new honchos knew about us was that we had already released an album and it hadn't sold. They made it clear to us that even if they were required to honor our contract, they would put no money behind promoting our album, and the record would die on the vine. So we came to an agreement for them to buy us out of our remaining contract at about $30K per band member, and we were dropped from the label's roster like so much trash. Our managers, agents, and attorneys followed suit, and we soon found ourselves back at square one, with me acting as the band's manager, booking our shows at local clubs and sending out mailers to our small group of local fans. Being the control freak that I was, I was happy to jump back into this role, but I don't think that Adam and Jesse were too pleased with it.

I'm sure that the disappointment of all this played a factor in the interpersonal problems we started having within the band as well. It seemed that we were all starting to irritate each other in ways that we hadn't before. From my perspective, I started seeing Adam's teenage attention deficit transitioning into the cockiness of a self-centered young man. He seemed less inclined to compromise or follow anyone else's lead, and he was often coming off to me as arrogant and overly competitive. I had seen this proud side of him in his sometimes-contentious relationship with Alex Greenwald (the handsome lead singer of the band Phantom Planet, which had been our friendly musical rival on the LA scene), but now I felt it more from him within the band as well. It also appeared to me that he just assumed everyone around him would follow and support his every whim. Due to his natural charisma, a lot of his friends would do just that, but as someone who was trying to work with him in a creative and professional capacity, I was growing more and more irritated by his attitude.

I also felt that it was becoming more difficult to get him to focus on anything that wasn't immediately gratifying. Call it ADD, or call it egotism, but I just found it frustrating. His short attention span could often render our band rehearsals scattered, inconsistent, and rather brief. After setting up and just schmoozing for the first hour of a three-hour booking, we would jam for a bit and run through a few songs, before Adam would invariably get bored and want to take a break or just leave early. And he only wanted to play a new song if it was already sounding good—if it was proving difficult to crack or needed more work, he wanted to ditch it and move on to something else that came more easily. It's a testament to his talent and the chemistry of the band that good material often came out of sheer inspiration, without much perspiration. I don't remember us even running through our full set lists very often. We would just play the new songs a couple of times, work on the transitions from one song to the next, then call it a day. I would often try to encourage a better work ethic for the band, but it would mostly fall on deaf ears.

I had one particularly frustrating argument with Adam regarding the nature of talent, in which he contended that he didn't care about ability that was gained through practice and hard work. He believed in "natural talent"—you've either got it or you don't. After one shortened rehearsal, I tried to argue my point as constructively as I could.

"Look, dude, I just want us to be the best band we can be. There's a lot of natural talent in this band. And our chemistry is truly special. But haven't you heard the saying 'Genius is 10 percent inspiration and 90 percent perspiration?' Aren't you inspired by the stories of people who have had to work for thousands of hours and overcome incredible odds to become great?"

"Honestly, no," he responded, to my surprise. "No, I mean I think that's great for people who don't have talent, but it's not inspiring to me. I'm inspired by truly great, natural ability. I think that's the most awesome thing, when somebody is just naturally amazing and driven. Look at Kobe; the dude is nineteen years old, and he's already the best player in the league. You can't teach that. And you can't practice that. It's in his DNA."

Adam seemed to see himself in the raw, young Laker star, who had made a splash in the NBA pretty soon after getting drafted out of high school, but who hadn't fully refined his craft to the level that he would reach later in his career. I found this maddening. It's a given that Adam did have natural talent (and obviously Kobe did too), but that didn't mean he didn't have to work really hard to make the most of that ability. I saw his arguments as self-serving and really just lazy.

"Yes, but Kobe is a selfish player . . . and he's undisciplined," I argued. "He's never going to be *truly* great until he matures and becomes a championship-caliber player. That takes a lot of *hard work* and sacrifice. Sure, they're winning games now, but they're not going to win *titles* until Kobe can learn to be a team player. He's got fucking Shaq on his team. Pass the frigging ball!"

"Look, I could practice the guitar every day for hours like every other geek at Guitar Center, and I'm sure I would get better technically, but that's not what makes an artist great. It's just not," he contended. "It's a nice story, but it's not what people want to listen to. It's not what people pay money to see. People want to see greatness. And you're either born with that shit or you're not. You either have a vision and a fire in what you do as an artist or you don't. It's as simple as that."

"I've always been more of a Magic Johnson fan myself," I countered, knowing Adam was a die-hard fan of the 1980s Lakers as well. I thought maybe this could be a halfway point between us in this argument. "Magic was a guy who could make his whole team great, just by being unselfish and creating opportunities. He figured out how to win by making everyone else on his team look good!"

I wasn't exactly being subtle. Of course, to be fair, the young Kobe grew and matured into the extremely dedicated, hardworking champion the world came to know and love, and Adam's inspiration from him gained a whole other level of meaning later in his career.

Also, to be fair and balanced about the conflict between us, I can admit that my way of going about things with Adam at that point was often equally immature, and it could irritate the hell out of him as well. So the frustration was surely a two-way street. I don't like to think that I was being competitive, but my ego was certainly at play more than I might have admitted. For instance, I began trying to stake my claim in some of the songwriting and creative control again, even handing Adam revised lyric sheets for songs he had written. He was well aware that the lyrics needed to improve from *The Fourth World*, and he had begun making efforts to write his songs about real experiences that actually mattered to him, but for some reason I thought that I had some jurisdiction in this area . . . and I most certainly did not. My lyrics were terrible. If anything, I knew a little more about English literature and journalism than Adam did, but I knew nothing about how to write a pop lyric. Not so subtly, I would give him books of poetry as gifts, and I would prepare my edits of the lyrics, printed out for band rehearsal. To his credit, he did take a few of my suggestions to heart just to appease me, but for the most part he was getting more and more annoyed when I would inject myself to that degree. I don't blame him. I was really just pushing back at him in a rather childish way.

So we found ourselves with a bit of a rift developing within the band. Every show we played and every demo we recorded had an entirely new and different style than the previous one, and if you asked each member of the group what kind of band we were, you might get two, three, or four different answers. Mickey was still on a British kick (everything from the Who to Pulp), but he was also listening to more obscure and avant-garde music by artists influenced by the Velvet Underground. I had fallen in love with Fiona Apple (both her deeply confessional songwriting and the brilliant studio creations of musician/producer Jon Brion and drummer Matt Chamberlain). Jesse was deeply inspired by the forward-thinking visions of Radiohead, and he had started taking piano lessons to incorporate more of his classical influences. And Adam just wanted to write his sentimental love songs of mirth and pleasure, perhaps to become the next Dave Matthews (whom every college girl and her mother loved at that time). I think that we all still believed that we had something bonding us together in terms of chemistry, but it was being stretched and strained by the searching that we were all doing at that point in our lives.

My frustration with Adam (and the group in general) was making me more inclined to define my identity separately from the band, so I started thinking about other ways that I could find some fulfillment on my own. I wasn't exactly in good academic standing at UCLA, after spending the better part of my time there working on the Reprise album, but I decided to pursue reenrolling and finally declaring a major. After having to do some petitioning to drop a couple of classes that I had just completely blown off during the height of the *Fourth World* sessions, I managed to get my transcript in order enough to enroll for the fall of that year. Mickey had applied and gotten into UCLA's theater department, so he started attending at that time too. We actually even took a screenwriting class together that summer. Not to be outdone, and equally fed up with the dissension in the band, Adam and Jesse packed up all their stuff one day and went to New York together to do a semester at a music school on Long Island called Five Towns College. I was pretty resentful of that decision, thinking that they were sending a clear signal to me and Mickey that they wanted to do their own thing, and sensing that they were moving further and further away from Kara's Flowers.

Although their departure (and the uncertain future of the band) was disappointing to me, going back to school and doing some soul-searching allowed me to take pride in my individual pursuits again, and I quickly began to enjoy college. I declared an English major, wanting to stay within the arts and humanities but not focus on music for a while. Perhaps I was still driven by the failure of my ninth-grade English class to finally prove myself as a man of letters. It was also a way to give myself a real challenge: the English program at UCLA was notorious for being very difficult and requiring a ton of reading, something that never actually came that naturally to me. I read rather meticulously, making sure I digest every word, so consuming massive quantities of literature every week seemed like a daunting task. I really wanted to extend myself further into uncharted territory, however. Having a new goal, a new task at hand, and something that set my sights a little further beyond what I would have previously tried, made me feel inspired and rejuvenated. But what the future would bring for the band was anyone's guess at that point . . .

I just happened to run into Brad Delson on campus the day I was dealing with my transcript/reenrollment situation. He was finishing up and getting his degree, just as I was starting up again. I asked him how things had worked out with that group he had put together, and he said they had just finally signed a major record deal, with Warner Bros., of all labels. I was surprised but very happy for him and Dave. Apparently, they had auditioned guys from all around the country to be their new lead singer, and they had found this guy from Arizona who could really scream. Brad invited me to come check them out at the Roxy that weekend, and I humored him, but I fully expected the band to be as amateurish as they had been a couple of years earlier. However, when I arrived at the venue for the show, I saw their big, professional banner advertising "Linkin Park," and when they kicked into their first song, they looked and sounded like a very polished and heavy rap-rock band. Then their new front man, Chester Bennington, let loose one of his signature screams, and I thought to myself, "Oh . . . I get it now."

Brad also invited me to attend his graduation party, and although I wouldn't know anyone there, I decided to go and try to be social. That wasn't like me, but I was trying to embrace a more outgoing side of myself.

by changing my attitude. What I had once looked at as a "phony" putting on a happy face and being outwardly social, I now viewed as better approach toward living my life. I really wanted to embrace a positive energy and to bring that energy into my new relationships. made a very conscious decision at that point to take the proverbial out of my ass, trying to be as open-minded and optimistic about new ple and new experiences as I possibly could.

Andy and Barry lived just down the block from each other on a stretch Glenrock Avenue in Westwood, which housed a big circle of their UCLA nds just off campus. I was astonished at how many interesting and gaging people there were in this one small community of college kids. dy lived in a three-bedroom apartment with five other roommates, most whom were really silly and fun as well; Barry lived just up the street in other apartment with a similar setup; and up and down the street were partment buildings filled with truly wonderful and sociable people. There ere actors and comedians in the group (Kelvin Yu has gone on to win an Emmy for writing television comedy). There were musicians and singers (Sara Bareilles has gone on to write and record massive hit records, tour the world, and even write a successful Broadway musical). There were cool surfer dudes from down south, "hella good" Bay Area kids from up north, and they were all part of this very friendly and inspiring community. I was enamored immediately.

I also decided to loosen my previous ban on "partying" around this time, because on occasion alcohol became a convenient way to facilitate this new, fun side of my personality. I wasn't drinking every night, far from it. At most I was going to the clubs two or three nights a week, but when we went out, I went pretty hard, priding myself on the ability to mix four and five different kinds of liquor in one evening. But I wasn't drinking to escape any pain or to drown any sorrows. Alcohol was just a way to enhance all the good feelings I was having and to "let loose," so to speak. Having been a guy who often had difficulty feeling present and committed to the experience of the moment, I found that a little buzz seemed to cure me of my self-consciousness for a time.

Besides, I had just moved back in with my parents afte
touring, my girlfriend Taryn had just gone off to colleg
Pomona, and now Adam and Jesse were gone, leaving n
the moment, so I was looking for opportunities to go c
new friends.

I ended up seated at a table with some very welco
dents whom I was just meeting for the first time, includin
guys named Andy and Barry, who were the absolute life of
was clearly the affable clown or the mascot of their circl
the whole table and even the tables on either side of us wit
antics. I could also see right away that he and Andy had a
dic chemistry between them, as if they had been writing part
improv troupe together. As it turned out, they had been perfor
campus as a three-piece comedy band called the Bicycling Mari
with another friend of theirs named Jason. I was intrigued with
utes of meeting these guys. There was just something very en
warm about their sense of humor and personalities.

Barry was taking everything on the table and making a prop
for his shtick, and at one point he started encouraging the rest of
involved, making a party game out of it. I had never really been
improv, but these guys were so enjoyable that I decided to step ou
comfort zone. I think they were surprised when I could keep up wit
quick wit and even take it to another level of silliness, and I could
their eyes that they knew I was a kindred spirit.

Meeting Andy and Barry was the catalyst for some pretty profe
changes in my life. There was something so innocently fun about tl
that inspired me to find a lighter side of my being. Having been a pre
miserable teenager, and having not even really enjoyed life on the ro
in a band with my best friends, I suddenly realized that a lot of my ow
unhappiness had been self-imposed. I recognized that if my expectation
of the world (and of the people in it) were always pessimistic, my cynicism
would become a self-fulfilling prophecy. It was something of an epiphany
to accept that I could choose to be a happier and more positive person,

simpl
act of
just a
more
So I
sticl
peo

of
fri
en
Al
ol
a
a

When Adam and Jesse came home from New York after that semester, they found a new man in me. I don't know if it was apparent to them right away, but I was in a much better place mentally, and I was more capable of putting my frustrations aside in order to talk about how (or if) we were going to proceed as a band. We needed to talk, and we did. I told Adam that I was coming over, and we sat down for about an hour, to really get it all out openly and honestly for the first time in a while.

"I guess I called this meeting because I just want to see where you're at with everything," I opened. "You guys picked up and left for New York all of a sudden, and we haven't talked much since then. I don't really know what you're feeling about the band at this point."

"Yeah, I mean, Jesse and I have definitely talked about it a lot, and I don't know . . . we certainly enjoyed writing on our own for a little bit . . . but there's still something with the four of us that is worth trying to maintain," he said half encouragingly, half reluctantly.

"Okay . . . I mean, I agree . . . I just think we're in a weird place right now . . . I don't think any of us are very clear about what we're doing. I mean . . . do you want me to write with you guys again?"

"I want you to be my drummer," he said bluntly. I didn't like the way he said "my" drummer, but I let it slide for the moment. "Honestly, I guess I have just been having some trouble with the way you try to get in the middle of the songwriting sometimes. Jesse and I have a thing together that works . . . And I want you and Mickey to be involved in the arrangements . . . of course . . . but honestly, no, I don't want you to 'write' with us."

This was hard to hear, but I understood. They did have a special bond together as songwriters, and I couldn't really compete with it. And I could also understand how it could be frustrating to deal with my attempts to do so. "But you still want to be in a band with me?" I asked matter of factly.

"I still think you're an awesome drummer, and I still think that we have a unique chemistry together, so yes, I do . . . but I just think that we're best when Jesse and I write the songs."

I paused for a moment to think, making sure that I would express myself clearly.

"I feel the same way about our chemistry as a creative unit, but I'll be totally honest . . . it's kind of hard for me to just follow along with whatever you and Jesse want to do. I feel that I have more to offer than that, and I don't like to think of myself as just a 'drummer.' I also think that we've always been at our best when we're a democracy, with ideas coming from all directions."

"I can see that . . . and I do think that we all bring something to the table . . . but I guess I'm just feeling like I want our roles to be a little more clearly defined at this point."

It was a difficult and uncomfortable conversation, but we were able to reach an understanding. I accepted that injecting myself into the writing chemistry between him and Jesse was counterproductive, and he accepted that my input to the creative process was more than just being "his drummer." This agreement and compromise allowed us to start to move forward with a new phase in our friendship and collaboration, and I know that it was very helpful to put everything out there on the table honestly.

There was a significant turning point, however, at which it became clear that we were rededicating ourselves to each other as a band. Shortly after we started things up again together, Rob and Bob Cavallo called a meeting with Adam and Jesse at Hollywood Records, where the two of them had taken up the helm as president and head of A&R. Immediately after this meeting, Adam called me and Mickey, inviting us to join them at the apartment in West LA that he and Jesse had just moved into together. We showed up there a half hour later, and we could tell immediately that their mood was tense for some reason. Both Adam and Jesse clearly had something on their minds. We all congregated in Jesse's new bedroom, and Adam started the conversation.

"Listen, guys, Jesse and I just had a meeting with the Cavallos over at Hollywood Records," he started. I would have been very excited by this news if I couldn't tell that there was more to it. They were both still very serious. "They want to sign us to a new record deal . . . just me and Jesse."

My heart sank. Mickey and I both took a deep breath, fidgeting as this bombshell sank in. Breaking up the band to isolate the meal ticket was so common in those days that it was a record industry cliché, but you never think it's going to happen to you. I knew that Rob had been around the four of us enough to know that we were a group full of big personalities with big opinions, and it might seem to him that it wasn't a workable situation, but I was still extremely insulted and angry to hear of this betrayal.

"And what did you tell them?" I asked hesitantly.

"We thought about it for a long time, and it was a really hard conversation to have . . . and a difficult decision to make," Jesse said. "But we decided that we're not going to break up the band. We started this thing together, and we're going to make it to the top together."

My emotions were all over the place in that moment. I was still very angry at Rob for stabbing us in the back in that way, but I was also deeply moved by the level of love that Adam and Jesse showed by saying they were choosing to continue with the band in its original lineup. This was an incredibly profound statement of loyalty and commitment, especially considering that we had no other leads for another record deal at that point. I expressed my anger at Rob so that they could hear it—"SERIOUSLY . . . FUCK THAT GUY!"—and as soon as I said it, it was off my chest, and we could just celebrate this amazing moment of rejuvenated band spirit. Adam and Jesse understood that this was both difficult and inspiring news to digest, so they could appreciate how mixed my emotions were.

In a strange way, this was the kick in the butt that we needed to redouble our efforts as a band and as a partnership. I think all four of us felt a renewed sense of dedication to one another, and it definitely helped us foster a better working relationship. I don't think I had really felt that Adam and Jesse actually wanted to continue with Mickey and me as a creative unit until I witnessed this remarkable show of dedication.

I decided at that point that it was only fair for me to take the new positive attitude I had adopted elsewhere in my life into my relationship with Adam. As frustrated as I had been with him before he and Jesse left for New York, I was ready to do my part to make our friendship and partnership work. Petty disputes or frustrations based on ego and competition were just totally counterproductive. I also realized that the same axiom about my unhappiness applied to this relationship: a lot of what was frustrating me was actually self-imposed. Expecting someone to change their basic nature is just setting yourself up for disappointment and frustration: we all have our strengths, and we all have our faults, and you often have to take the good with the bad. The fact of the matter was that, for all our differences, Adam was a very important person in my life, we had been close friends for a long time, he brought a lot to the table in terms of talent, and I wasn't prepared to walk away from all that. I loved the guy. So, if I allowed the things that irritated me to make me miserable, I had no one to blame but myself. I had to either accept those things and embrace him for everything that he was or move on. I chose to embrace him, and it made all the difference. He chose to embrace me right back, and as a result, the renaissance in my personal life started to correlate with a rebirth in the band's life as well.

chapter 9

the renaissance

I n the fall of 1999, Andy invited me to move into his apartment in West-wood as his new roommate. I was elated to join my funny new friend and his buddies in their three-bedroom setup on that delightful stretch of Glenrock Avenue, brimming with new opportunities for fun and adventure. Sure, I had to accept some nonideal living conditions ("slumming it," so to speak) in order to enjoy the fruits of this arrangement, but my new positive attitude made it relatively easy for me to go with the flow. I shared a bedroom with Andy that was about the size of a closet, and the apartment in total looked and smelled like a trash heap.

The other two bedrooms housed three more guys and one girl, all of whom would soon become close friends of mine as well. In one room there was Shawn Tellez, a charmingly handsome young man from Orange County who had a way with the ladies, but who also had low-grade narco-lepsy, the smelliest feet you've ever encountered in your life, and a little bird that would sit on his head and shit in his hair. His roommate was another good-looking kid, named Jason, who was pretty shy at first, being a little younger and straight out of Sonoma wine country, but who would come out of his shell in time. In the third room there was Travis, an adorable little surfer dude who would amuse us all by stripping down to his underwear and doing uncanny impressions of various wild animals (and who was also known for having enormous balls, which he would take out at parties after some encouragement from the crowd). His roommate was Erica, who made her own clothes with a sewing machine, and she was crazy enough to want to live in that filthy dump of an apartment with us five "gentlemen."

I took it upon myself to scrub and sanitize the revolting bathroom and kitchen the first day I moved in, saying to myself that I'd rather they be clean than wait around for someone else to clean them. After all, not a lot of college kids are as obsessively neat as I was. The bathroom looked like it hadn't been disinfected the entire year these guys had lived there before me, but I was just so excited to be living with all these truly entertaining people around me that I was willing to do whatever it took to make it a livable environment. And these guys were truly disgusting. The couches were ones that had been thrown away, then brought up from the street, covered with filth. The carpet was affectionately referred to as "the pube rug," because they didn't even own a vacuum. The bathroom was caked with scum and littered with dirty surfing equipment, and the kitchen was covered with dirty pans and grime, with lord knows what else growing in the cabinets and the refrigerator. I had to spend the entire first week doing housework just so I could sit on the couch and walk on the carpet without my shoes on. However, none of this could take away from the fun I was having with these guys. This was my true college experience, finally.

As if six of us weren't enough, we also had an honorary roommate in my close friend Jordan, whom Barry and I had met in the English program. She was a very smart, cool, artistic chick from Venice, who had a sense of humor and wit that gelled with mine immediately, and she quickly took to our group of friends as well. She crashed on our couch most nights of the week, and she, Barry, Andy, and I quickly formed a quartet of best friends, spending all our free time together. Our various backgrounds created an interesting blend of personalities in our little group.

It didn't take long for Adam to notice the excitement we were enjoying there in Westwood. After we had that honest conversation to begin the new phase of our friendship, I started inviting him to join us for midnight basketball, and he even started crashing on our other couch some nights. He worked his charm with the group, dating a couple of the cute girls on the block, but it also meant that he and I were spending more time together again. We would go down to Westwood Village to watch Laker games over a pitcher of beer, we would hang out and joke with all my new friends, and we just started having fun as buddies again, the way we used to when we started the band. The weird thing is that, on top of all that, we had both started listening to a lot of the same music during the time that we had been apart. Stevie Wonder became the centerpiece of a lot of our new inspiration, and we both got into some hip-hop and R&B as well. He was obsessed with Lauryn Hill, and I was listening to tracks produced by artists like the Neptunes and Timbaland. We were both really into Questlove's beats on D'Angelo's new album *Voodoo*, as we were also getting turned on to older R&B like Marvin Gaye and Al Green. The former weirdness surrounding conversations about our influences quickly evaporated as we shared a new passion for these styles of music, inspired by the possibilities they could bring to our own music. As a result, some of our new songs had a sultrier feel, emulating these more soulful grooves.

Whereas before the break we couldn't seem to get on the same page, all of a sudden, the band had a more unified vision for what we were trying to do with the new music we had begun writing. Jesse was playing the piano more at this point, and he was incorporating some of his jazz and classical compositions into the R&B-influenced stuff as well. This really opened up our sound to a fresh area of inspiration, which made our new music much more interesting and unique. We were no longer bound by the predictable four-chord structure of the pop-rock music from our previous incarnation, and we felt freed up to explore different genres that were unique and exciting to us. Our set list was still a little too "all over the place" for people to figure out exactly what kind of band we were, but at least we all felt that we were moving in the right direction.

A transitional moment in discovering our reborn sound came in the form of a nine-song demo/EP we titled the *Stagg Street Recordings*. We recorded the whole thing in about a week, printed up CDs, and started selling them at shows, so that our revitalized fan base could get a sense of the new material. The disc was definitely overly eclectic in style, every track sounding like a different band (not to mention that the recording was a little lo-fi), but there were a few songs in the bunch that reflected the more soulful approach we were starting to incorporate. The Stevie Wonder influence was apparent on a couple of songs in particular. Another track titled "As Things Collide" became popular with the crowd living around me in Westwood, as the era of ripping and burning CDs was in full swing.

Trying to hustle and make things happen for Kara's Flowers again, I grabbed the enthusiasm of the moment by promoting the band around campus. I printed up flyers for our shows and distributed them everywhere I could think—I put them in newspaper boxes, left them in common areas, and just passed them around to students as much as I could. I encouraged our friends to burn CDs and spread the music, wanting to build a fan base the old-fashioned way, by word of mouth. It seemed that my personal experience of school, my social experience with my new friends, and my life in the world of Kara's Flowers were coalescing and synergizing into something I couldn't have anticipated: a sort of renaissance of all three worlds working together to create a rejuvenated spirit in everything that I was doing. Sure, it was sometimes a struggle to make time for everything, and I remember writing some of my papers at 4 AM after a night out with my friends or a rehearsal with the band, but I was really feeding off the energy I was getting from all these new inspirations, so I was able to get everything done when I needed to.

The one casualty of my jam-packed schedule, unfortunately, was my relationship with Taryn, who was off at Scripps College. Some weekends I would make the drive out there to visit her, but most times she would come into town to see me. However, with my booming social life at UCLA and everything else going on, she would often complain that it seemed I wanted to spend my time with my friends more than her. It wasn't that we fell out of love or that anything went sour in the relationship; I was just so engaged with what I was doing around campus that our relationship had taken a back seat for me. I understood that this was not fair to her. I also took the fact that my passions were lying elsewhere at that point as a sign that it was time to move on. It was extremely difficult to break up with Taryn, and I know that I broke her heart, but it was the right thing to do in the long run. My life was just branching off into a lot of different directions, and I was in no place to try to maintain a relationship with someone I could only give a small fraction of my attention.

On top of all the shows the band was booking in Hollywood and elsewhere around the city (and even some down in Orange County), I managed to get us a weekly slot at the only bar in Westwood that allowed live music. It was called the Westwood Brewing Company, and it would play a significant role in the next phase of our lives. Brew Co., as we called it, was a popular spot for the Thursday-night party crowd, and more importantly, it was where the hot girls hung out. Even the bartenders and cocktail waitresses were very attractive young women. Given the built-in crowd, I told the club's managers that I guaranteed we would have a line down the block within a month if they let us have Thursday nights. And we did just that. The first week, it was mostly just my group of friends in attendance, but within one month the club was turning people away at the door because it had reached capacity. Hundreds of college kids were lining up down the street, just waiting to get in.

Doing an extended residency at Brew Co. was not just good promotion; it was a great opportunity for us to work on our chops as a live band. We had to fill a whole evening of entertainment each week, so we decided to do two separate hour-long sets, going from about 10 PM until well after midnight. We started jamming and improvising more in our set, incorporating a lot of covers, which we had never really done before. For the first time, it was our responsibility to provide the party for the evening, and we relished the opportunity. We included some grooving crowd favorites like

Stevie Wonder's "Boogie On Reggae Woman," the Rolling Stones's "Beast of Burden," and Rufus featuring Chaka Khan's "Tell Me Something Good," to supplement the material from *Stagg Street*. We brought friends and other musicians onstage to jam with us, and overall it became just a really loose party vibe, which was very conducive to our growth and development as a band. This seemed like the perfect intersection of all of our influences to me: Adam and Jesse got to indulge their jam-band fantasies; we were beginning to incorporate our new, more soulful appeal; and we could rock out anytime we wanted to in the set. More than any of that, though, it just felt like a big night out with all my friends. We didn't sound like the Beatles anymore, but we had found our Cavern Club.

During one of our rehearsals around this time, Jesse started playing one of his new jazz progressions, to which I quickly put a grooving beat. The feel of what we were playing inspired Adam to write a melody and lyric on the spot (about one of the lovely ladies he was dating in Westwood). In the chorus he sang, "That may be all I need / in darkness, she is all I see / come and rest your bones with me / driving slow on Sunday morning, and I never want to leave." This very romantic lyric coupled with our jazzy and soulful groove quickly made "Sunday Morning" a crowd favorite at our live shows. I can admit now that the beat I put to Jesse's progression was probably at least a little inspired by Jamiroquai's "Virtual Insanity," which was a big hit on the radio at the time. However, the larger inspiration for all of us was Stevie Wonder, whom I know Jamiroquai was extremely influenced by as well. So I don't feel at all bad for coming up with a similar groove! All good music takes a little from here, a little from there, right?

In the spring of 2000, I signed the band up for UCLA's big talent show, the Spring Sing, realizing that it would garner an audience of thousands at the varsity tennis stadium. I'll admit that we did not take this event as seriously as we probably should have at the time. Because we had been signed to a major record label, we considered ourselves above the fray of most of the other amateurs who would be performing. We attended very few of the many rehearsals, and we probably picked the wrong song for such an event. I think we already had "Sunday Morning" in our arsenal by then, and we should have played that, but instead we picked one of our longer, more involved arrangements, in an attempt to show off our chops. We hadn't considered that there would be other artists on that stage who might offer something more immediate.

One of my hilarious new buddies, Josh Covitt, was a member of the comedy troupe that hosted the event, doing sketches between the musical performances that were much more impressive than I had expected from a school talent show. Immediately, the show seemed more professional than I was anticipating. Josh went on to perform in the Upright Citizens Brigade and do a bunch of funny commercials and other acting gigs. But the thing we really hadn't predicted was that there would be other musicians who were more remarkable than us. Most notably, my friend Sara Bareilles completely stole the show. She won not only best individual performance but also best ensemble performance, as well as best overall performance. She sang one of her beautiful original compositions, and her a cappella group Awaken was more engaging than our rambling six-minute jam session. Sara was *not* a diamond in the rough at that early stage of her development. She was a well-polished singer, musician, and songwriter, even then.

Our lackluster performance at Spring Sing was really just a miscalculation on our part; we thought that we were appealing to a college crowd that loved Dave Matthews Band and therefore would appreciate a long, intricate song. We just forgot to practice it! But I think we took from that experience an important lesson: most crowds just want to hear a good song, sung by a good voice, and performed with sincerity. That's what Sara delivered that we did not, so it was a teachable moment for us, for sure.

Despite that one misfire, the buzz from our reinvigorated fan base was getting around town, and we started attracting attention from the industry again. One of the first people to take notice was Sheryl Crow's manager "Scooter" Weintraub. However, he was a little noncommittal about his interest. I played him the demo that we had made of "Sunday Morning," and his only comment was that it sounded too much like Sting and Dave Matthews Band. Granted, that early demo had a saxophone solo (played by Adam's dad, Fred Levine) in place of what would later become the third verse!

Also around this time, an old friend of ours named Jordan Feldstein entered our professional life. Jordi's dad, Rich, had been our business manager since the Reprise album, and I knew Jordi from playing soccer together as a kid, but Adam had actually remained very close with him since growing up together. The last time I had seen him was when Adam and I went to his little brother Jonah's bar mitzvah, but now he was interested in getting involved with our band as a manager.

When Jordi stepped into the fold of our band, we could tell right away that he was a real go-getter. He was just my age at twenty-two years old, and he was a junior agent at one of the major booking agencies at the time, but he wanted to branch out on his own, to take on our band as his first foray into artist management. This was a bold move for a guy who was just getting his feet wet in the entertainment business. Sure, he had grown up around it, having Rich as his dad, but now he wanted to stake his career on a band that had no record label and certainly no guarantee of success.

We had only a slight hesitation about letting Jordi manage us, based on his lack of experience, but he certainly made up for that by showing us his commitment on day one. When we met to interview him for the position (upstairs at Brew Co.), he showed up with a bunch of boxes of brand-new Motorola StarTAC flip phones. This was a big deal in those days; I don't think any of us had cell phones yet, certainly not the nice ones he gave us. After walking in with these impressive courting gifts, he said to us, "I need to be able to reach you guys 24/7." What a baller move! Scooter Weintraub didn't stand a chance after that. We were in with Jordi 100 percent.

Jordi's excitement about the band was infectious, and it pushed us to take a big leap forward in finding our new direction. One fateful day at band rehearsal, we were talking about the hip-hop tracks to which we were all listening, when we agreed that Aaliyah's "Are You That Somebody?" was the hottest track on the radio. I half-jokingly suggested that we write a song directly influenced by that track. Sure, we had started playing some jazzy progressions and, sure, we had started incorporating groovier beats, but the idea of directly emulating a hip-hop track seemed ludicrous for a band like us. The band was actually excited by the idea, however, so Jesse suggested that I come up with a beat inspired by that track, to which he would come up with a piano riff, similar to how we had written "Sunday Morning." The beat to "Not Coming Home" was literally the first thing I played, and the riff that would be the basis for that song was the first thing that Jesse played. Adam sat down with his lyric pad and wrote the melody and lyrics while we jammed on that groove, and we wrote "Not Coming Home" in all of about thirty minutes. We had written songs quickly before, but this time it felt almost as if we were channeling something. That moment of inspiration was a huge turning point for what we were trying to do with our music from that day forward, and it became the template for a series of songs that came in quick succession after, including the tracks "Through with You" and "Secret."

Jordi could see that we were onto something, so he wanted to get us into the studio to make a demo ASAP. Only, he wanted to make sure we did it right, so he pulled some strings to get us back into the $2,000-a-day Conway Studios with a top-notch producer at the helm. Given the expense, Conway had seemed totally unrealistic for us ever since we recorded the basic tracks for *The Fourth World* there. But Jordi was a man of action, and he wanted to be sure that everything we did was top-shelf.

Normally an unsigned band wouldn't have access to the kind of producer that a record label would hire for them to make their album, but Adam was living with three rather connected friends in a house in Los Feliz at the time: Sam Farrar (son of producer/songwriter John Farrar), Savannah Buffett (daughter of Jimmy Buffett), and Will Nash (son of Graham Nash). Both Jimmy Buffett and Graham Nash had a long history with session drummer Russ Kunkel, who came highly recommended as a producer for us, along with his engineer son, Nate. Russ was an inspiring guru for the recording. He had a total Obi-Wan Kenobi vibe, which was exactly what we needed in order to harness the "force" of our band. Nate was a very talented engineer/mixer to boot, and the session that transpired would create a new five-song demo we called "the Conway Five."

Working with a famous session drummer at the helm (and one who was most known for his incredibly smooth beats and grooves) was very encouraging to me, given where I was in my development. Russ wasn't the kind of drummer I had listened to growing up, but as we were making the transition to more groove-oriented music, his calm consistency both as a musician and as a *super*-chill presence in the studio really allowed me to sink into the vibe that we were trying to achieve with the new material. Originally, Jordi could swing only a couple of days at Conway with the Kunkels as a pro bono, one-off session, but when word got back about how inspired and unique the session had been, Graham Nash himself offered to put up the dough to finish the session properly. I don't know how much money he shelled out exactly (maybe $10–$20K I would guess), but we ended up working at Conway with the Kunkels for a full two weeks, recording the four new songs that marked our new sound: "Not Coming Home," "Through with You," "Secret," and a future B-side called "Ragdoll." To round it out, Nate worked his magic on a greatly improved remix of "Sunday Morning" to complete the five-song disc. This recording was a massive step forward for us creatively. We played around with the use of space in a way that we never had before. We focused on groove and vibe, working in an atmosphere unlike anything we'd created before as well. Every night during those two weeks, we had a bunch of our friends at the studio, and the session took on the energy of a big party. All the good vibrations that we had been feeling in our personal lives were present in the studio for the recording of those songs, and you can hear it on the tape.

The Los Feliz house full of music royalty became party central that year. It seemed that the entire up-and-coming hipster scene of Silver Lake and the surrounding areas could be seen hanging out and partying at that place any night of the week. Even young Hollywood celebrities like Jake Gyllenhaal, Natalie Portman, and Ashton Kutcher started making their way into those gatherings. This created an interesting dichotomy for me, from one side of LA to the other. On the Westside, my college life in Westwood was in full swing, with my big circle of friends representing more of the collegiate experience. But on the other side of town was this new community of Hollywood hipsters and artists who hung out at "the Lowry house" (as it was known, due to its location on Lowry Road). Just as I had grown up at the intersection of LA's diverse neighborhoods, I was once again strad-dling two worlds on either side of the city. At first, it didn't seem that these two worlds would mix very well. And when I started bringing my West-side friends over to the Eastside parties, sure enough, they stuck out like sore thumbs. I'm pretty sure that most of the hipsters thought my friends were just a bunch of preppie jocks, "cheese-dicks," and no-style schlubs. But over time, the band and their cool friends started to warm up to the salt-of-the-earth quality that my college buddies were bringing, and it began to coalesce into one big lovefest, with our band at the center of the scene.

The introduction of the Conway Five to this big, young-Hollywood crowd was game-changing. We started playing those new songs in our set, and they were infectious. At first, there were looks of shock and disbelief when we would break into the Michael Jackson–inspired harmony in the chorus of "Not Coming Home." We had all grown up with MJ and Prince in the 1980s (like everyone else), but it was pretty audacious to emulate the King of Pop, especially with a Timbaland-inspired beat underneath, and even more especially when done with live drums and guitars by four white kids from Brentwood High School. This unique combination of influ-ences created a buzz around town pretty quickly, and our shows started to become a place to spot young celebrities. At one show at the Viper Room, all the hobbits from the new *Lord of the Rings* movie showed up!

Many of my friends and roommates on Glenrock graduated in the sum-mer of 2000, so I moved out of that apartment and into my aunt Michele Lee's house in Holmby Hills, staying close to Westwood to finish up my last few quarters. This arrangement was almost too good to be true. Michele had had a long, successful career, starting on Broadway in the 1960s and acting in film and television up through the '90s, but now she was back in New York, doing a play again on Broadway. Placed in the position of house-sitting, I had the run of her massive estate, and I really took advan-tage of it. I started having my own barbecues and pool parties there, trying to outdo the hipsters in Los Feliz. I heard through the grapevine that Adam thought I was a little spoiled and undeserving of this level of luxury, but who was he to talk? Savannah and his other rich friends were paying for him to live rent-free at that amazing old-Hollywood house in Los Feliz. We were all living the good life at that point!

It was during the time I was living at my aunt's house that I met Shantell. I was originally introduced to Shan, a bartender and server at Brew Co., through a mutual friend named Amber, a slightly crazy (or a lot crazy) girl who also worked there and whom Adam and I had both "dated" for a brief moment. Adam wrote the lyrics to the very sexy song "Secret" about a jaunt to Las Vegas with Amber, which ended with them pulling the car off the highway somewhere in the desert. Apparently, Amber was playing the demo of that song to all her friends (including Shan) on a girls' trip to Vegas, and that had been Shan's first introduction to the band. Amber also claimed that the 311 song "Amber" was about her. I have no idea if that is true, but it tracks.

Shan had been serving us drinks at Brew Co. for some time, but for whatever reason I hadn't pursued her yet, even though she was absolutely stunning, with big, hazel eyes like a Disney princess. I was dating a few other girls around that time, and my attention was pretty scattered from everything else going on in my life. However, one night, as I was loading in for our regular Thursday-night show, Shan walked in the front door just as I was walking in the back, and we caught each other's eyes. It was the first time I had really seen her out from behind the bar and not wearing a Westwood Brewing Co. T-shirt and apron, and I was stopped in my tracks by her beauty, staring at her while I still held two big drum cases in my arms. She waved at me, and I thought to myself, "Who is that??? I think I would remember *her*!" I paused for a moment, just looking into her eyes from across the room, and then she gave me a little knowing smile, recognizing that I had become mesmerized. I finally put my drum cases down and walked right over to her.

"Hi, I'm Ryan," I said with a big smile forming on my face.

"I know. I've been serving you your food and drinks for months," she said with a coy little grin, telling me she wasn't holding it against me too badly.

"Really? Here? Wow . . . I'm sorry. I guess I've just been distracted get-ting ready to play and stuff." I tried to cover my embarrassment. I'm sure I was blushing.

She laughed it off. "It's okay. You're talking to me now."

"Yes . . . I am." I was hypnotized by her eyes and her lips as I talked to her. I found her face strangely calming and exciting at the same time. I had never had this kind of confidence talking to a beautiful woman before. "Listen, I've gotta set up for the show now, but can we talk after we finish? I really want to talk to you more."

"Of course we can . . ." She was still grinning as she walked away up the stairs to the other side of the restaurant. I had that much more reason to play my best that night.

When we wrapped our set for the evening, I was finally able to walk over to the table where she and her friend had been sitting, and I asked if I could get them a drink. She had a better idea.

"Why don't you grab your friend over there, so Fran has someone to talk to, and the four of us can go somewhere a little quieter?"

When she said that, she was looking at Barry, who was entertaining everyone around him as usual, but I grabbed him and asked if he wanted to join me on this impromptu double date. He was more than happy to oblige. The bar that we went to ended up being equally noisy, so I then decided to invite them all back to "my place," so that we could actually hear each other.

The four of us jumped in my Ford Explorer, and we rode through West-wood toward Holmby Hills. Shan was in the passenger seat next to me, and I could see that she looked a little confused as we were driving into a more and more outrageously expensive neighborhood. I decided to let my little charade go on a little longer. We pulled up to my aunt's big, empty man-sion, and I clicked open the huge gate into her front courtyard. There was a shocked silence in the car for a moment.

"This is *your* place?" Shan said, with a little skepticism in her voice.

"Yeah, this is my place . . . ," I said casually. God bless Barry for not ruining my little ruse yet. I gave Shan a little glance and a smile to let her know that I was just pulling her chain, but I didn't say anything about it just yet. I think she was beginning to figure out that I was just house-sitting, but I thought maintaining a little mystery would be fun.

The four of us spent the next few hours sitting on the bed of one of the guest rooms, talking about everything we could think of. Barry was his usual, amusing self, but he actually played it a little cooler than normal, allowing both of us to talk to our respective dates a little more. I appreciated that. Somehow, in the midst of the conversation, the topic of 1980s music came up, as we reminisced about our childhoods. It was then that Shan revealed her love for *Headbangers Ball*–era hair-metal bands.

"*You liked Mötley Crüe?*" I said, stunned by her admission.

"Of course! I was obsessed with Nikki Sixx. He was so hot!" she said. "My best friend was more of a Guns N' Roses girl. She was in love with Slash."

"That's amazing! Oh my god, you guys were such cool girls! I was more of a Tommy Lee guy, of course. His stick twirls made me want to be a drummer!" I was giddy.

"Yeah, I liked Blas Elias from Slaughter more. He was a very pretty man. He had amazing hair! I don't know if he was a good drummer, but I was totally in love with him." She laughed. "We all thought that the bad boys in those bands could be set straight if they just loved us enough," she said sarcastically. I thought that was adorable.

"Have you ever noticed that half of those bands were just doing a really bad Led Zeppelin impression? Like Slaughter, for instance—that dude was just trying to sound exactly like Robert Plant. And most of the drummers were just doing a terrible John Bonham impression." I didn't know if I was losing her with this question. It was one thing for her to like '80s power ballads—it was another thing to throw down the Zeppelin gauntlet.

"Yeah, but none of them were as good as Led Zeppelin, so you couldn't really tell," she said quickly. That was it. I was smitten.

Shan became a fixture in my life from that day forward. We talked every night on the phone, until we finally had the opportunity to have our first proper date, for which I just brought in some food, and we ate and talked all night. After that first evening alone, we started spending pretty much every night together. She would come over right after she got off her shift at Brew Co., and we would just hang out, usually until the sun came up. We really opened up to each other pretty early on in our relationship, and it was clear that we had a much deeper connection than I had ever experienced before. She was not perfect, and neither was I, but we seemed to understand and have compassion for each other in a way that felt very satisfying and comfortable. She was more complicated than Taryn, but she certainly wasn't as complicated as my first girlfriend! I felt that I had found the right mixture of someone who could understand the darker sides of me and someone who had the maturity required for an adult relationship.

Shan had had a rough background growing up, with all kinds of traumas that I won't go into, but she really impressed me with how tough and independent she was. Not coming from privilege like a lot of the people I knew, she had literally worked her way through college at UCLA, graduating cum laude in the process (she was extremely smart on top of being stunningly gorgeous). Very nobly, Shan had put off a University of Washington graduate program in social work, in order to take sole care of her dying father, just a couple of years before we met. However, you wouldn't guess that she had a rough past, judging from how fun she could be with me and my big group of friends. They took to her immediately, as she could hang with us like one of the guys. I loved the fact that my friends really seemed to like her and liked us together. That meant a lot to me.

One night, after she had been out with some of her friends for most of the evening, she came over late, and we were standing in my aunt's kitchen for a moment, when she hopped up on the counter, sitting with her legs hanging over the edge. She gestured for me to come to her, and I sauntered over close, putting my hands on her legs and my face close to hers. She looked deep into my eyes as if she were looking into my soul, and I took a deep breath, soaking her in as well. We weren't doing anything particularly special that night or in that moment, other than just really looking at each other and feeling each other's presence.

"This can't be happening . . . this wasn't supposed to happen," I said.

"What wasn't supposed to happen?"

"I can't be falling in love with you already."

She gave me a little smirk. "Gee, thanks! What do you mean? You don't want this to be happening? You don't want to be in love with me?"

"No, no, I just mean I was supposed to take some time . . . I wasn't supposed to fall in love with anyone for a while . . . with everything going on in my life . . . but I don't have much of a choice about it at this point . . . I'm in love with you."

She smiled without the smirk this time. "I love you too . . ." She paused, her eyes welling up a little bit. "I actually think I love you more than I've ever loved anything in my life, if that's possible," she confessed.

"I love you more than anything too."

That romantic phrase became the thing we would say to each other every time we said goodbye, or every time we wrote a card or a letter to each other: "I love you more than anything."

Within a few months, I decided that it was time for me to move out of my aunt's house, and Shan and I moved into a one-bedroom apartment in West LA to begin a new life together as a young couple in love.

I now had everything I wanted in my life at that time . . . except for a record deal. Riding the buzz that we had created around Hollywood, Jordi started shopping the Conway Five to all the major labels in the industry. As a result, we were flying back and forth to New York on weekends and breaks to do showcases on both coasts, but believe it or not, they were all passing on us. As much as they liked the band and the unique sound we had started to create, most of them just couldn't figure out what they would do with a band like us. Most record labels are only interested in a sure thing: a known commodity that they can plug into a certain radio format and market to a specific audience. So the feedback we got from a lot of the label execs was "You need to figure out if you're a rock band or a pop/R&B act, because we don't know how to promote what you are now." Pretty shortsighted, right?

We had all but given up on any of the major record labels taking a chance on something different, when one small upstart named Octone Records came calling for us. They had seen us at one of our Viper Room shows, and not only did they *not* want to change our sound to fit a certain marketing strategy but they wanted to create a whole campaign specifically designed to build a grassroots following. They wanted to do it the old-fashioned, organic way. This was a breath of fresh air for us, after the disappointment of the sink-or-swim Warner Bros. experience. Octone consisted of only three guys at the time, and they were not exactly what you would call our type of dudes. They were sharks, on the hunt to stake their claim in the record industry with a huge catch that they could hang their name on. But that meant that they were just as hungry as we were, and they had just as much to prove. So, even though these guys seemed like the kind of suits that exist on the polar opposite end of the record industry from the creative artists like us, we had a feeling that they could deliver on their marketing plan, and that was all that really mattered at that point. We would much rather be teamed up with guys who were in it to win it than fat cats who were just throwing more darts at the wall to see what sticks. In their pitch, the Octone guys said they would put us on the road for a year before they would even release the album, which was a big commitment to a slow and steady buildup of our fan base and media presence. It would be a long crusade, during which they would work on one radio station at a time, like the independent labels used to do in the 1950s and '60s. This was music to our ears.

chapter 10

what a maroon!

I n the midst of the excitement of the Conway Five, the cool scene at the Lowry house, and the weekly shows at Brew Co., a new musical friend became more prominent in our lives. James Valentine was a jazz-trained guitar wiz, who had come out to California from Lincoln, Nebraska, with his progressive rock band Square, and we took notice of his impressive chops the very first time we saw him play. Reel Big Fish's front man, Aaron Barrett, had introduced us to Square, encouraging us to book them as an opening act, and when they joined us on the bill at the Chain Reaction in Anaheim, we watched James perform for the first time. Square was a three-piece band with just keyboards/vocals, drums, and guitar, but they made a big sound (kind of a cross between Rush and Ben Folds Five, if you can imagine that). However, there was a lot of space in their arrangements for James to fill with his epic guitar solos, and he did so with awe-inspiring technique and flair. Adam, Jesse, and I looked on with glee as we watched him rip a massive, five-minute, over-the-top, jazz/fusion solo right at the apex of their set. It was self-indulgent for sure, but James and his band-mates definitely had the place rocking, and the three of us had goose bumps.

James had started coming to the parties in Los Feliz, jamming with all the musicians there whenever he could and ingratiating himself into the scene. He'd accepted the job of guitar tech for our Conway Five recording session, just because we wanted him around and because, as a starving musician, he needed the cash. Adam and Mickey had stopped showing up for our Thursday-night Brew Co. shows, so Jesse and I decided to invite James and Sam Farrar (Adam's housemate and bassist of Phantom Planet) to sit in with us on a few occasions, in order to fill our commitment with an extended, improvisational jam session. It was exciting and fun to play with musicians who had a very different feel than I was used to, but it also made me realize what an innate chemistry I had with Adam and Mickey. We had been playing together for so long that we just naturally slotted into a certain groove and feel together. But now I had to stay on my toes a bit more, in order to try to blend with these very skilled but very different musicians. The sets were an interesting departure for me, because James was a technically trained, progressive-jazz geek, complete with a pedal board full of effects loops and other fun stuff, and I was actually following him most of the time, rather than the other way around. I had never really played to a metronome at that point, so I'm sure I was out of time with his loops, but it was a learning experience.

I suppose I need to explain why Adam and Mickey stopped showing up to the Brew Co. shows at that time. Granted, we were playing a lot of important showcases around town (and on both coasts), and also granted, the demands on Adam were greater than those on the rest of us, given his role as the front man and lead singer. However, this was another point of contention between us that caused me a lot of consternation. He claimed that he wanted to save his voice for the "important" shows we were doing (meaning the industry showcases in Hollywood and New York), and Brew Co. had ceased to be his top priority. But I felt that he was just being a diva. He even declined to show up for one of our headlining concerts at the Chain Reaction in Anaheim, which resulted in the rest of us doing an entire set karaoke-style to a packed room, with some of our hard-core OC fans getting onstage and singing songs off *The Fourth World* with us.

Mickey, having become a consummate Eastside hipster, followed suit by not showing up to the Brew Co. shows either. I think he figured that if Adam wasn't going to be there, then it wasn't worth his time. To my perception, the Westside scene wasn't cool enough for his style and taste, but I might have just been projecting my own disdain for elitism. I was really angry about their disregard for the fan base we were growing on that side of town, but I did my best to take it in stride, because we were in fact playing some very important shows for industry folk at the time, and I didn't want to make too big of an issue out of it. I guess my new attitude of acceptance allowed me to let it roll off my back a little bit easier than it might have in the past. I expressed my frustration to Adam a couple of times, especially after the Chain Reaction debacle, and then I let it go. Inviting James and Sam to come jam with us at Brew Co. was my way of making lemonade out of the situation, and I think Adam was actually a little jealous that we had a fun show without him. So he actually showed up unexpectedly at our next show at a frat party in Westwood (not to sing, but just to pull out his guitar and jam with us and James).

It was one night at the House of Blues in Hollywood that James's involvement with our band took a big step forward. Singer-songwriter Sophie B. Hawkins had offered us a slot to open for her there (anyone who came of age in the 1990s probably remembers her big hit "Damn, I Wish I Was Your Lover"). Playing that venue was a big deal for us, and the show would be a huge opportunity to perform for a new audience, so naturally we wanted to sound our best. In a lot of ways, we were still a garage band, pretending to be a more polished pop/R&B act, so we were looking for any way we could class up our set and create a fuller sound. Jesse was playing the keyboards more of the time now, and Adam was starting to experiment with performing more as a front man without his guitar, so whereas we used to have a two-guitar lineup, we were now performing with no guitar half the time. So it made sense for us to ask James if he would consider sitting in for the gig to pick up the slack. James was so proficient on his instrument that he had his parts ready to go on day one, and just the presence of a musician of his caliber in the room really brought the sound and feel of the band up a notch.

For that first show with us, James stood upstage next to the drums with Jesse's keyboards out in front of him, which looked pretty weird from the audience perspective. Beyond that misfire in visual presentation, the show was a huge step up in sound and performance value. James slotted perfectly into what we were doing, and his vibe and feel fit ours like a glove. We were keenly aware of how difficult it could be for a new element to fall right into the chemistry of a group that had been playing together for eight years, so we certainly didn't take the magic of that show for granted. As a result, we decided that we needed to have James in our band one way or another. The only problem was that he was still a member of the band Square with his two best friends from Nebraska.

James started playing every show with us after that, including the showcase we did for Octone Records, and it was clear that he was becoming a part of the formula. I think he was in a bit of denial about it, however, due to his guilt over cheating on Square. We could tell that he wanted to be in our band more than anything—he was feeding off the excitement of our chemistry and the buzz we had created around town—but he was acting as if it were just a fun thing to do for a while. We had bigger plans for him, however. So, one day, Adam and I invited him to Brew Co. for a beer and a big talk. My beautiful new girlfriend Shantell served us a round of pear ciders (that's about how manly we were), and the three of us sat by the window in Westwood, talking about James's involvement with the band. I think he knew what was coming, and he looked both excited and nervous.

"You belong in our band, dude," Adam said. "It's your destiny, bro, you need to accept it. You need to quit Square today and join our band. It's time."

James's face was turning four different colors as he digested this bold statement.

"Wow . . . I . . . I guess you're right," he said.

"You know I'm right, dude! We need you. And you need us," Adam said. "It's time to move up to the big leagues, James. Get on the train, homey!"

"I know, I know . . . and this is amazing, it really is," James said, looking like his mind was running a hundred miles an hour. "It's just tough . . . I've been with those guys for so long. We all came out here to live the dream together. I would be breaking their hearts."

"I know it's hard, man," I said, trying to be the understanding, compassionate one, "but you're not doing them any favors by staying in a band that's not making you happy. You have a great opportunity here, James. You know it's what's best . . . for all of us."

"I know . . . I know." He was gulping down air as if it were painful to swallow.

"Listen, dude, I know you need a kick in the ass right now to do what you already know you want to do," Adam said. "This is what you're gonna do, bro—you're gonna go straight down to Anaheim right now, pack up your stuff, and you're gonna move up to the Lowry house today. You're gonna start working with our band full-time, starting immediately."

James was stricken with guilt, but he knew this was something he couldn't pass up.

"Yeah? Okay . . . yeah . . . Yeah, that's what I'll do . . ." He gulped again, turning pale.

And that's exactly what he did. He went down to Anaheim and started packing. The next day, Jesse went down there with his station wagon to help him gather up his stuff, they drove back up to Hollywood, and we played a show at the Viper Room together that night. Our new label execs called a meeting just after sound check to ask us if James was officially in the band or not, and he literally had to make his final decision right there on the spot. They were about to draw up the contract that week, and it was "put up or shut up" time. Sweating bullets, he said he was in, and we played our first show as an official five-piece that night.

The only problem was that James had chickened out of telling the other two members of Square that he was quitting the band! Believe it or not, his two Lincoln, Nebraska, compatriots drove all the way up from Anaheim to see the show that night, and they were standing in the audience at the Viper Room, not knowing yet that James had decided to accept a position in our band. Adam was also not aware that they hadn't heard the news yet, so he introduced James as the new member of our band onstage in the middle of the set. I could plainly see the looks of shock and anger on these guys' faces from where I was sitting behind the drums. I know James felt truly horrible. He was a very sweet midwestern boy, corn-fed and raised on scripture. He had no intentions of hurting anyone. But he was jumping on a high-speed train with us, so he just had to hold on for dear life as it was leaving the station.

Around this time, Adam grabbed the musical direction of the Conway Five and ran with it, recording a series of exciting new demos at the Lowry house with Sam Farrar as his production collaborator. The darker and sexier edge we had begun with "Not Coming Home," "Through with You," "Secret," and "Ragdoll" was coming through more and more with these new R&B-inspired tracks, such as "Shiver," "Tangled," and "The Sun." Many of the lyrics to these songs were inspired by Adam's tumultuous relationship with Jane—some of them more romantic and sexual, some of them expressing the frustration of their hot-and-cold affair. With this collection of beat-driven tunes that expressed the many dynamics found within one tempestuous relationship, we now had a definitive sound and a consistent lyrical flow throughout this larger set of new material.

I was impressed that Adam was stepping up to the plate in terms of work ethic. The inspiration of the moment had infected all of us with a sense of urgency and excitement for what we were creating, but Adam really took it upon himself to reach for the brass ring. Every week he seemed to churn out more and better demos, and the band rehearsals were becoming synergistic endeavors again, as we pushed our sound further to the limits of our potential. The energy among the five of us was not unlike the creative chemistry we'd felt in the early years of the band, only now we had more focus in defining our own unique sound and style, and we had the drive to work tirelessly in taking our music as far as it could go. Adam was continuing to grow cockier in the midst of it all, but now he had reason to be cocky. He was writing potential hit songs, and he was becoming the front man we needed with each passing show.

I remember having a conversation with Adam before one show at the Whisky around this time, in which my dad and I encouraged him to experiment more with his stage persona. He had grown more confident and more expressive as a performer over time, but with our new, sexy style of music, I thought he should push the envelope as far as it could go to find his ultimate performance. We talked about Prince and how dynamic and sexual he was onstage, using his guitar and mic stand like phalluses, and bringing the erotic quality of his grooves and lyrics to a fever pitch when performing a song like "Darling Nikki." Adam decided to just go for it that night, and he was humping everything onstage! His guitar, his mic stand, his amp, the stage monitors . . . nothing was off-limits. It was as if he were trying to squeeze every last ounce of sexuality from his being. Our families were pretty uncomfortable with that performance, but I think it was very liberating for Adam. By pushing himself to the limits of his comfort level as a performer, he was able to scale it back and find the sweet spot between his more reserved self and this totally unrestrained character he had indulged. I think sometimes you have to go too far before you can find just right.

We were convinced that we were ready to go into the studio and make an album of the caliber of Prince's *Purple Rain* or even Michael Jackson's *Thriller*. That was the level of confidence we had, and these were the kind of conversations we were having among ourselves. Of course, the record label was doing what record labels do, telling us we needed more hit songs before we could record the album. So Adam started recording more demos with a definitive bent toward commercial pop, generating some of the more tender love songs like "Must Get Out" and "Sweetest Goodbye." At this point in our career, we had no hesitation about going for the Top 40 with all of our ambition. *Pop* had ceased to be a bad word, because some of our biggest inspirations—the Beatles, Stevie Wonder, Michael Jackson, Prince—were artists who crossed over to the mainstream with catalogs of massive pop hits. We just wanted to make the best pop album we could possibly make: one that would transcend the fashion of the moment and ascend to the heights of these timeless hitmakers.

One night in Sam Farrar's studio, James was playing a bossa nova pattern he had just written, inspired by his affection for Brazilian composer Antônio Carlos Jobim, and Adam could hear a pop song even in that lick played in a long-outdated style; that's how in the zone he was. He stayed up all night reworking James's creation, and by morning he had the demo for the song "She Will Be Loved." I remember Adam being over the moon about that track, driving across town to my apartment on the Westside to play it for me and Shan with eager anticipation of our responses. Shan was not easily impressed by the things we were doing in the band (one of the things I was very attracted to about her), but when we first heard it, we both had the same reaction: (1) it's a little cheesy, and (2) we *love* it, and it's going to be a massive hit.

We were thinking at the time that "Not Coming Home" could be a good first single to introduce the band, that "Sunday Morning" could be a big crossover hit, and that "She Will Be Loved" was the eventual ballad that would blast the album into the stratosphere. So we were itching to get into the studio, to effectively channel all that enthusiasm into the recording of the album. But the label execs were still pushing us to write more songs, looking for that one, true, first single. We thought they were crazy, and we were getting rather frustrated with their breathing down our necks. So we decided to go back to the drawing board and do one more band demo session, the way we had done the Conway Five, just to appease them. To be honest, this session felt a little less inspired and a little more like we were forcing it, but it would produce the first two songs on the album and the first two singles: "Harder to Breathe" and "This Love."

"Harder to Breathe" came out of sheer frustration over having to appease the record label. The main groove of the song came from a rather busy riff that we had originally written as an instrumental in "Not Coming Home," but for the sake of putting a melody over it, we made it dumb. "Make it dumb" was a musical concept of which we had become fond after enjoying headbanging hip-hop tracks such as DMX's "Party Up (Up in Here)," which seemed almost silly in its simplicity yet had everyone jumping up and down in unison. Sometimes the simplest choice, stripped of all cleverness, has the most impact. So we made the verse groove very straightforward, without any clever polyrhythmic accents or harmonic embellishments. Then Adam wrote a lyric about the anxiety of high expectations (to which I could relate immensely), punctuated with the palpable frustration he was feeling over having to churn out more music on command. We didn't realize it just yet, but that song would be the perfect introduction to the band, incorporating all the elements, past and present. It had the angst of our teenage beginnings, emphasized with a rock edge. It had the soulful groove of an R&B track, only played with more of an aggressive energy. It had the melodic and lyrical hook of a pop song, coupled with a youthful "fuck you" attitude, all of which would deliver the goods to our young audience. The label execs didn't realize that the lyrics were about them, so they loved it! We didn't agree with their plans at the time, but they were confident that they had their first single.

The progression for "This Love" was originally just one of Jesse's many interesting piano compositions (another one that we had all liked right away but couldn't figure out what to do with). It had some very intriguing chord changes, but it wasn't until we came up with the Dr. Dre–inspired beat and arrangement that the song started to evolve and take shape. Adam then wrote that big payoff of a chorus progression and melodic hook, which provided his ultimate inspiration for the lyric: it would become the exclamation point to all the songs he had written about his relationship with Jane. It would be the ultimate breakup song, encompassing the whole span of emotions that range from the joy of a burgeoning relationship to the pain of its ending—from the delight to the sorrow of a passionate but doomed romance. "This love has taken its toll on me / And I have no choice, 'cause I won't say goodbye anymore."

With the label finally happy with our list of songs, the next step was finding a suitable producer. The first person we interviewed for the job was famed funk, disco, pop, and soul icon Nile Rodgers of the band Chic, who had produced and written huge hits with a long list of very successful artists in the 1970s and '80s. I have to hand it to Octone—this was a pretty inspired choice for the crossover record we were attempting to make. We had a lot of fun jamming with Nile (his funk guitar rhythm is second to none), and he regaled us with many great stories from working with artists like David Bowie and Madonna. However, Nile's asking price was a little too steep for our budget, so it just didn't work out. We were disappointed, but we still had high hopes of finding just the right fit. The only problem was that a lot of the producers in whom we expressed interest were out of step with what the label wanted. Because our roots were in rock, Adam, Jesse, and Mickey felt that we needed a more urban-, hip-hop-, or R&B-style producer to give us some cred in the world into which we were attempting to venture. On the other hand, the label thought that if we went too far with making a slick R&B record, we would lose some of that edge and live energy we carried from our rock background.

I think I can say without offending him that Matt Wallace was not our first choice. Sure, we all liked his work with Faith No More, but the label was most excited about his recent mix of the song "Meet Virginia" by Train, about which we were not as crazy. This was not the cool, urban-cred guy for whom we had hoped. Even upon meeting him, we thought he seemed less like a cool, young record producer and more like a suburban dad, complete with male-pattern baldness and a Tommy Bahama Hawaiian-style shirt. We just couldn't see it: How could this middle-aged white guy be the man to deliver the kind of record that would cross the bridge for us? But Octone was convinced that Matt was our guy, so we adjusted our expectations and got to work.

The task for Matt was no small one. Ours was a band with big personalities and even bigger opinions. Everyone in the group had his own vision for what the record would be, and what it should sound like. I think most bands usually have one or two very loud voices who tend to dominate the discussions, but we had a whole slew of type-A control freaks, all wanting to put their stamp on what the record would become. Adam, Jesse, and Mickey were all pretty adamant about it sounding very produced; they even wanted to loop the beats, to make tracks that could compete on the radio with hip-hop, R&B, and even the biggest Top 40 pop. On the other side of the argument, James and I felt that we should maintain more of the band element in the recordings, more prominently featuring the live drums and guitars and recording more in the fashion of the rock band we were at our core. I personally liked the idea of being heavily influenced by modern hip-hop tracks and old soul records, but I wanted to play and record in a style consistent with our roots, like the Chili Peppers did when incorporating funk and rap into their rock arrangements. My vision was to take inspiration from the Neptunes and Timbaland beats, but then play them like Chad Smith or John Bonham would. I had heard somewhere that Bonham was inspired by funk grooves by the Meters when he came up with some of his beats, but of course he played them like the badass rock drummer that he was. Sure, we wanted to compete with even the Top 40 pop stars, but we were a real band with real organic soul, and that element was what should set us apart from them. Fortunately, the record label was on James's and my side in terms of approach, favoring the live arrangements probably even more than we did.

So Matt Wallace had to deal with record label executives breathing down his neck to deliver what they thought was a serviceable promotion for the band, then he had to listen to five young, passionate, slightly crazed musicians barking at him with 150 different ideas every hour. He had to sift through all the noise of our passions, discerning what was real inspiration and focus and what was just a big argument over nothing. And we argued a lot. We argued about everything. So, looking back, I actually don't think that adding another young, enthusiastic voice to the mix would have been a very good idea after all. As it turns out, we needed the "fatherly" presence of Matt Wallace to balance our energy.

Around this time, we started seriously considering renaming the band. We had been wanting to change the name for years, going back to before we even signed our first deal with Reprise. We went through every imaginable moniker in those days, coming close to naming ourselves the Roundabouts, believe it or not, before realizing we couldn't agree on anything that had meaning to us other than Kara's Flowers. In promoting *The Fourth World*, however, it became increasingly frustrating every time we had to correct people who had misunderstood or mispronounced the name. When

Adam would say "We're Kara's Flowers" from the stage, many in the audience would think he said "Cars and Flowers" or "Carson Flowers." And most commonly, when people saw it written down, they would say Kara like "Kerra," with a soft vowel sound, which we hated. More importantly, though, the name Kara's Flowers didn't seem to represent how far we had come and how much we had changed from the Reprise record. So it was time for a fresh start, with a new name to go with our new sound. After going through a whole litany of more names and getting our hopes up only to find out they were already taken (and endless arguments with Jesse, who for some reason wanted us to be called Mosetta, whatever that meant), we finally settled on the name Maroon 5, much to the label's delight. We swore an oath not to talk about the origin of the name, and it became this mysterious topic that we would never fully address in interviews. I haven't heard the band talk about it much since, so I will respect the oath we took. The secret of the Maroon 5 name lives on!

Amid all the excitement of our new record contract, I finally graduated with my degree in English from UCLA in the summer of 2001, so the timing worked out pretty well. As proud as I was of the band for pulling ourselves back together, rediscovering our passion and chemistry, and earning a second shot at our dreams, I was equally proud of myself for having stuck to my goal of graduating from college and for finally proving to myself that I was the man of letters that my ninth-grade English teacher couldn't see. Of course, my parents were ecstatic that I now had a degree to fall back on if the crazy dream of rock stardom didn't work out, but they were equally proud of me for having the gumption to go back and finish school without their prodding.

To celebrate, all my best UCLA buds—Andy, Barry, Jordan, Travis, both Jasons, Shawn, Kelvin, Sara, and Shan—and I had a big, tacky, celebratory night starting at the Hooters in Santa Monica (yes, if memory serves, I do believe that even the future icon of female empowerment Sara Bareilles was in attendance for all the beer, chicken wings, short shorts, and boobs that Hooters had to offer). After we got a good buzz there, we continued on to the Pope Room at the nearby Buca di Beppo Italian restaurant for more decadent food and drink. The next day, my parents threw a barbecue party in their backyard with the whole band and all their families joining my UCLA crew. We were celebrating my graduation, but it felt like we were celebrating a lot more than that.

I had stretched out my $30K buyout check from Warner Bros. over the preceding three years, not needing to get a job that whole time due to my rather frugal nature, but I didn't have enough money to last me beyond graduation. So Rich Feldstein's business firm was nice enough to give me a job in its accounting office until our advance from Octone came through. It was a bit ironic and humbling to be doing filing for the office that was supposed to be doing my taxes, but I was very grateful for the opportunity, which allowed me to pay my rent and focus on the music we were getting ready to record. The moment of truth was approaching, and we were well aware that it was "put up or shut up" time.

chapter 11

the making of
songs about jane

Right out of the gate, preproduction for the new album would be a lot different than it had been for *The Fourth World*. The era of digital recording had taken over the industry almost entirely by 2001, so we would now be recording on computer disks rather than on analog tape. Everything we laid down would have to match up to the grid within the program Pro Tools, so there would be no more just pressing "Record" and letting it fly. We would need to play everything to a click track (a digital metronome), in order to sync to the program's internal clock, so our rehearsals in preproduction would become largely focused on that skill set for the first time. As if my own level of perfectionism weren't enough, I now had to live up to literal perfection, maintaining metronomic rhythm throughout the performances. This, of course, was making me very anxious, even before we started recording.

On top of that, we would be auditioning programmers, who would come in with their MPC sampling machines and jam with us, to show us how they could add to the sonic landscape of our recordings. Having had no experience with that way of making music, I found this a very foreign process, but Adam had been utilizing this kind of sound generation in his demo sessions with Sam Farrar, so his expectations were beginning to lean in the direction of looped beats and hip-hop samples. However, the four (and now five) of us in the band had mostly operated as an organic garage band up until that point (and I'm pretty sure Matt Wallace had no experience with a sampler or a programmer either), so we were really just fumbling around in the dark with this stuff.

The night before we began rehearsals, we all gathered in Jesse's small living room in Culver City, and we listened to a bunch of great records for inspiration. Some of the music we played for each other was intended to inspire the kind of soul and feel we would try to achieve with the album, and others were references for the new hip-hop and R&B recording styles that we would attempt to employ. We listened to Herbie Hancock's *Head Hunters*, focusing on the steady grooves, very dry 1970s drum sounds, and experimental use of analog synthesizers. We danced to Stevie Wonder's *Songs in the Key of Life*, in total awe of the elaborate musical arrangements and soulful performances from start to finish. We bobbed our heads to Jay-Z's *Hard Knock Life* and Missy Elliott's *Supa Dupa Fly*, keying in on the hypnotic drum loops and complex, polyrhythmic arrangements of Timbaland's productions . . . And then we listened to Michael Jackson's *Thriller* in its entirety, swearing that we were going to make a record akin to that pop masterpiece: a track list of nothing but hits, one after another.

Inspired by the relentless catchiness and soul of *Thriller*, we had one rather audacious goal overriding everything we did: Every single element you hear needs to be a hook. Every lyric, every melody, every guitar line, every piano part, every bass line, every drumbeat . . . everything. We wanted to make a record so undeniable that if you "put the needle down" at any point, you would be drawn in by a musical phrase that would be infectious. So we dissected every arrangement and every musical element down to its essence, playing with the space and placement of every note as they played off one another. We were *not* going to settle for a guitar or a keyboard just strumming the chords like a normal pop-rock band would. Every lick had to be a signature. I began to wonder if my perfectionism had rubbed off on Adam, because he now would settle for nothing short of an absolutely bulletproof pop masterpiece. More likely, though, it was his intense competitiveness that drove him to seek conquest over everyone else in popular music. It was no longer good enough to just compete with the alternative rock bands or even the pop acts of the moment. Our sights were set on creating a generational album like *Songs in the Key of Life*, or even the highest-selling album of all time, *Thriller*.

It bears repeating that we as a band argued about everything like a big Italian family around a dinner table. We debated everything from the tempo of the click track to the tone of the snare drum, from the distortion of the guitar to the wah-wah pedal on the clavinet. And you could feel the tension rising as we approached the first week of recording. Our arguments were still very respectful and never ventured out of the bounds of the creative debate, but the feeling and the intensity were different than in previous sessions. The failure of the Reprise album that we'd experienced as teenagers had left us with a powerful lesson about how precious this opportunity really was. At ages twenty-three and twenty-four now, we were under no illusions: it was most likely our last and best chance to make a hit record. Thankfully, the task at hand was more under our control this time. We were working with about a quarter of the budget we'd had with Warner Bros., but we were on top of every element of it, and we had the promise of our small label to promote the album for a year on the road. Sure, we felt the anxiety of performing under all the pressure, but we also had the confidence that we would do everything in our power to make it great.

Another big part of the preproduction process was writing bridges for most of the songs. I don't think we'd ever written a proper bridge before this; we'd mostly just thrown in some kind of musical interlude to get back to the last chorus. It became a running gag every time Matt Wallace would ask, "Have you guys thought about writing a bridge for this song?" No, we really hadn't. But it made a lot of sense now that he said it! So most days involved a moment when the rest of the band would take a little break to allow Jesse to come up with one of his interesting and inspired progressions. Then Adam would write a melody and lyric for the new section, and voilà! We had a new bridge, and the song was that much better. Sounds easy, right?

When we started the recording session at Rumbo Recorders, I had one week to track all my drum parts. There was also no room in the budget for a drum tech, so I was relying on my very limited understanding of tuning to get whatever sounds I could out of my very limited equipment. This process was intense for me, and my general level of anxiety was higher than it had been in previous recording sessions, because my perfectionism was no longer only self-imposed. Whereas in the past we had just thrown down the basic tracks with a producer at the controls, who would help me decide which takes to use, we now had the whole band in the control room, just listening to me play to a click track and pointing out every beat in every measure that was off the grid even slightly. I could feel everyone looking over my shoulder, which made me more anxious and defensive of their comments and criticisms. We had all given each other a lot of leeway with developing our own parts in the past, but now it felt like we were drum tracking by committee.

It also felt a little like it was backwards day, because Adam was the anal one and I was arguing for the value of human imperfections. Because he had been employing programmed drumbeats in his demos with Sam, he had become accustomed to a high level of consistency and evenness in the rhythm track, and his expectations had risen as a result. Per his request, we put the drums in one of the isolation booths to get a very dry drum sound, of which I was not a fan. I couldn't really understand the appeal of a "dead" drum sound, other than to try to achieve a retro 1970s aesthetic. I love the sound of a live drum room with all of its natural reverb and decay, so this technique felt stiff and quite literally dead to me. And we even tried looping some of the beats for the first time, editing every track to within an inch of its life. I had very mixed feelings about all of this from an artistic perspective. Sure, I wanted the songs to compete on pop radio, and that meant making everything as tight as a mosquito's ass, but I also felt that something was being lost in the process. That live groove, that thing that set us apart from the other pop acts, was getting a little squashed by this meticulousness. And the fact that I felt this way is saying a lot, coming from an obsessive-compulsive perfectionist!

And the meticulousness didn't stop there. Everything we recorded was held to the same scrutiny, as we all piled into the back room of Rumbo Recorders for the bass, guitar, keyboard, and vocal overdubs. Every stroke of every bass line, every guitar strum and piano strike, was matched up with the drums, measure by measure. Then we added "ear candy" to every track, experimenting with any idea that could make the songs sound like pop hits. While the other guys were doing some of their overdubs, I was upstairs in the lounge with a laptop and a microphone, recording shakers, tambourines, handclaps, and even my breathing (which actually made it onto a couple of the tracks). It's kind of funny to think that I recorded some of those tracks all by my lonesome, especially because I didn't even really know how to use Pro Tools much beyond pressing "Record" and "Stop" at the time. But we didn't have time to dillydally, so we were all trying to contribute in any way we could, doing whatever we needed to stay under budget. We were throwing the kitchen sink at this thing, and we would just have to sort it all out in the mix before it became a finished product.

The mood was tense. Even as we strove for perfection, there was an overriding sense that we were blowing it, big time. I remember Adam saying at one point that he thought we had messed the whole thing up, that the record sounded "crispy," as he put it. I tried to remain outwardly optimistic, but inside I agreed. I thought it sounded stiff and clipped, that our novice attempts at making hip-hop tracks had rendered the thing rather lifeless. My dad even made that very same comment when he came to listen to the recordings during overdubs. He had no experience with the kind of music by which we were being influenced, and he had no reference point for the ways in which we had been going about trying to achieve it, but he immediately remarked that the tracks sounded very flat, lacking the mojo that our band chemistry usually delivered onstage and on record.

Matt Wallace, who had two kids at home, was working long hours trying to keep up with our manic focus, but he would inevitably have to go home at some point, leaving us to our own devices and insanity. As a result, he and I had a regrettable moment one night, amid all the tension. We were discussing what had been done and what needed to be done, and I said something like "Well, if you were here with us when we were doing it, then maybe you could help," implying that he was spending more time with his family than at the studio. Under the stress of everything, Matt glared at me and said, "Fuck you, man! Seriously, fuck you!" You could hear a pin drop in the room after that, as everyone looked around nervously.

As much as we really didn't want to hear from them at the time, the Octone execs came to the studio around this point to also say exactly what we had been feeling about the rough mixes: they sounded stiff and lifeless. This feedback was aggravating and infuriating to hear from our record label, because no artist likes to get that kind of call from the "suits," but it was also something of a relief, given the stress we had been putting on ourselves. We now had permission to loosen up a bit and let the recordings breathe. We didn't have to try to make our drums and guitars sound like drum machines and synthesizers. And even better, the label was willing to increase the budget a bit to remedy the situation.

Our studio time at Rumbo Recorders was ending at that point, and we had most of the songs "completed," but we went back to the drawing board on about half of them, re-recording the drum and bass tracks at another studio. Can-Am Recorders had been the home of Death Row Records previously, and there were very visible bloodstains on the wood floors, from where Suge Knight and his cronies had their pit-bull fights. That was a rather dark and ominous thing to walk into the first day, but once we put down rugs and set up the drums, the session took on a much looser energy than the previous one. We now had the help of some professional drum techs known as the "Drum Doctors," who brought in some amazing vintage gear and set it all up really nicely tuned for me, so all I had to do was just play. Whereas the first week of drums had been high-pressured, overanalyzed, and stiff, this week was loose and fun, with really great vintage drum sounds. I just played live takes of "This Love," "Shiver," "Tangled," "Sunday Morning," and "Through with You" on top of the existing tracks, and they immediately felt much more grooving and vibey. Of course, I'm biased when I say this, but I think those live performances saved the record.

It wasn't by design, but the fact that some of the tracks on the album retained some of that clipped first pass of drum edits, while others ended up with a bigger and more open feel, gave the album a unique sonic dimensionality. Tracks like "She Will Be Loved," "Must Get Out," and "Sweetest Goodbye" have that very looped and edited feel to them, while the ones like "Shiver," "Tangled," and "Sunday Morning" have a much more expressive performance quality to them. Even the tonal qualities of the drums are very different from one track to the next, which makes the whole album a more dynamic listening experience than it might have been, had it been done all one way or the other.

"Tangled," in particular, turned out to be an interesting opportunity for me to express myself. The first pass of the song was missing something—it lacked a discernible drum hook—so in my live overdub I dove deep into my inspiration from Missy Elliott's *Supa Dupa Fly* to create a new and more unique drum groove for the verses. The tempo of the track was a perfect canvas on which to play a beat similar to one of Timbaland's programs, so I just tried to do my best impression. Of course, playing my new beat on a big vintage kick and snare gave it a different spin than what you would hear on one of Missy's records.

"This Love" became an interesting hodgepodge as well. We had originally intended for that track to have a very sparse arrangement with a shaker-driven feel, using the Neptunes's beat on Mystikal's "Shake Ya Ass" as the template for the groove, but once I did my live take on top, the recording felt a little too loose for a pop radio single. So it took a remix from Mark Endert (who had mixed Fiona Apple's first album) to sort through everything we had put down in our multiple ideations, turning it into the pop track it became. Similarly, "Harder to Breathe" required a remix from Michael Barbiero (who had mixed Guns N' Roses's *Appetite for Destruction* and Metallica's *Black Album*) to give it the full rock edge it needed. I was half joking when I sang that high, screaming harmony in the choruses, but apparently Barbiero really liked it, because he made it louder than everything in the final mix!

Somehow, amid all this close attention to detail, we managed to enjoy having our friends around for some of the sessions, as we did for the Conway Five. Shan came by with a batch of fresh cookies and a blender a few times, making margaritas for everyone. I remember all my buddies from UCLA showing up at different times to hang out as well, as we tried to keep the vibe as social and fun as we could under the circumstances. We were much more under the gun this time, so we weren't exactly letting loose with the party atmosphere in the studio all the time, but we did make time to go out and socialize after hours, often at Les Deux or Las Palmas in Hollywood or the Brass Monkey karaoke bar in Koreatown. As much as I had made my peace with Adam by this point, he could still be aggravating to me on those nights. He usually decided where we would go, but he would often change his mind ten minutes after we got there, and we would all have to get back in our cars and follow him to the next spot. Some nights, we would follow him around to three different places, before we realized that he was just trying to find some girl with whom he wanted to hook up, and we were all just following him around on his personal quest. This kind of thing didn't seem to bother our friends that much, because we were all having fun in the process, but my personal history with Adam could make it more irritating for me. I suppose I could have just split and gone home if I didn't like being a part of his entourage, but I guess I wanted to be a part of the adventure just like everyone else. It was hard to not love the guy. He was a young man who followed his passions unapologetically. Sometimes he could lack consideration, but he was always fun, entertaining, and charismatic, so it's understandable why everyone was so willing to follow him around.

In the midst of making the album, I also wanted to bring my friend Sara Bareilles the kind of attention I thought she deserved from the industry. Up until that point, Sara had done all her songwriting alone at her keyboard, so I figured she needed some help putting together a proper demo. She was happy to take me up on my offer to produce the session, and we settled on a song called "Come Round Soon" to arrange and record together. I enlisted Jesse as my engineer and partner for the session, which went very smoothly, and it got me thinking for the first time about a future in producing. If I had been more entrepreneurial, I would have started my own label right then and signed her to it! But I was about to go on tour with Maroon 5 for an indefinite amount of time, so the best I could do was to pass the demo around to the industry folks to whom I had access. Eventually, our manager Jordi would decide to take her on, representing her as he had us, and Jordi did what he had promised again, delivering a major record deal and setting her up for the successful career she ended up having. I don't take any credit for Sara getting the attention she deserved, however; I truly believe that would have happened anyway.

I don't know if anyone knows this fun fact, but the future star of *The Office* and *Parks and Recreation* Rashida Jones actually sang backing vocals on both the Conway Five and *Songs About Jane*. She was a friend of the band, whom we had all thought was extremely cool (on top of having a major crush on her), and her sultry voice turned out to be a really interesting and sexy compliment to Adam's higher-pitched male timbre. She can be heard most prominently on the demo version of "Secret," but the record label ultimately thought that having a female voice too prominent in the mix on the album would be confusing for our audience. I thought it was great, though. The blend of Adam's and Rashida's voices together reminded me of Lindsey Buckingham's higher timbre blending with Stevie Nicks's huskier tone in Fleetwood Mac.

Rashida actually performed as one of our backup singers for a show in the Conway Five days. I was rather intimidated, due to her pedigree as the Harvard-graduate daughter of Peggy Lipton and Quincy Jones (she had a very confident air), but I got up the guts to ask her out on a date . . . And she just flat-out turned me down. She was very nice about it, but I definitely got the feeling she was just out of my league!

Another memorable story from the *Songs About Jane* era involved none other than the great actor of our time, Leonardo DiCaprio. As the buzz around our band continued to grow, more and more of young Hollywood were showing up at our shows. One night, we played a pretty exclusive showcase at our old haunt the Troubadour, with a club full of family, friends, and industry folk in attendance. The Troubadour is a great place to see a band, but it has an even better view from the stage, because you can see literally every face in the audience, no matter where they're sitting or standing. As I took the stage that night, I looked up at the balcony where Adam, Jesse, and I had started the band almost a decade earlier, and I saw my parents sitting right in the front row of benches up there. Unmistakably, the face sitting right next to my mom was that of massive Hollywood A-list star Leonardo DiCaprio.

Leo, who had been the obsession of my previous girlfriend Taryn (and every other teenage girl in America when *Titanic* came out in the 1990s), had put together an impressive streak of excellent movies by the time he came to our show, but he was on the verge of crossing over into cinematic royalty with his first Martin Scorsese film, *Gangs of New York*. He was so famous by that point that he had to don a look similar to that of Neil Diamond at my Little League games: hat down low over his eyes, shaggy and unassuming in his presentation. But it was undeniably Leo, and of course, he had a group of very attractive women by his side.

When we got done with the show, my parents and Shan came backstage to say hello, and I immediately asked my mom, "So, you were sitting with Leo, huh?" She looked confused for a second, and then she said, "*Oh my god!* Is that who that was? He gave me the middle finger!" I was stunned by this revelation, and of course I needed to hear the context. My dad was actually on crutches at the time, having just had back surgery that morning to repair one of his many softball injuries (he never quits), and the two of them had gotten to the show early to ensure they had a comfortable seat on the balcony. Leo showed up just as the lights were going down, and he tried to nudge them over to make room for himself on the bench (I'm sure to avoid getting tangled up with fans in the general admission). As mild-mannered and shy as my mom is by nature, she's a mama bear when it comes to protecting her family, so when he was literally nudging them over to make more room, she was just protecting my injured dad when she turned and asked, "*Do you mind???*" And Leo responded by flipping her the bird.

I, of course, found this hilarious, and I knew this was a story we would be telling for years. There was no animosity or anything like that; it was just funny. So fast-forward to the touring years, when every interviewer asks you the same questions over and over, and we would often tell that story to answer the usual question "Do you guys know any celebrities?" It was just an amusing anecdote to fill an interview, and it reflected no grudge of any kind. However, I guess word got back to Leo's camp that I was furious at him for having flipped off my mom.

It wasn't until 2005 that I met Leo at an Oscars after-party at Prince's house in Bel-Air. The band and I were some of the early arrivals to this super-A-list party, and when Leo walked in, he came right over to us.

He put both his hands on my shoulders and said, "Man . . . apparently, I flipped off your mom? I'm sooooooo sorry, man! I meant no disrespect . . . I love moms! I love my mom! I'm sure you love your mom! I'm sure your mom is great! I'm so sorry!"

It was adorable.

I felt bad that he had gotten the impression that I was actually angry at him, so I tried to alleviate his worry the best I could. "It's all good, man! I wasn't mad; it was just a funny story to tell in interviews!"

He kept apologizing. "Are you sure? Are you sure, man? Are we good? Are we good, man?"

What a mensch. I really wanted to be his friend after that.

Of course, a buddy film was not in the cards for me and Leo, but the story got even funnier that night as the evening progressed. Everyone at the party was getting drunker and drunker as more incredibly famous people showed up, and at one point the legendary Joni Mitchell walked in. Joni Mitchell is not somebody you expect to see anywhere, ever, let alone at Prince's Oscar after-party, so we were obviously pretty excited. But we were standing within earshot of Leo when she walked by, and we overheard him say to his friend drunkenly, "Did you see who that was??? That was *Carly Simon*! Oh my god, *Carly Simon*! I can't believe it!"

I don't know what was funnier . . . the fact that he mistook Joni Mitchell for Carly Simon . . . or the fact that he was that excited to see Carly Simon.

chapter 12

get in the van

As we put the finishing touches on the album, Adam felt that it needed a title that genuinely reflected the lyrical arc of the songs included. He argued that it must be called *Songs About Jane*, because any other name would just be dishonest. We knew that not every song was about Jane, but Adam asserted that there were elements of that relationship in every song and the title encapsulated an overall theme of the collection. We were all happy that Jane's name could sound like a stand-in for anyone who's ever been in a frustrating relationship (like a Jane Doe). So we agreed on the title, but we still weren't convinced that we had hit the mark with the recording. The resulting collection of tracks, which was an amalgam of our many influences (and in some cases our immaturities), didn't sound the way any of us had imagined it would. I suppose that's a good thing. A good compromise is when nobody's happy, right? We were also just so inside of it, having spent every day obsessing about every detail, that it was impossible for us to hear it objectively. All we could hear were the imperfections or the things we would have done differently. However, for better or for worse, it was an accurate representation of where we were as artists at that moment, and the label execs felt they had a record they could market, so it was time to move forward.

I think most fans who came to know the band through *Songs About Jane* probably don't realize that we were actually two years deep into touring in support of the album by the time it really took off in 2004. We played over five hundred concert dates between 2002 and 2003, and that's not including the promotional acoustic shows at radio stations, record stores, and distribution centers all across the country. When you consider that most high-profile bands will usually do somewhere between fifty and one hundred shows in a touring year, you start to get a sense of how long a haul that campaign was for us. And then when you add in all the photo and video shoots, interviews, meet-and-greets, fan-club events, and radio and TV appearances, along with the travel associated with all these things, you might start to understand just how exhilarating and exhausting our lives were for those years.

When I describe my touring years to people I've met since, most of them imagine a glamorous setup in a big, luxurious tour bus, complete with decadent hotel suites and five-star service. While that may be the way the band rolls these days, that was certainly not the case in 2002. With the exception of a big RV fiasco during the summer tour, we spent all of that year (and half of the following) driving ourselves around the country in a standard passenger van. It was our first time back on the road since '97, and once again it was just the guys in the band accompanied by a tour manager/soundman named Ron, with all our luggage and musical gear packed in the trailer behind us. We split the driving between Ron, Jesse, James, and me, but I would guess that between 1997, 2002, and 2003 I personally drove a van and trailer all the way around the continental United States more than five times over.

As we prepared for an indefinite amount of touring, Shan and I accepted the fact that I would not be living in LA again any time soon. So it made no sense to maintain an apartment together when I had no income other than my per diem and she was still working as a bartender and waitress. Once our lease ended, we moved out of our apartment in West LA, and Shan moved back in with her old roommate Fran, this time in West Hollywood, in a neighborhood not far from my parents' house. A few of my UCLA friends—Shawn, Jason, and Barry's friend Gene from Pittsburgh—moved into another apartment in the same building, so at least I would have a warm welcome to celebrate my homecoming on the few-and-far-between occasions that I was there. Shan and I were both very sad that I was leaving, knowing that we wouldn't be able to see much of each other for an indeterminate amount of time, but we both tried our best to maintain a brave face, toughing out a long-distance relationship.

Before the final mixes of the record were even finished, the band ventured out on the road in February with a vague notion that the album would be released at some point later in the year and the first single, "Harder to Breathe," would be promoted to radio some time thereafter. We found ourselves with more options for tours than we'd had in '97, and our itinerary quickly filled up. The first shows we played were in support of Michelle Branch, who had a big hit called "Everywhere" at the time, and it was just that: you couldn't turn on the radio or MTV without hearing or seeing it. We were all excited to head out and play these shows, as they were sure to have packed houses of enthusiastic pop fans waiting for Michelle. One of the funniest things that James Valentine has ever said was only about an hour up the I-5 freeway on the way to our first date with her in San Francisco. We had just finished a grueling year, slaving over an album we were prepared to promote for at least a year (if not multiple years) on the road, and we were all getting amped up for the first leg of an indefinitely long tour, joking and musing about life on the road, but we inevitably hit our first lull in the conversation. We sat quietly for about a minute or two, and then James broke the silence by saying, "I don't know, guys . . . I'm just looking forward to getting back in the studio and making some new music."

That first tour was a great beginning for us. We played for five hundred to a thousand people every night for a month or so, and we were just starting to hit our stride performing our new material. The audiences seemed to like us right away, so we were feeling pretty optimistic about the future. It was on the next tour opening for Nikka Costa, however, that things really started to heat up. Nikka's music was more in the vein of what we were doing stylistically, and her band showcased some really funky hip-hop/soul musicians with a reputation around the scene. Beyond being great players with a lot of style and feel, her band members struck me as performers who could actually rock out while playing that kind of music. For some reason, we had assumed that we needed to play in a much more restrained way in order to be funky and grooving, but watching Nikka's band play hard each night inspired us to perform our new sound in a slightly bigger and more bombastic way. So, whereas the recordings in the studio had been pretty controlled to fit that medium, we began to utilize more of our rock roots again live.

Watching these more accomplished musicians play every night, however, I also started to feel some of the impostor syndrome that I had first experienced in '97, perhaps to an even greater degree this time. Although the guys in Nikka's band (and the other opening act, Tre Hardson from the Pharcyde) were often complimentary about my drumming, I really felt that I was just faking what these guys had actually been trained to do. One after another, these very cool and talented musicians told us we had great arrangements and a really soulful pocket, and the awesome bass player in Tre's band even told me I had "a heavy foot" on one of the first nights we played together. I actually didn't know whether that was a compliment or not at first, but I figured he meant it as such! While all this positive feedback was encouraging, and I did feel confident that our band had a unique chemistry and sound, I also thought that my lack of rudimentary training placed me on a rung below the caliber of musicians on that tour. And it made me feel that I was not personally capable of certain things and that this deficit might hold us back at some point in the future. The impostor syndrome was a bit mightier in my mind than the impact of the praise, so a certain level of self-doubt was starting to work its way into my psyche.

My general attitude and mood were still pretty upbeat during that time, however. My "power of positive thought" approach had been so successful in creating a renaissance in my personal life that I was sure a similar kind of willpower could make this endless touring cycle an enjoyable proposition. And it worked again . . . for a time. The Nikka Costa tour was awesome. We had a blast. Her very cool, very diverse crowds responded to our music immediately, and we received a lot of love and enthusiasm everywhere we went. This was a big change from the mostly white punk/ska crowds for whom we had played in '97, and we were just fine with that considering that we never really fit in with that scene anyway—we had been wanting to play to a broader fan base with our new sound. Knowing that fans of Nikka's funk/soul music were responding well to what we were doing reassured us about the potential of the album we had made. Up until a certain point, we had still thought of ourselves as a garage band doing an impression of a soulful pop/R&B act (at least I had), but now we knew that we could cross over to a bigger audience outside of alternative rock.

After the Nikka tour, but before releasing the album in the summer of that year, we set out to canvas the country on a solo tour of every major distribution center in every region of the country, as an attempt to "rally the troops." Our small indie label, Octone Records, had attained distribution through BMG (by way of Clive Davis's new J Records imprint), but the label execs had their work cut out for themselves to get us noticed by the marketing staff of this large conglomerate that would be working and promoting our album. These two months were among the most exhausting—and deliriously fun—periods of my life.

Octone had a plan to send its radio rep out with us to visit every one of the BMG regional distribution offices around the country (there were about twenty of them, I think), but he would also personally go into every local radio station and promote the first single in person along the way. That tour went a little something like this: After driving all night (or all morning), taking shifts behind the wheel, we would pull into a city like Dallas, we would brush our teeth in the parking lot of the distribution office using our water bottles, and we would pull our acoustic instruments out of the U-Haul, go upstairs, and give a groggy-eyed show to all the local reps. After that, we'd often go to the local radio station and do the same thing again. Then we'd go to the venue, pull out all our electric gear, and set up for sound check, after which the reps would take us out to dinner to schmooze (hanging with the artists was the perk of that job to which most of these guys looked forward). After dinner, we'd put on a rock show for the troops, and they would want to stick around to buy us drinks and schmooze some more, having just been turned on by the loud version of our show. When we'd successfully wooed our new soldiers of fortune, we'd then pile back into our van, drive all night (or sometimes sleep for a few hours at a motel, then drive all morning), pull into a city like Atlanta or Boston or Seattle or wherever else would become a major market for promotion, and repeat the same routine.

I was definitely not complaining about the relentless schedule at the time, though. We were being treated well by these often-enthusiastic label reps, and we were playing our own headlining shows on the road for the first time, which was exhilarating unto itself. I had mentally prepared myself for the fact that it would be a whirlwind tour and that I wouldn't have any time to myself for a while, so the feeling of these long days and weeks ended up being more similar to the fun I had when I was living on Glenrock Avenue than to the slog of the '97 tour. The power of positive thought was working. And all the acoustic shows were actually a lot of fun, despite the frequent delirium of having just awoken in a van in the parking lot. Playing the bongos and singing harmonies with my musical brothers felt very intimate, especially because we were often playing for only a few people. And knowing that we were wooing and conquering one local rep or one radio programmer at a time provided a small sense of accomplishment along our slow journey upward.

We ended that promotional tour in New York City with a show at the famous Village Underground in downtown Manhattan, and the man himself, Clive Davis, showed up to see us. This was a *big* deal. Clive was responsible for the careers of everyone from Janis Joplin to Bruce Springsteen to Whitney Houston to Alicia Keys (and many other iconic artists along the way). Octone's affiliation with his new J Records label was only that up until that point: an affiliation. But Octone had told us that if we reached a certain level of notoriety via word of mouth, modest record sales, and industry buzz, J Records would then come in with the big guns to help take us to the next level, by financing a global marketing campaign run by its much larger promotional staff. Considering that our entire record label consisted of three people at that point, Clive's attendance at that small club show in the Village meant that there was some serious heat coming off our band, even before the album or single dropped. Adam was a little nervous, and he didn't have one of his best shows vocally, but the word from the top was that Clive had enjoyed the set and he was curious to see how we would do when we had a single and album to promote later in the year. We tried not to let it go to our heads, though . . .

Those early tours took us right through the spring, but before we could embark on a summer tour, we needed to have a video in the can for the release date that would come in July. So we arranged to shoot the flick for "Harder to Breathe" back in Los Angeles at the end of May. We were all looking forward to capturing our live energy on film, and we went along willingly with the label's idea to make it a mostly performance-based video, shot at our usual practice spot, Swing House Rehearsal. We had made only one video before this (for "Soap Disco" on *The Fourth World* in '97), and this one had a much grittier, low-budget feel to it, so we weren't sure if we had hit the mark with it when it was done (as we had wondered with the album as well). We shot the whole thing in one long day, giving our best mimed impressions of our usual stage performance, but it didn't feel like a particularly special shoot. However, I can see now that the stylistic choice of a simple, stripped-down performance was the right introduction to the band. And by giving the film a slightly "edgier" look, the director, Marc Webb, serviced the intensity of the song, which worked to alleviate some of the associations that might have come with the glossier singles to follow.

I have to hand it to the Octone guys; they made a pretty shrewd decision to market us to rock stations first, using "Harder to Breathe" as the vehicle, even though they knew they had potential pop hits deeper on the record. I think most labels would have just blasted "This Love," "She Will Be Loved," or "Sunday Morning" right away, going for all the marbles without restraint. Although "Harder to Breathe" would take a year to peak on the charts (and it was never as big a hit as the later singles would be), it set us up well to be taken more seriously than just another pop one-hit wonder. However, I wasn't crazy about the fact that the costume designer put me in a poncho for the shoot. I didn't know whether to consider that racist, being the only Mexican in the group! I hadn't encountered anything like that since that one time in middle school, but the poncho seemed like a little too much of a coincidence. The other guys were razzing me when I contested the fashion choice, so I eventually relented and wore the damn thing. It wasn't worth fighting over. Adam called me "Poncho Villa" for a while after that, however (eye roll).

We had been on the road for the better part of five months by the time we came home to regather for the record release and summer tour, and it was really beginning to take its toll on my relationship with Shan. There's no way to say this that makes me sound like anything other than a typical male douchebag in his twenties, but the idea of being tied down to someone whom I was going to see for only a couple of days every couple of months had me feeling that I needed more freedom. I also wanted to believe that I was cut out for the rock-star life, because reality dictated I would have to get used to it. I had signed up for the carnival ride, so now I would just have to put my hands in the air and try to enjoy it.

I guess that just shows how different my current mindset was from my attitude on the first tour in '97. Rather than being homesick all the time, I was trying to adapt and embrace my situation. I was definitely thinking about Shan a lot of the time, and inside I wanted nothing more than to be with her, but I also wanted to indulge myself in whatever adventures the road might offer. To any objective person, the idea of trying to maintain a relationship with a twenty-four-year-old guy who was touring nonstop, playing concerts around the country for attractive, young audiences, would seem pretty untenable. Perhaps my first girlfriend had been right that dating musicians only brings heartache—they'll just go off on tour and break your heart! So Shan and I needed to have a big talk before I left again.

We were both very open and honest about our feelings. She was very sad, but she also understood where I was in my life, and she was willing to wait for me. She was clearly not happy that this was a phase I needed to go through, but she knew that telling me no was not really an option. She could tell that I had made up my mind that I was going to have my proverbial cake and eat it too. So we came to an agreement that we would just hold no expectations for our relationship at that point. I would live my life on the road, I would call her when I wanted to talk, and we would see each other when I was in town. As it worked out, we would continue to talk almost every day and see each other every time I was in LA, but we just wouldn't talk about what I was or wasn't doing out on the road.

The band and I were thrilled to book a spot on the Jeep World Outside Festival tour that summer, with Sheryl Crow, Train, Ziggy Marley, and O.A.R. headlining, but we made the mistake of thinking that traveling around the country in an RV would be an improvement over the van. Management informed us that our budget still wasn't big enough to move up to a bus, but they asked if we'd rather have an RV, given that we'd be out in the middle of nowhere at these festival campsites. Nobody bothered to tell us that the RV would quickly begin to stink of piss and ammonia, it would break down constantly, and Adam and I would be sleeping head to feet on a couch about three feet wide. For some reason it hadn't occurred to us that the one queen bed in the back bedroom wasn't going to be enough for seven guys. Our tour manager Ron and guitar tech Shawn (a different Shawn, although my UCLA buddy Shawn Tellez would eventually join our crew as well) had to sleep on the driving chairs at the front, and James actually volunteered to use a sleeping bag on the floor of the kitchen area. The new guy always gets screwed.

We were having a lot of fun, though. This was our first big outdoor festival tour, and it almost felt like summer camp. We would wake up every morning out in the countryside, where we joined the other artists and crew in the catering tent for breakfast (which felt pretty luxurious compared to the truck stops to which we had grown accustomed), and there was a real sense of community, as if we were one big circus traveling around the country together. However, it wasn't quite as glamorous for us as a festival tour might sound. We were playing on the second stage out in the parking lot during the middle of the day, so we only performed for a couple hundred people, while the rest of the crowd was watching O.A.R. or Ziggy Marley on the main stage. But because our album and single were released at that time (after a big record-release party at the old Tower Records on Sunset Boulevard), we slowly crept up the list of bands on that tour, from opening to headlining the second stage, over the course of those two months. So we could really see how much progress we were making, day by day, week by week.

The album sold about 5,000 copies the week it came out, and then it dropped off to 500 the next week (which was expected, because all the people who had been waiting for it to come out bought it the first week). But then we watched it go up to 1,000 the following week . . . and to 1,500 the week after that . . . and to 2,000 after that . . . It was gaining a little bit of traction with each passing show and each radio play. Octone would give us weekly reports on how many spins "Harder to Breathe" got across the country at each radio station that had added it to its playlist, and the numbers increased incrementally as promotion grew and developed organically. And Octone also gave us breakdowns of how many copies the album had sold in particular cities, so we could see that after we played for a good crowd in Charlotte, North Carolina, for instance, there would be a spike of a couple hundred records sold in that city alone. All of this gave us the kind of reinforcement that we needed to keep up our morale after the six . . . seven . . . eight . . . months we had been touring so far.

One moment that stands out to me from that summer, however, was a disappointing and embarrassing one for Adam. When we started the tour, we were introduced to the headliners, but we had begun to wonder if and when they would actually come see our daytime set, which was outside the main amphitheater. It took about a week for Sheryl Crow to finally come see us play. A couple of songs into our set, we could see that she and her assistant were walking down to the soundboard to check us out. I know Adam had been nervous about playing for her, given that she was a very big star when we were in high school. I don't know if it was nerves or just bad timing, but all of a sudden Adam's voice just went out completely, and he could barely sing a note. This wasn't the first time that this had happened, as his voice could be a little temperamental when we played shows night after night, but it seemed pretty coincidental that it happened right at a moment of elevated pressure and anxiety. After trying in vain to work through it, he turned around to me and mimed stabbing himself in the stomach, as if he were committing hari-kari. Sadly, we watched Sheryl Crow as she turned around and walked back up toward the catering tent. Adam was pretty distraught after that.

I was obviously disappointed that we hadn't made the best impression, but I also felt badly for Adam. He was really upset, and I could see how much pressure he was under to perform well every day. I guess I had kind of taken for granted how much of our success was weighing on his shoulders, and I hadn't really considered what that can do to your ego when you're in that situation day after day. When everything goes well, you feel like you're flying high in the clouds, but when it goes badly . . . it can be devastating. This one rather minor calamity helped me understand what I had perceived up until that point as occasional diva behavior. Whenever he complained about the state of his voice, not wanting to perform at times that weren't as important to him (like at Brew Co.), he was actually very nervous about having to be at his best when it *really* mattered, and this was weighing heavily on him, I think. I don't want to project my own psychology onto him too much, but I have to imagine that this show and the few other times that this sort of thing happened were isolated instances of "the yips."

This one event actually had a pretty large impact on Adam's approach to touring and performing from then on. He stopped drinking and smoking on the road entirely, not wanting to compromise his voice, and he started doing vocal warm-ups before every show. I was impressed that Adam used that setback as motivation to step up his level of professionalism. If you think about it, an embarrassing moment like that could be devastating to your self-confidence and have disastrous implications for your ability to perform well in the future. But instead, he went the other direction, working that much harder to overcome this sort of challenge and get back up on the horse, so to speak. Perhaps he had more in common with his idol Kobe Bryant than I had given him credit for.

chapter 13

the man in the arena

We were still living pretty much hand to mouth by the fall of 2002, and we would continue to do so well into 2003. I think the average person probably assumes that when you sign a record deal, put out an album, and tour the country, you're at least making a pretty good income. The reality is that making albums and videos is expensive. Keeping a band on the road that is not yet selling out their own shows is expensive. Vans, U-Hauls, gas, food, lodging, crew, equipment . . . it all adds up. So, after the initial advance (which was pretty small this time), all of the record label's funds go to this long marketing crusade they call touring. On top of that, record contracts are structured such that you need to recoup most of that cost out of your small share of the record sales before you see dime one. So, without doing a bunch of math, that means that you basically have to be selling hundreds of thousands of records, have to have songs you wrote blowing up the airwaves, or have to be selling out pretty large venues, before you actually see another check going into your bank account.

My frugal dad raised a pretty sensible young man, however, so I was saving up my per diem whenever possible! We would each get twenty dollars a day for all our food costs, but the venues were required to either provide us a meal or give us a small stipend to buy ourselves dinner. And sometimes, if we were really lucky, the motel or hotel would provide a breakfast of some kind. And whereas the other guys would see their twenty-dollar per diem and immediately think to themselves, "Where's the closest record or vintage clothing store?" I would pocket as much of it as I could, until I'd saved up a few hundred dollars by the end of a tour. I don't really know why I bothered doing that, though, because without fail, Adam would spend his whole week's per diem in the first few days, and then he would come to me for money.

"I don't save up my money just to give it to you, Adam!" I would say to him.

"Come on, Ryan, don't be a cheapskate. I'll pay you back when we get next week's per diem."

"And then you'll be out of money again, and you'll be coming to me for more! It never ends, Adam!"

I think the guys thought I was just being a miserly Jew, but the stereotype doesn't hold, because Adam is Jewish too, and he can't keep a dollar in his pocket for more than an hour!

These kinds of spats were all just part of the brotherly relationship we had at that point. After nine months of constant touring, Adam, Jesse, Mickey, James, and I pretty much had our own language with one another, and just the five of us were enough to keep ourselves entertained. Anyone who came in close contact with us in those days was amazed at the sense of humor that we shared, having spent so much time together for so long. We could riff off of one another as if we had rehearsed a routine. James's midwestern charm added something new to the mix of our personal chemistry as well, as we felt we had to indoctrinate the newest recruit.

I also remember James saying that he was impressed with how we handled disagreements within the band. As I've said, we could argue about almost anything, but we would always resolve our disagreements and make peace before the day was done, just like a healthy, married couple . . . only there were five of us. James had never seen that lack of dysfunction in a band before. He said that most guys in bands just hold on to hidden resentments for years. I felt lucky to have that kind of special relationship with three (and now four) other guys with whom I was sharing this very unique experience. It was not lost on me that there was something very special about where we were in our lives, and where we were going.

After the big summer festival tour ended, we played some more dates on the West Coast opening for O.A.R. to begin the fall before we would head out east for our first college arena shows, opening for John Mayer in November. John was already a pretty big star by the time we crossed paths with him, and he was becoming something of a blues guitar hero as well as a teen heartthrob (two things that don't necessarily always go together). James had originally met John when they did a summer semester at the Berklee College of Music together a few years prior, and James decided to reach out to John when our album was finally ready for release. John loved our sound immediately and graciously offered us dates on his tour, just as he was reaching the apex of his big breakthrough album *Room for Squares*. His fan base was already much larger than that of most of the artists for whom we had been opening, so these would be our first shows on arena and amphitheater stages, playing directly before the headliner.

My only image of John before meeting him was that of a very skilled and soulful guitarist, who sang the kind of love songs that teenage girls wish their boyfriends could sing to them. Despite his status as an up-and-coming blues man, he seemed the romantic type to me. But our first impression of John could not have hit further from that mark. About twenty minutes before we were set to take the stage in Temple University's basketball arena in Philadelphia, John introduced himself to us, standing in the big, open freight area behind the stage.

"Love the record, guys. 'This Love' is my favorite song of the year, hands down. It's going to be a huge fucking hit." He had watched us play in sound check from the back of the arena, but this was our first up-close interaction. "You guys are going to be famous within a year; trust me, you'll be headlining places like this, and all these teenage girls will be screaming for you, while I'm back home twiddling my thumbs . . . "

"Relationships are hard, man," he continued. "Do you guys have girl-friends back home?"

We were taken aback by this question out of nowhere. He went on talking before any of us could answer.

"Do you know what the difference between men and women is? When I'm in a relationship, I just want to get that car out on the highway, man . . . I just wanna put it in gear and get some miles behind us, you know what I mean? Just hit the open road and see where it takes us. But women, they wanna pull the car over at every stop and inspect the engine for problems. 'Are we low on oil?' 'Is the brake fluid leaking?' I mean, I'm like, 'Come on, let's not analyze this to death, please! It's just going to drive us crazy, right?' I'm like, 'Let's see where we can take this thing before we go to the mechanic every week!'"

It didn't occur to me until later (after watching him do this kind of thing several times with several different groups of people) that John sees himself as a stand-up comic. He can talk to a circle of people standing around him for half an hour, entertaining everyone and himself at the same time. He just hadn't thought to inform us that this was what he was doing. It was hilarious, especially because we were literally a few steps away from playing our first arena show for 12,000 people and we were all pretty nervous. With the exception of a few radio festivals back in '97, this was at least five times the size of the average audience for whom we were used to playing. I suppose it's possible that he recognized the anxiety of such a momentous occasion and he was trying to ease the tension by shaking us up with a ridiculous story. However, I suspect he just likes to do his shtick!

My parents had decided to fly to the East Coast to spend Thanksgiving with me at my aunt Bea and uncle Carlos's house in Virginia, and the trip would double as an opportunity for them to catch our first arena shows, so my dad had actually driven from Virginia to Philadelphia for that show. While we were setting up, he grabbed the video camera we had in our van, and he was taping all of this backstage before the show. I don't know where that tape is today, but it exists somewhere. He was doing interviews with the band and even introduced himself to John, who broke into a whole routine once he saw the camera rolling. My dad had the same reaction, thinking, "Is this guy nuts?" He then came to the same conclusion that John was just doing his shtick.

My dad was filming us at the side of the stage as we prepared to go up and do our opening set, but then John stopped us and told us to hang back for a bit. The arena had only filled up about a quarter of the way so far, and even though the schedule said it was time to play, John wanted to make sure that we had a good crowd there to see us. This was a very thoughtful thing for him to do, one that few headliners would do in support of the opener. He really did want us to have the full experience and maximum exposure to his big, young audience. And once the room had filled in a bit more, he actually went out to center stage to introduce us. Again, he didn't have to do this, but he did it, to make sure that his fans were paying attention to us. The lights went down, the spotlight went up, and John went to the mic.

"Hi guys. Welcome to the show. I'm going to play for you guys in a little while, but before I do . . . I want you to enjoy this first group. These guys are my favorite new band of 2002 . . . and they're about to become your favorite band of 2003. Ladies and gentlemen . . . Maroon 5."

The audience screamed as the stage went black, and John walked back down the steps toward us. He wished us a great show, and we climbed the stairs out into the darkness. As the cheers died down, we took our place beneath the powerful lights that slowly rose to illuminate us, and we prepared ourselves to launch into our set. Believe it or not, the place actually felt a little empty and cold from where we were standing. Being onstage in an arena is different than you might expect: it's hard to get any real sense of the crowd because the spotlights are all aiming at your face, and the rest of the arena just looks like outer space. I guess that's why artists started asking fans to hold up their lighters (or cell phones) in the darkness. And it sounds strangely quiet onstage, because the huge speakers are out in front of you and all of that sound just sort of disappears out into the abyss, creating a distant echo off the back wall. That's why a lot of artists will wear in-ear monitors, which we did not yet have ("in-ear monitors" are basically just very efficient earplugs and headphones, which block out all outside noise while providing a very clean audio mix so that you can hear yourself clearly in a venue like that). Without in-ears, the sound onstage dissipates pretty quickly, and then all you can hear is the reflection and rumble bouncing off the walls around the room. And because we couldn't see anyone out in the darkness, the first couple of songs in the set kind of felt like we were playing to an empty arena.

As we settled into our performance, however, we could feel the energy in the room slowly start to ramp up. When we reached the breakdown moment of the set, when I would loop the beat to "Sunday Morning" while Adam talked to the crowd, Adam told me to stop for a minute.

"Wait, wait, wait! Can we just stop for a second? . . . Can we get the house guy to pull up the house lights for a second? . . . I wanna see you guys! I can't see you guys!"

I stopped the beat as they raised the house lights, and when they did, we got our first glimpse of a fully packed arena. Adam then said what I think we were all thinking. "HOLY SHIT!!!!!!"

"HOW YOU FEELING TONIGHT, PHILLY???" he asked after a brief pause.

The uproarious screams and applause had a sound and volume we had never heard from a crowd before. I remember looking out at the very top of the arena, where a few people right up against the back wall were waving their hands over their heads. They looked like little ants from where I was sitting, and I just started laughing to myself. This was flat-out surreal. I couldn't help but feel totally giddy in that moment, just like we did the first time we went onstage in a club together as kids. People will sometimes ask, "When was the moment that you knew you made it?" Well, I don't think you could say that we had "made it" yet at that point, but it was definitely a moment in which I thought, "Wow . . . this is something that most people never get to experience," and I could certainly feel the awe of it as it was happening. About 12,000 people were screaming for our band, and most of them had just met us. Closing out that show felt like we had really accomplished something. All the work we had done was finally starting to pay off.

As we walked offstage to thunderous applause and legions of screaming teenage girls who had just become huge fans of Maroon 5, Adam strode
right up to my dad's camera, and he exclaimed, "WE'RE GONNA BE FUCK-
ING STARS!!!!!!!" My dad laughed and looked at me, beaming with pride. I
smiled at him and winked. We're gonna be fucking stars . . .

The following show was a similar setup with John Mayer at George Mason
University in Virginia, and Shan flew in from LA to join me and my family. Sure, we were not technically "boyfriend and girlfriend" at this point
because of the arrangement that we had come to regarding our relationship, but we had been prominent in each other's lives for a couple of years
by then, and I wanted her to be there to experience this momentous occasion with me. She arrived while we were at sound check, and when I came
backstage to find her, she informed me that she had already met John while
she was waiting in the wings, and he was very . . . friendly. I didn't know
what to take from that, but I soon found out, when we went to the catering
hall for dinner. After we got our food and sat at one of the cafeteria-style
tables, John walked in and sat at the end of the table, right between her and
me. He then proceeded to spend the next twenty minutes looking only at
her and launching into the exact same shtick about men wanting to take
the car out onto the highway and women wanting to stop and look under
the hood. Shan and I were kicking each other under the table. I, of course,
had told her about our bizarre first meeting with him, but now she was
getting a firsthand reliving of it. It dawned on me that a lot of girls were
probably attracted to this level of confidence and lack of self-restraint, but
Shan just found it hilarious (at least that's what she told me!).

After Thanksgiving with my family, Shan rode with me in the van up
to Connecticut in the snow to see the end of that string of shows. John
actually came onstage to perform with us at a show near his hometown
in Wallingford, plugging in his Fender SRV Strat to jam with us on "This
Love," much to the delight of his huge indoor amphitheater crowd. I think
he just wanted to jam with us, but again, it was not something he had to

do, and it definitely made the audience pay attention, so we really appreciated the gesture. The feeling in the room was electric, and it felt more like what we'd imagined headlining a big tour would be like than anything we'd experienced before.

We toured with John a couple of more times after that, and every time Shan was around, he would just stare at her or talk to her as if I weren't even there. If I didn't know that Shan loved me so much and was so dedicated to our relationship, I suppose I might have been jealous or bothered by it, but I just thought it was hilarious and amazing to watch. It was often as if I didn't even exist. Shan would just blush and go along with it, but the two of us would laugh about it afterward. I'm sure she was flattered that a big pop star was obsessed with her, but she was never one to gloat or rub something like that in my face.

At a later date, when the band was in New York for a private event, John invited me and James to his apartment for an after-show get-together. He was playing us his demos of the songs he had just written for his new album, and at a certain point James went down to the kitchen to fetch more drinks, leaving me alone with John.

"Hey, man, I wanna apologize for being sticky on your girlfriend," he said to me.

"It's all good, man. If anything, I'm flattered that you're so infatuated with her. You're a big star!"

He seemed surprised to hear that. He made a face as if to say, "You mean you're not worried that she's going to run off with me?"

He then said, "It's not that I want to steal her from you, man, it's just kind of like . . . I'd like to go to the factory where they made her and have them make me one, too."

As if that weren't enough, when the first single from John's second album, "Bigger than My Body," came out, the girl who starred in the video was a doppelgänger for Shan!

We finished off 2002 with a tour opening for Vanessa Carlton, and sure enough, we had completed one very full year in support of our album, just as our label execs had promised. The only thing was that we weren't even close to done yet. "Harder to Breathe" was only a moderate hit at certain radio formats by that point, and the album was just very slowly creeping upward in sales from week to week. The label guys decided we were only about halfway to where they wanted us to be in order to consider the next level of promotion. The game plan was to continue to build on the modest successes we had gained, and when the time was right, they would kick the album up to the parent company, J Records, for help from the great Clive Davis. We would then promote the second single, "This Love," and release the album internationally, complete with all the bells and whistles of a major-label marketing campaign. In other words, the media blitz was only going to start after we had already done two whole years of touring, and 2003 would turn out to be an even bigger whirlwind before that would happen.

chapter 14

try harder

About a year into touring on *Songs About Jane*, I started showing the first signs of problems with performing. They were subtle, but the other band members were noticing them. From time to time I would miss a beat, or I would obsess so much about one part of a song that I would end up botching it. I don't know if the audiences spotted these things, because I'm sure they passed quickly, but the band definitely did, and they started bringing them to my attention, pointing out spots where I'd flubbed. The guys weren't actually being derogatory about it; they were speaking more from a place of concern, but my first reaction was to become defensive, thinking they were being overly critical.

"Did you hear that? . . . What happened there exactly?" Adam asked as we sat in the back of the van, pointing out a moment in the previous night's recording when the drums stalled for a beat.

"Eh, yeah . . . I don't know." I shrugged, trying to think of an excuse for it. "It was just a flub . . . I just had, like, a twitch or something, and I didn't come back in for a split second. It wasn't a big deal."

"Yeah, but why does that happen?" Jesse asked. "Sometimes you'll miss the snare and just hit the rim, and we don't get a good backbeat. Are you losing focus? Or . . ."

"No, no, I'm definitely not losing focus," I assured them. "I'm concentrating hard on what I'm doing. It's just . . . I don't know. It won't happen again, okay?"

"We just want the show to be as good as it can be," Adam said. "We need to figure out why stuff like this happens and try to fix it. We're at a level now where we can't really afford to not be at our best."

"Yeah, I know, I get it, okay?" I said testily. "I don't know . . . I feel like I'm getting out of practice for some reason. The only time we play is onstage, so I'm only playing our set over and over. I think my body just gets stiff and my arm kind of freezes up . . . I can work on it, I guess . . . I'll just warm up more in sound check."

They were somewhat appeased for the moment, and I didn't drop a beat for a while after that, but later in that tour Jesse brought up another issue to me.

"Ryan, I was listening to you playing in sound check, and the bass drum just sounds inconsistent. It's like you play it harder on some hits and softer on others. It just feels kind of out of balance. I don't really understand it . . . You didn't used to play that way."

"Well, I'm human, okay, Jesse? I don't know if I can hit it exactly the same every time. I'm not perfect."

"I think you can, if you work on it," Jesse said. "Maybe just practice that in sound check too?"

"Yeah, I can try to work on it, I guess . . . But I don't know if I'll ever be perfect at it."

"Don't say that . . . you can do whatever you set your mind to."

Obviously, I knew that the standard of performance had risen since our garage days and the band could no longer tolerate flubs and miscues, but I couldn't help but get a little testy when these were pointed out to me. However, my defensiveness was really just a front for my internal self-criticism. Inside, I was getting very angry at myself, knowing that I was causing myself these problems. But my perfectionistic mind could only think of one recourse to address the issue: *try harder*. However, in reality, the problem wasn't a matter of effort—it was just the opposite: I was over-thinking to the point of giving myself a mental block; I was giving myself "the yips" again.

As a result of my increased pressure to perform well, I also started edging closer to my drums, feeling that I needed to get right on top of them to control my playing more. However, this tendency had the opposite effect. With my legs now squished up against the pedals and my arms not fully extended in hitting the drums, I was getting more bound up, making my movements even more difficult to control. It was maddening. I felt as if the harder I tried, the harder it was to play well. I would grip the sticks stiffly and bear down to aim the direction of their flight, but in doing so my arms would get very tense, causing my muscles to cramp and my joints to lock up. I heard another drummer once refer to something called "sour foot," meaning that you just feel like you don't have as much control of your kick pedal one day. Well, I pretty much had sour foot every day, causing me to pull my drum seat closer to the pedal and jam my leg up, causing that inconsistent dynamic to which Jesse had referred.

My tendency toward obsessive-compulsiveness, which the band had mostly just laughed and teased about in the past, was also becoming more apparent to those around me. I was never self-conscious about it before, thinking of it as just a little personality quirk about which we all could have a good laugh, but now it bothered me when it was pointed out. I remember James noticing that I always positioned the logos on my cymbals facing me, needing to touch each one of them before I could play. I hadn't noticed that I was doing this, but I was definitely aware of how much time I would spend trying to get my drums set up and tuned just right. It was becoming extremely frustrating to me because, strangely, what felt right one day would feel totally off the next day, and I would have to spend a lot more time and energy trying to get myself comfortable behind the drum kit. But what I was really feeling was panic over my inability to perform to the level of perfection that I (and now the rest of the band) expected, and all the machinations of setting up my drums were just my way of trying to reclaim the control I felt slipping away.

I wasn't the only person in the band having a hard time on the road, as the touring life dragged on through our second straight year. Mickey went through a phase in which he was really questioning if this was what he wanted to be doing, and it was really getting him down. Mickey is a very smart, intellectual guy, and his taste in most things can be "artsy" (for lack of a better term), so performing for the mainstream pop crowds wasn't exactly his cup of tea. He didn't like the idea that we were quickly becoming a part of the world of mass consumerism (rather than a cooler/hipper world of art and intellectualism), and you could really tell from his lack of enthusiasm onstage. He would often stand without moving his feet the entire show, just staring down at his shoes.

Adam and I discussed our frustration with Mickey's demeanor, wishing that he could better appreciate the unique opportunity that we were being given and the fact that most people would kill to be in his position. In retrospect, I can see that it wasn't disregard or lack of consideration on Mickey's part, however; he was actually depressed. Often he wouldn't come out of isolation all day, and when he did, his mood was very low and quiet. Adam and I called a band meeting with him to address the issue one day in Memphis. We talked to him about what we had been noticing and how we were feeling about it, and he acknowledged that he had not been giving it his all. He said that he missed his scene back home and regretted that he wasn't able to do some of the things that were more fulfilling to him, but that he did in fact appreciate how amazing what we were doing was, and he promised that he would try harder to enjoy it. We were happy to hear him affirm his dedication to the band, and believe it or not, that one conversation was enough for his general attitude and disposition to improve pretty significantly.

Jesse could be up and down in his mood as well. He would start most tours with a couple of weeks of supreme optimism in classic Jesse form: he wanted to take our band to an extraordinary place of significance, to turn people on to better music and art, and to effect positive change in the world (both Mickey and Jesse were pretty sociopolitically motivated by this point). He could be rather grandiose in his notions of what we could do as a band in this regard, wanting to create charities and write socially conscious lyrics that would raise awareness of important issues. However, somewhere in the middle of each tour, he would get disillusioned and take a turn for the dark, after which he would start to feel that what we were doing was rather meaningless. He would talk about going to India or some other faraway place to take up Buddhism or something else that he would find more meaningful than playing pop music. I could get frustrated with Jesse at these times, but looking back on it, I feel for that passionate young man. He was a true idealist, and the world can be frustrating and disappointing at times.

When Jesse would get into these disheartened states, I would try to encourage him by telling him that what we do as a band is actually really beautiful.

"We make people happy, Jesse," I would argue. "People listen to our music not only because it brings them joy but also because they can relate to it. Human connection is the most important element of any art, and people are really starting to connect to our music."

"Yeah, but I want us to be like the Beatles," Jesse would say. "I want us to promote peace and love . . . and compassion. I want our songs to be about something more than just a relationship . . . and our videos to be more than just a performance. I want to create real art like Radiohead . . . Look at Coldplay, even. They promote important charities at every appearance they do . . . Remember when Eddie Vedder wrote 'Pro-Choice' on his arm on *MTV Unplugged*? I wish Adam would do stuff like that . . . or get involved with activism like Bono."

"I'm not really comfortable doing that kind of thing," Adam chimed in. "I think as an artist you have to stay within your jurisdiction. Don't get me wrong, I love that there are guys like Bono out there bringing attention to important causes, but I'm not really a political person. I think about girls and relationships most of the time, so that's what I write about. That's what I know. And that's what I'm good at. I think it would be kind of inauthentic if I tried to write a song about world peace or something like that."

"Yeah, and not every band has to be U2, and not every singer can be Bono," I contended. "We can still do great things—support charities and raise money for causes that we agree on—but people come to our shows to be moved by the music and just enjoy themselves. It's actually pretty amazing that we can provide that for an audience. That's our gift that we have to offer people, and that makes me feel really good! We're putting that out into the world."

This sort of conversation seemed to make Jesse feel better for the moment, and he would close out the tour in a better mood.

Somehow, we were all able to work through our issues for the time being, and we continued to perform relatively well through a lot of 2003. Things were really looking up for us in general. We were still playing in support of bigger headliners for the first half of that year, but it was clear that many of the people in attendance had already become aware of our band. For the first time, fans in the crowd were mouthing our lyrics back to us—an honor that we had only imagined before then—and it felt marvelous to see. After a few more successful tours supporting Guster and Jason Mraz, we went out on our first full-size, twenty-thousand-seat arena tour in the spring, supporting Matchbox Twenty and Sugar Ray. Rob Thomas was very kind to us, even buying us a bunch of nice cameras as tour gifts. He was a big fan of our band, and many nights he would stand at the side of the stage to watch our set. He complimented me on my drumming style, even asking if I would consider playing on the solo album he was planning to record. I was deeply honored by this request, but it also made me a little nervous. I was sure that he would notice that I wasn't as adept as he had believed from watching our band onstage. The thought of getting into the studio with this very successful artist and embarrassing myself was a rather scary prospect.

I also hit it off with another well-known musician on that tour, who had a reputation for being a party animal on the road but was a lot of fun to hang out with at the side of the stage. He and his girlfriend liked me and

Shan as a couple, too, so they instructed me to be good to her. He implored me, "Don't be like us, man. We fucked up our relationship a long time ago. I'm a total dog on the road, and when I come home I have to slap the gardener's dick out of my girlfriend's mouth."

I don't know if this joke had an effect on my thinking, but sometime around then I began to consider recommitting to my relationship with Shan. The freedom for which I had asked hadn't been as fulfilling as I had imagined, and it was clear to me that no casual fling in some small town was going to compare to the connection I had with the intelligent and beautiful woman I loved back home. However, I had in fact indulged in a few ill-advised flings during our time apart, and the guys thought that I should tell Shan about them before I asked her to recommit. So I called her from the road, just a couple of days before I would be coming home for a few days, and I owned up to everything. She was understandably upset, and she was hesitant to jump back into a committed relationship with me.

I went straight to her apartment when I got back into town, and when I got there, she looked like she was already on the verge of tears before I even said anything. I tried to reassure her as much as I could, but I could see that this was going to take time. She was even more upset than she'd been when I'd told her I wanted my freedom, and the knowledge of my dalliances was causing a new level of distrust that hadn't been there before. She still loved me, and she wanted to be with me more than anything, but she was beginning to believe that I was going to continue to break her heart in the future.

It was on the Guster tour that we got our first real tour bus. For the first week we rode around in a run-down, silver Eagle left over from the 1980s, which was inhabited by spiders that crawled in our bunks, but we quickly upgraded to a relatively new, black Prevost, which was a big step up in lifestyle for us. Having a bus also meant we had a bus driver, which meant we no longer had to drive ourselves all over North America, we could sleep through the drives on our own little bunk mattresses, and we had lounges in the front and back to hang out comfortably, watch movies, or play video games (we even had a pet goldfish in the front lounge for a little while). Of course, this meant that the video game guys (Adam and my old roommate Shawn Tellez, who was now our assistant tour manager) stayed mostly in the back lounge and the artsy cinema guys (Mickey and Jesse) hung out in the front lounge for the most part. James kind of went back and forth between the two, but I was torn. On a friend level, I was a bit closer with the video game guys, but I hated video games! Especially the really violent ones that they loved the most. I can't tell you how many nights I had to try to fall asleep to the sounds of extremely realistic gunshots and explosions blaring from the game *Halo* right next to my head.

We had twelve bunks on the bus, which was enough for the band, our small but growing crew, and our bags of luggage stowed for easy access, and it was now a little easier to bring our girlfriends on tour with us from time to time. When we were still in the van, Shan and I had to lie butt to butt on one of the rows of seats to try to get comfortable enough to nap, but now we had a bunk into which we could squeeze two grown adults. Having women traveling on the bus with us was a pretty different scene than you'd see on most band buses, and the roadies couldn't understand it at all. They thought of touring as if we were a bunch of sailors living in a submarine, who would dock from time to time and pillage the local fare. But we liked having the feminine energy with us, so we encouraged each other to bring our girls. Shan started joining me for a week every two months, Adam started bringing his girlfriend Kelly at the same time, Mickey would bring his girlfriend Z, and Shawn even brought his girl Gisella with us at times as well. We had as many as four women traveling with us at one time. The road crew even complained to us about it, saying that they lived on the bus, too, and it was cramping their style. We felt pretty firmly that this was the way we wanted to roll, so we told them that they were our employees, and they would just have to deal with it or find another job. They started treating our girls nicely after that.

Being on a bus also meant that the "Odd Couple," Adam and I, were 100 percent full-time roommates, cohabitating in the same small space (without ever separating to different motel rooms), so the differences between our personalities started to become a minor issue again. He would leave half-empty water bottles all around the place, he would throw his dirty socks on the floor of the hallway between the bunks, he would chew his food with his mouth open, and in general he would just work on every last one of my pet peeves, one after another. But our little arguments about these things were really just brotherly spats more than real animosity. The positive feelings I had for all my compatriots far outweighed any petty disputes we had with one another. And we were still having a lot of fun together. The silliness of our teenage years would arise in the delirium of long hours, days, and weeks on the road together, and those moments are some of my favorite memories. I do remember, though, on at least a few occasions, watching Adam chewing with his mouth open and asking him, "Are you serious???" He would look at me as if to say, "What's wrong with you?"

The summer of 2003 included another huge, outdoor, amphitheater tour, this time with John Mayer and Counting Crows co-headlining, as well as a series of radio festivals. Somewhere in the middle of that summer, we played a one-off daytime rock festival near Dallas, which led to a rather unusual evening with none other than future first daughter Ivanka Trump and her boyfriend Bingo (yes, you read that right . . . Bingo was his name-o). We had been introduced to Ivanka by way of Savannah Buffett, who grew up within this circle of extremely wealthy children, traveling between Manhattan's Upper East Side, the Hamptons, Palm Beach, Florida, and so on. This group of heirs and heiresses could act obnoxiously spoiled a lot of the time, but they could also be entertaining and gracious in moments. Most of these kids had more money and resources than anyone you could possibly imagine, and they just seemed to be parading through life, looking for any opportunity to outdo the last party or the last decadent expenditure. However, Savannah had informed us that the Trumps were not actually in the same league as these other very wealthy industrial families. As most of the world now knows, Donald Trump had gone bankrupt several times over from his involvement in his Atlantic City casinos, and he was now what Savannah described as "TV money," referring to his modest resurrection on the show *The Apprentice*. She said this dismissively, as if TV money were not real money, not compared to the actual billions that these other families were worth.

Bingo was one of these extremely rich kids, and he was just finishing up college at Southern Methodist University at the time. When he and Ivanka showed up backstage at our show in Texas, Bingo was immediately the life of the party. He had grand plans for how he wanted to take us out and show us the town. He suggested that we rent a stretch Hummer limo, go to a strip club, and party harder than we'd ever partied before. Ivanka had a much more restrained demeanor than he did, but she seemed fine going along with whatever he suggested. Sure enough, the night was just as decadent as he had described. He wasn't able to find a stretch Hummer limo on short notice, but he did get a limo of some kind, we did go to a strip club (in which he was able to get an entire section closed off for just our group), and he did bring the party in more ways than one. He passed around "party favors" and bought lap dances for everyone, insisting that we all just go crazy that night. This guy was a wild man, pure and simple. I had never been a part of debauchery on this scale, and he seemed to revel in blowing our minds with the level of depravity and decadence.

However, at one point in the night, I was actually able to sneak away from the Bingo show and have an interesting one-on-one conversation with Ivanka. As we sat on folding chairs outside our tour bus, I asked her what her plans were for the future.

"So, Bingo's graduating . . . what are you doing now?" I asked.

"I'm getting my degree at Wharton," she answered confidently.

"Very impressive. What kind of business do you plan to go into?"

"Real estate," she responded quickly.

"Ah, the family business, huh?" I asked, grinning.

"Yes, exactly," she said. "I'm very proud of what my family has accomplished in real estate. My grandfather and my father have contributed so much to New York City, and I can't wait to make my imprint on the Manhattan skyline as well."

This statement felt like a pre-rehearsed sermon on the merits of the Trump family, but I was struck by the grandiosity of her ambition. She went on.

"I'm very proud of my parents for how they pulled themselves out of financial ruin to remake their fortune. I remember walking down the street with my father one day when I was young, and he pointed to a homeless man and said to me, 'That man has more money than me,' because he was in so much debt at the time. My parents could have folded up and been totally destroyed by that, but they worked very hard to reclaim their place."

I hadn't said anything to the contrary, but for some reason she felt that she needed to give me her pitch in defense of the Trump family and the Trump Organization. Her lecture seemed to be in total lockstep with the branding strategy that the world has come to know for everything Trump: talk big and apologize for nothing.

I was actually pretty impressed with Ivanka at the time. In comparison with the other uber-rich kids I had met (who mostly just wanted to party hard and talk about the frivolous pet projects on which they were "working"), she sounded very ambitious and focused. However, it was only in retrospect that I realized just how media-directed her whole presentation was. This wasn't an off-the-cuff conversation she was having with a new friend. She was delivering statements that had been prepared as PR for the family brand, and I just happened to fall in earshot. And then Bingo tried to eat our goldfish.

chapter 15

cracks in the ceiling

By the middle of 2003, we were starting to book late-night TV appearances, playing "Harder to Breathe" on *Last Call with Carson Daly*, *The Late Late Show with Craig Kilborn*, and a few others. We were getting offers left and right, so we just had to fit them into our already jam-packed schedule wherever they fit. At one point, after flying all the way back to Los Angeles from the East Coast, we were informed as we stood at baggage claim that we had just been offered a spot on the *Late Show with David Letterman* and we would have to jump back on another plane to fly back to New York immediately! Talk about exciting and exhausting! I did my best to let the exhilaration of this mind-blowing opportunity overtake my discomfort with the last-minute change of plans, quickly shifting into "flying by the seat of my pants" mode for this adventure (what other choice did I have, really?).

Most late-night shows are prerecorded, so my big fear of live television didn't come into play yet with these performances, but playing for this large a television audience for the first time was definitely nerve-racking. I remember finishing our performance on *Letterman* (on that ice-cold Ed

Sullivan Theater stage where the Beatles had played in 1964), looking over at Paul Shaffer and the band for approval, and getting a big thumbs-up from their drummer Anton Fig. That was a huge honor, and it was very encouraging.

Around then our promotional plans were beginning to expand internationally, but before we could go to Europe for the first time in the summer of 2003, we had some important business to attend to with our record label in New York City. J Records was kind enough to put us on the bill for a private event that Alicia Keys would headline, entertaining all the CEOs of the major companies associated with BMG International. It was as if the heads of the Five Families were in New York to see this show at the Millennium Hotel, featuring Alicia Keys, Maroon 5, and Gavin DeGraw. This would be our big coming-out party, as these were the people who would sign the checks to promote the album all over the world, when the second single, "This Love," dropped in January. And we didn't disappoint. We played one of the tightest and most energetic sets ever at that show, and it was a smashing success, with all the label and distribution heads promising us we were going to be big stars.

After a few more dates in the US, we flew overnight to London, where we were scheduled to play a show that very same night. I was too excited to sleep on the red-eye, and I was still wired when we got into the city, so while most of the guys went to their rooms to get some more sleep, I headed out right then to see London for the first time. BMG UK had put us up in a pretty swanky hotel called the Grosvenor House, which sits right across from the beautiful and famous Hyde Park, so I found myself right in the middle of everything I wanted to see. I walked straight through Central London to Buckingham Palace, Trafalgar Square, Big Ben/Parliament, and Westminster Abbey. It was all very romantic for me, seeing a new foreign city by myself, as if I were a college student backpacking through Europe. And just having that little bit of freedom to do my own thing separate from our usual 24/7 entourage felt like a breath of fresh, British air. However, it didn't dawn on me just how tired I was going to be when I tried to perform that night without any sleep.

When we all met up to head to the concert venue in the cool, Bohemian neighborhood of Camden, I was already starting to hit the wall. I drank some Red Bull to keep me going, but by the time we went onstage, I was a total wreck. I could hardly see straight. Somehow, I got through the show running on fumes, but I promised myself I wouldn't make that mistake again. But I did. I woke up before the sun the next morning, and unable to get back to sleep, I decided to do round two of my London walkabout. The other guys had been more excited to partake of the nightlife and the shopping than the historical sites, but having studied English literature, I was more interested in Shakespeare's Globe Theatre than whatever nightclub or clothing store was trendy that week. I figured I could see a lot more of the city if I ventured out before anyone was awake, so I got up, got myself some coffee, and took the tube across town to see the Globe, the Tower of London, Tower Bridge, and St. Paul's Cathedral. However, the jet lag came back to haunt me again once I finished this early morning jaunt. I tried to take a short nap when I got back to the hotel, but we were scheduled to meet up for a photo shoot at noon, and I just kept watching the clock, seeing the minutes that I wasn't sleeping tick by. We met in the lobby to head toward the shoot site in East London, and I *really* hit the wall this time. I was about as tired as I've ever been in my life, and we were just starting a long day of press, including fittings and makeup, setups at multiple sites, and a handful of interviews, all capped off by an evening of schmoozing with our local reps. I was miserable and exhausted.

The next day we started a stretch of tour dates opening for Matchbox Twenty, and the jet lag just wouldn't relent. The worst of it hit me the night we were set to play none other than the legendary Wembley. Of course, when we had seen the name Wembley Arena on our tour itinerary, we were all giddy with anticipation, because most rock stars will invoke "Wembley" when imagining the ultimate in concert grandiosity (with flashes of Freddie Mercury strutting around the stage in front of 100,000 people at Live Aid). However, what we had envisioned was actually Wembley Stadium, which had been recently demolished and lay in a big pile of rubble just next to the arena that we were scheduled to play that night. Wembley Arena looked more like a big, empty airplane hangar than a concert venue, but it still promised a very large audience to whom we could introduce our music, and it was still called "Wembley," so we were still pretty excited! However, I remember all too well lying on my back on the floor of our dressing room that evening, trying desperately to rest before we went onstage in front of 12,000 Brits for the first time. Imagine performing for that many people (who have never even heard of your band) when you haven't slept more than a few catnaps in a week. Well, I did and, again, I got through it with the last drops of adrenaline I had in my system, but I couldn't really enjoy it at all. In my memory, the crowd response was rather tepid, but that could have just been my perception, given my foggy state.

I finally got over the jet lag by the time we left the UK and headed for the continent, and getting some more rest allowed me to start enjoying performing for audiences in new countries. The crowds in Germany seemed to take to us right away, and I vowed to soak up their local fare as much as I could, eating schnitzel and bratwurst and drinking local brews. Our sound guy Mark became my partner in crime for outings around these cities, because he enjoyed that kind of thing more than anyone else in the band or crew, and my overall experience of touring overseas greatly improved once I adapted to the time zone and found a buddy for sightseeing.

After finishing that string of dates in Europe, we headed back to the States to segue right into our first real headlining tour of North America, without any substantial break. Headlining was what we had been working toward for more than a year and a half on the road, and it was finally coming to fruition. We would be doing fifty-two shows in sixty days, in one-thousand-person capacity venues like the House of Blues all over the United States and Canada. Everything was starting to come together for us, just as I was beginning to get really exhausted. Before we could start that tour, though, we needed to shoot another video, this time for our second single, "This Love." The song was slated for radio release in January, and these were the only days into which we could fit the video shoot.

y very first birthday, in the backyard of our family home in Carthay Circle, with my parents, Gina and Kenny. I swear I have a memory of this moment, but maybe it's just from seeing it on our mantel my whole life.

My family enjoying a lovely vacation in Hawaii when I was three years old and my brother, Josh, was six.

Posing with my parents after my sixth-grade graduation ceremony, at which I had my first anxiety-inducing experience with public speaking. I was very proud but slightly embarrassed by the number of awards I received that day!

Tournament of Champions in Malibu, California, representing Beverly Hills Little League. Look at the torque on my arm! The leverage in my legs! I was a beast at twelve.

My brother, Josh (*left*), and I shared most things growing up, including our deep affection for the show *Knight Rider*. Just look at how happy we were together when we met David Hasselhoff at ages nine and six. I guess the Hoff and I shared a bond, too—over cut-off Everlast sweatshirts!

Josh and I jam on the beach in Cabo San Lucas, Mexico, in 1994, while my mom, Gina, lounges and enjoys the music.

On the Brentwood School football field, where many a pep band show was held. Josh returned from college to join me and the boys in 1994.

The original four members of Kara's Flowers (with our friend David Richman), performing at our first pep rally in the Brentwood School gym. We played Rage Against the Machine's "Killing in the Name" at a school assembly. Talk about inappropriate!

Performing with the pep band on the Brentwood School football field.

At one of our first club shows in 1994, Jesse's dad, Bob, held a photo shoot in front of the Anti-Club at sound check. (Jesse, Mickey, Adam, me)

Performing onstage in the earliest days of Kara's Flowers in 1994–95, when I played with wild abandon, creating sonic thunder!

Unloading my great white whale of a Jeep Wagoneer for our first demo recording session. (me, Jesse, Adam)

Our first recording session in a professional studio, making a demo at Room 222 on Hollywood Boulevard. (Larry Goetz, Jesse, Mickey, me, Adam)

Kara's Flowers goofing around in my teenage bedroom. I would like to say that our sense of humor was dissimilar from that of Beavis and Butt-Head . . . but I would be lying. (Adam, Mickey, Jesse, me)

Recording the album that never came out on Omad Records at the legendary
Sound City Studios in Van Nuys, California. (Jesse, Adam, Mickey)

I embrace my bandmates after a successful showcase performance for record label executives in 1996. (me, Adam, Jesse, Mickey)

The glamorous life of a touring band in 1997 . . . huddling around a laptop in a motel room. (Mickey, Jesse, Adam)

Performing on UCLA's Bruin Walk in 1999, during the *Stagg Street Recordings* era of Kara's Flowers.

Celebrating my graduation from UCLA, the culmination of a wonderful time in my life. (Jesse; Shantell; Shan's little brother, Chad; Gina; me—top row; Andy Coyne— top row; Jason Fields; Adam; Kenny; Travis Leete; Barry McLaughlin)

My parents sent Shan and me to Hawaii as a graduation present
in 2001, right when our love affair was in full bloom.

The girl made famous by a Maroon 5 album, Jane Herman, with Adam in my parents' backyard in 2001.

Celebrating in my parents' backyard in 2001 with the newest member of our band, James Valentine. (Adam, James, me, Mickey, Jesse)

Playing the beat to the song "Secret" during the first week of recording S*ongs About Jane* at Rumbo Recorders in Canoga Park, California, in 2001. My drum kit was stripped down and shoved into a small overdub booth, to emulate the dry, punchy sounds of a hip-hop production, à la Questlove of the Roots.

Adam and Jesse recording the organ overdubs at Rumbo Recorders in Canoga Park, California, in 2001.

Having my college buddies at the studio helped lighten the mood from the intensity of our attempts to capture greatness on the recording of *Songs About Jane*. (Me, Travis Leete, Jason Fields, Adam)

Playing and singing my backing vocals at the *Songs About Jane* album release party at Tower Records on the Sunset Strip in summer 2002.

Playing the second stage on the Jeep World Outside Festival tour in summer 2002, introducing our new album *Songs About Jane* to eager audiences around the country. (Adam, me, Jesse, James)

Performing onstage at the Roxy Theatre in Hollywood, California, in 2002, looking energized and ready for our never-ending tour.

Backstage at one of our first shows opening for John Mayer in late 2002. Spirits were very high! (Adam, Mickey, James, Jesse, me)

Shan flew out to the East Coast to see me perform with John Mayer in late 2002 . . . and got a lot of attention.

At LAX for a red-eye flight. I took these photos with the camera Rob Thomas of Matchbox Twenty gave each of us as an end-of-tour gift. James is sporting his as well. (James, Jesse, Mickey, Adam)

Adam typically had a lot of energy. Just check out the look on Mickey's face. (Me, Adam, Mickey in background)

Adam and I sightseeing on a day off in Amsterdam in 2003. Adam was in search of a tattoo parlor he had heard of.

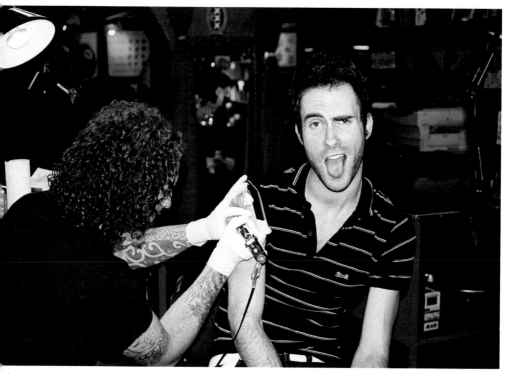

dam went all the way to Amsterdam to get a tattoo that read "Los Angeles" on his arm. One of his first attoos ever, it was inked in an underground parlor attached to a small museum of freaky things in jars.

Big summer tours have a very communal feeling to them, because everyone is camped out at the festival site all day. Dan Vickrey and Adam Duritz of the band Counting Crows wandered into our dressing room on this tour in the summer of 2003. (Dan Vickrey, me, Adam Duritz, Adam)

This is one of my favorite photos of Shan. I took it with my new camera on the set of the video for "This Love" in fall 2003.

On the set of the video for "This Love" in Los Angeles in fall 2003, the production team took my brand-new, custom drum set and rubbed sand all over it, so I had to breathe through that one for a minute!

One of our many delirious, early-morning radio visits, this time in New York City during our first headlining tour of the US. (Me, Jesse)

On the set of *Top of the Pops*, filming at the BBC in London in early 2004. (James, me, Adam, Jesse, Mick

Shan, Kelly, and Z joined us again on our crowded tour bus in early 2004, this time for our first headlining tour of Europe. (Jesse, me, Mickey, Shan, Kelly McKee, Mike Colon, Z Berg)

Shan giving me a massage on tour to release some of the tension caused by my injuries. (Matt Flynn's wife Heidi, me, Shan)

Performing AC/DC's "Highway to Hell" to close out a fan club show at the Troubadour in 2004–5.

James and I scream the chorus of AC/DC's "Highway to Hell" to close out the band's first headlining show in Tokyo, Japan, in 2005.

Posing at a Japanese TV station in 2005. We were getting used to having a lot of cameras aimed at us at all times. (James, me, Mickey, Adam, Jesse)

The band performed at the Shoreline Amphitheater in the San Francisco Bay Area on the summer 2004 tour with John Mayer, but I could only watch from the sidelines. (Jason's friend Ryan Hudson, Shan, Jason, Adam, Kelly, James, John Mayer, Jesse)

Shan and I trying to enjoy ourselves in 2005 at one of many concert after-parties. I was feeling pretty low at this point in my life, and the drink in my hand was beginning to become a fixture. It was getting harder and harder to pretend I wasn't drowning. (Me, Shan, Sam Farrar, Stephanie Eitel Farrar)

I pretended I didn't have a care in the world on the set of the "Sunday Morning" video at London's Abbey Road Studios in 2005, but I had to fake my way through the performance, as I was barely able to hold a beat at that point.

My UCLA buddy Sara Bareilles joining us for a party at my house in Los Feliz in late 2005.

As Shan and I settled into a more "normal" life after I left the band, we traveled to Europe a few times between 2007 and 2012. I took this selfie on a lovely day in Salzburg, Austria, in 2008.

Adam was nice enough to ask me to perform Paul Simon's "Me and Julio Down by the Schoolyard" with the original Maroon 5 lineup, as he and his new bride, Behati, walked down the aisle at their wedding in Cabo San Lucas, Mexico, in 2014. This was the rehearsal the day before. (Me, Mickey, James, Jesse)

My mom, Gina, and I share a love of music. Here we are enjoying a concert at the Hollywood Bowl in 2014, as I continue to try to move on from my life in the band.

My dad, Kenny, and I have shared a love for the Los Angeles Dodgers since I was a little kid. Finding recovery in 2016 helped renew my enjoyment of small things, like a good ball game with my pops, as seen here at Dodger Stadium in 2018.

About a year into my recovery, looking fresh and happy with Shan.

Josh and his wife, Amber, moved to Wisconsin with my two nephews, Beren and Otto, so we visit them whenever we can. Shan would have been with us this time, but she had the chicken pox! (Kenny, Amber Dusick, Otto Dusick, Josh, Beren Dusick, Gina, me)

I finally built my own little studio in 2016–17, just in time to find my new passion for psychology and helping people, but this room has continued to be a wonderful creative space to work and explore new ideas, including writing this book! Recovery brings some amazing things.

This production, directed by Sophie Muller, was a much more elaborate and stylized affair than the one for "Harder to Breathe," and we shot it over two very long days this time. Sophie had a beautiful eye for design, and we had enjoyed the visual style of her videos for No Doubt in particular, so we weren't surprised when we showed up to see a stunning set, complete with colorfully coordinated backdrops, set pieces, and clothing choices. The shoot went smoothly for the most part, but it wasn't very easy on my obsessive-compulsive mind. I had ordered my first custom-made drum set from DW Drums, complete with a satin cherry finish and gold-plated hardware, but when it arrived on set, Sophie immediately proclaimed that it looked way too shiny and new. So she had her grips throw it in the big sandbox that was our stage and rub dirt all over it. I understood the concept of a rustic, distressed décor, but this was my first Cadillac of a drum kit, and it literally hurt me to see them rubbing sand into every nook and cranny. The video looked great, though, and the performances we gave reflected the energy and passion of the music. Adam insisted that his current girlfriend Kelly be cast in the role of his tempestuous lover, and I'm glad that he did. Kelly was obviously a beautiful model, and their chemistry on film was undeniable as they rolled around on a bed together pretty much entirely naked, adding some much-needed heat to the video. It took a very full, exhausting two days to create that titillating short film, but when it was done, we finally had our first real buzzworthy clip.

Right from the get-go, our first headlining tour was both remarkable and worrying. The first few dates on the West Coast were a glorious success from a fan perspective, with packed, sold-out crowds screaming for us at a deafening volume and singing our lyrics back at us in unison. However, playing these full-length sets of every song on our album (plus a couple of new tunes and covers) was a much taller order for me than our previous concerts had been. Performing for ninety minutes shouldn't have been so taxing, but that was the price I paid for never having learned proper drumming technique. I would come offstage every night having sweat out about five pounds from exerting myself so much.

I began to regret that I hadn't learned the proper mechanics of drumming and I hadn't practiced to develop more physical endurance in the years before touring. After teaching myself to play as a teenager, I took for granted that drumming came so easily to me. I got defensive at the idea of learning more or practicing better ways of playing, thinking that I could just do things my way and it would all work out fine. I avoided these challenges out of pride and fear, personality traits of which I am not proud. (I suppose that makes me a hypocrite as well, because I did the very thing I argued against with Adam, relying on my "natural talent.") Of course, having to learn this lesson the hard way, onstage in front of our first sold-out crowds, was extremely uncomfortable for me. Holding my arms in a position to play became harder and harder as each night dragged on, and general fatigue began to set in. I became less able to focus on the sounds that we were making together as a band, as I needed to focus more on just how I was going to execute what I was doing personally. I felt a heaviness in my body and mind, as if I were trying to hold up the roof of a great big house, which we had been building over ten years of playing in the band. I could see that the ceiling of this structure was beginning to crack above me, and I had a growing sense of impending doom: I feared that these fractures would eventually bring the whole thing crashing down on me.

Early in the tour, we played three sold-out shows in three nights at the House of Blues in Hollywood. On top of that, we lined up a full day of press the first day, we performed "Harder to Breathe" on *The Ellen DeGeneres Show* the second day, and we did a radio appearance on KIIS FM right before the last show. I remember going to sound check on the third day, and my right arm felt like it was full of lead. I tried to hit the floor tom, and I couldn't get my arm to just pull the stick up and lay it back down in a normal way. It felt heavy and uncoordinated, and my hand was shaking. I was extremely concerned about this feeling, but I didn't tell anyone, wanting to just push it out of my mind and pretend it wasn't happening. I deluded myself into believing that maybe it would go away if I just didn't think about it.

I strained through the show that night by finding new arm positions that would allow me to cross over to the hi-hat during the verses and reach for the ride cymbal in the choruses. These mechanical changes were not improvements, mind you—they were actually quite worse. They just took the tension off certain muscles and placed them squarely on other joints, particularly my right (pitching) shoulder. When the show was done, we had to sign a bunch of autographs before we could celebrate with our friends in the Foundation Room, and I literally couldn't write my own name. Think of that: I couldn't sign my own autograph, but somehow I could contort myself into getting through a ninety-minute set playing the drums. That seems impossible. Well, I did it, but the ways in which I managed to do so were worsening the impact on my old pitching injuries, while creating horrible mechanical habits that would prove extremely difficult to break.

I started having to do some serious physical and psychological gymnastics to get through every show after that. I could see the cracks in the ceiling growing with each passing show, but there was no way I was going to admit that I couldn't keep holding that roof above my head for much longer. I was too proud, and too scared, to do that. So I just stuffed down the feelings that I couldn't hack it, tried to figure out any way I could manipulate my drum set and my body to get through the shows, and I soldiered onward. I also started relying more on coffee and Red Bull to muster the energy to overcome exhaustion and arm fatigue. This, of course, did not help the steadiness of my hand. Over time, things that had once been easy became more difficult, and I found myself adjusting my already-faulty drumming technique even more to play through the pain and lack of coordination. Every performance became a battle of will to overcome a body that just didn't want to cooperate with what I was asking of it.

I suppose if it had been the 1970s, I probably would have developed a huge cocaine or speed habit to get myself through the long days and weeks of touring, but believe it or not, that kind of lifestyle was not the norm in the 2000s (at least not to the extent that I'd expected). I did see some drug use on the road, but I was actually surprised at how professional most of the bigger artists were in regard to their performances. A lot of musicians I've known smoke weed, and some drink, but I never witnessed fishbowls of cocaine or pills in the tour buses or dressing rooms I visited. I suppose the era when people expected rock stars to be total drug-addicted fuckups ended when the corporate aspect of touring took over the industry. There's a lot of money at stake for a big tour, and successful artists have contracts with major promotional companies that would sue their asses off if they had a tour-ending meltdown. And audiences expect a quality show for the kind of ticket prices they're paying these days, so blowing a tour could literally mean the end of your career. As a result, I think most big-time performers were pretty businesslike by the time we entered the game . . . at least the ones who were still successful.

There was one other factor I haven't mentioned that might have played a role in my increasing exhaustion on the road, however. On top of the physical pain, the coordination issues, the sleep problems, and the self-doubt, I'm pretty sure that I was malnourished a lot of the time. I didn't experience the same stomach problems I'd had back in '97, but I (and maybe some of the other guys in the band as well) had a mild form of "man-orexia" at that stage of our career. We were doing photo and video shoots left and right, and the fashion of the day was to be very thin and boyish. My frame was a little bigger than that of some of the other guys in the band, so I thought that I looked too much like a grown man by comparison.

Although the "heroin chic" era of the '90s had transitioned into the boy-band phase in popular culture, the hipsters were still obsessed with a more emaciated rock-star look, which was a factor in the band's image. I even had photographers tell me that I looked "too healthy" and ask me if I could slump over because my posture was too good. This definitely played a role in my psyche, and I often ate just enough to get through my day, but not enough for the number of calories I was burning every night. It's easy for me to see now how insane that mentality was, but at the time it just seemed like part of being in show biz. I can only imagine how much worse that aspect of the industry is for women, who are quite literally told that they need to be skinny and "perfect" at all times.

The fact that I couldn't get much time to myself was also starting to wear on me again. We would ride on the bus through the morning until load-in time, so we would usually sleep in, but once we came into the club to get situated, we were going and going until late that night again. We had meet-and-greets scheduled with fan club members and industry reps, we had interviews and photo shoots with local radio and TV stations, and after signing autographs and socializing with the fans in the postshow hour, we all had to get back in the submarine that was our tour bus to head to the next city. The few "off days" were actually travel days, so we would spend them all together on the bus most of the time. On the rare occasion when we did have a real day off at a hotel, I would often just want to enjoy my own space as much as I could.

You might be asking yourself, "Did no one ever think that maybe scheduling a couple of days of recuperation into a tour would be a good thing?" Believe me, I asked that question several times. The answer was always no. The schedule was made several months in advance, according to what tour dates were available to us and what was financially prudent in maintaining the ongoing promotional campaign. And, if anything, more stuff was added to the schedule as it came up, rather than subtracted. For the first year and a half of touring, we were subject to whatever shows were offered to us, and it was our agent's job to figure out how to route us from one string of dates to the next, while incurring the lowest costs along the way. The record label was still footing the bill for most of those early tours as part of its promotional overhead, so maintaining the bottom line was essential. And when we finally became self-sustaining and profitable on our first headlining tour, our profit margins were only in the thousands (as opposed to the millions the band enjoys today), so every extra day of paying the salaries of the crew and covering the hotel bills for the whole entourage could eat pretty significantly into that bottom line. Touring is expensive . . . until you're making millions. Then you can do whatever the fuck you want.

My parents back home didn't seem to understand that I was actually really busy on the road, judging from the fact that my dad would get upset with me if I didn't return his calls in a timely manner. I would usually have to wait until after the show to call him back, but by then I was exhausted and didn't want to talk to anybody. I felt a lot of pressure to be "on" at all times, being all things to all people, so I could feel a little resentful of my dad's thinking that I could just drop whatever I was doing and talk to him as often as he would like me to (which was a lot). Shan ended up getting the short end of the stick many of those nights, because even when I had enough energy to make phone calls at the end of the day, I would usually call my parents back first (to be a good son) and then finally call my girlfriend once I was done with everything else. However, by that point I wasn't very talkative, so she would complain that I seemed to be only calling her out of obligation. The reality was that I really did want to hear her voice, but I was just totally spent by the time I had fulfilled all my responsibilities.

I don't mean to paint the picture that headlining was all miserable all the time. Despite the struggles I was having, I actually remember that tour fondly. After almost a decade as a band, we had finally become a national headlining act with a fancy tour bus and a growing legion of fans, things that most musicians never get to experience, and that fact was not lost on me. And more importantly, the five of us were as thick as thieves: we were a group of close friends doing something truly remarkable together. Sure, I was stuffing down my real emotions and internal struggles, and I was putting on a brave face to try to enjoy the experience with my buddies, but that didn't mean we weren't still having fun together. There were many days and nights on the bus when we laughed like we were still teenagers, and it would feel as if I didn't have a worry in the world for those moments. And there were some nights in cities and college towns around the country that we would tie one on and celebrate the success we were enjoying, feeling the grandeur of our accomplishment. My physical health and internal psychology may have been degrading, but I could still appreciate how special it was to have reached this incredible place with my musical brothers.

On top of that, we finally started making a little bit of money! We received our first publishing royalty checks at the start of that tour, and ironically enough, they were deposited into our accounts the night we were set to play the House of Blues at the Mandalay Bay Hotel in Las Vegas, of all places. Adam was literally standing at an ATM on the casino floor, dialing

Rich Feldstein's number on his cell phone and waiting to know the exact moment that he could take cash out of his account. I, of course, was thinking about practical questions like "How many royalty checks will it take before I can afford the down payment on a mortgage?" While Adam was thinking, "When can I go blow a big chunk of this hard-earned money on one crazy night in Vegas?" However, I should have known that Adam would never have bad luck gambling. I don't know what he did in a former life to be so blessed, but everything he touches seems to turn to gold.

Another highlight of our touring was the choice of closing numbers we would play at the end of each set list. We had always tried to pick a rather audacious cover song to end our shows, as a sort of send-off and celebration after we'd finished the job of delivering a tight set of our own music. In the Kara's Flowers days, I sang (or rather screamed) the Who's enormous rock anthem "Baba O'Riley" from behind my drum set, and on *The Fourth World* tour we closed with Queen's "We Are the Champions," a song that most bands wouldn't dare touch. Early in 2002, we ended our sets with "Darling Nikki," which offended quite a few innocent pop fans, the same way it did when Prince first released it in the 1980s. By 2003, it was Nine Inch Nails's "Closer," which had Adam screaming "I wanna fuck you like an animal!" to a roomful of mostly young women, who were all screaming it right back at us! James begged us not to play that one when we performed in front of his large Mormon family in Utah and Nebraska, but I'm not sure the song we replaced it with was a much better option. It was definitely funnier, though, given the context. This time I came out from behind my drums and went to center stage to sing AC/DC's "Highway to Hell." I don't know what would have been more offensive to the devout: animal sex or the wholehearted embrace of eternal damnation.

You might be wondering how an anxious guy like me was able to go to center stage and belt out a big number like that to a huge crowd, but for some reason, that was never a nerve-racking proposition for me. I actually really looked forward to it. I guess it was just because it seemed like a big party by that point in the set, and we weren't taking ourselves too seriously. We had finished the real work of trying to perform our own material as well as we could, so the pressure was off completely. It actually felt like that time that I played air guitar and lip-synced "Enter Sandman" with Adam Salzman, in front of a bunch of screaming middle schoolers at a Santa Monica bat mitzvah. Only this time it was the real thing, with real fans who had bought tickets to our show and were having the time of their lives! It may sound strange, but I was actually less nervous to do that every night than I was to play the drums. And singing that song at the end of each show of the headlining tour was another brief moment when all my troubles seemed to just float away and I could enjoy the splendor of what we were doing. However, I suppose it was rather ominous that I was screaming "I'M ON A HIGHWAY TO HELL" at the top of my lungs every night.

We had a few different opening acts on that first headlining tour, but the one who was playing right before us the entire time was Gavin DeGraw, who was about to release his first album on J Records. Gavin was an interesting guy, funny and charming but also intense at times, and I enjoyed his performances a lot. He was a piano man by trade, singing sweet, soulful songs at his keyboard, but his live show featured a rather remarkable rhythm section on that tour. I don't think you would mistake Gavin for a "rocker," but his drummer Matt Flynn certainly made him sound that way. I remember sitting at the side of the stage with Adam one night, and we both took notice of just how much Matt was bringing to the table with Gavin's music. We had watched a lot of very good drummers in other bands by that point, but Matt had something that none of the others had—he hit *hard*. Matt was a real rock drummer, in the old mold, like the drummers Adam and I loved when we used to watch *Headbangers Ball* as kids. I don't mean to say that he was glam in any way, far from it. I mean that he was a hard-hitting, heavy-grooving rock stud, in the line of John Bonham and Phil Rudd. He was very technically proficient as well, but what set him apart was the intensity of his thumping beats, which drove the music in a way we hadn't seen a drummer do in a while. I couldn't help but feel jealous of the ease with which he served up the kind of heavy intensity that I used to bring as a teenager. And it didn't help that Adam seemed to be fawning over and coveting the consistency of his energy and tempo. As if I hadn't already been self-conscious enough about my diminished state, I now had a veritable rock machine with whom to compete.

Somehow, a lot of the shows were still pretty good for me, though. I guess it was just the energy of the crowd that allowed me to deliver a decent performance most nights. A little more than halfway through that tour, however, I finally hit the wall completely. I just couldn't hold my arm in a position to perform anymore, due to the painful fatigue of my shoulder. We had made our way across the country to Florida, by which time I felt as if I were drowning onstage every night, trying to keep my head above the surface of the water long enough to gasp for air. So, on a show day in Tampa, I finally went to an orthopedist to check out my shoulder. The part of me in denial wanted to believe so badly that a doctor could give me a quick fix and clear up the problem, but the fatalistic side of me knew that whatever the doctor prescribed was not going to be a miracle cure—that the problem was broader and more to the core of my being. I don't know which idea was more worrying to me: that there was something really physically wrong with me or that there wasn't. Because if the problem wasn't my arm . . . then the problem was me.

The orthopedist did an MRI, told me I had inflammation and tendinitis in the shoulder, and gave me a shot of cortisone, and I played that night . . . terribly. The pain in my shoulder just felt more like a dull ache after the shot, but the mechanical discoordination did not improve at all, and if anything, I had less control over my right arm as a result. The show was a sloppy mess, my arm felt like it was just flopping around totally uncontrollably, and the feeling of drowning onstage was more intense than ever. Or to use a better analogy, I felt like a fish that had been thrown on the deck of a boat, flailing and flopping around in desperation. Adam and Jesse called a band meeting in the dressing room after the show to address the issue.

"Look, Ryan, I don't think I need to tell you at this point that there's clearly something wrong," Adam said. "It's obvious to all of us, and I'm sure it's clear to you. I think you really just need to go home and seek more medical attention to figure out what's going on and how to fix it."

"What? Go home? Now? How am I gonna do that? We're playing in Orlando tomorrow!" I replied testily.

"We just got off the phone with Ryland," Jesse said, referring to the drummer in James's old band Square. "He's available to fly in on short notice and play with us until you can come back."

I was taken aback and upset to hear that they had already found a solution for the immediate problem, but in a strange way it actually felt like a load off my shoulders. Perhaps it was just more delusion and denial on my part, but I suddenly embraced the idea that I could go back home for a little break, see an expert in LA who would know how to solve the problem, have an opportunity to chill out and spend some time with my girlfriend, and then be rejuvenated enough to go back out on tour 100 percent again. Sounds reasonable, right?

I stuck around for another day to help Ryland get acclimated, and then I watched the band play their first show with him in Orlando. The experience of seeing my band play with another drummer was extremely unsettling for me, almost like watching my wife with another man or something. So I decided then and there that I wanted to get this sabbatical over with as quickly as possible. I went home and saw the top orthopedist in Santa Monica, who told me I just needed to "have a cocktail and relax," to let the inflammation subside. So I rested for a week, getting massages, drinking wine, and relaxing in hot tubs, then I jumped on a plane to rejoin the band in Washington, DC, ready to finish the last couple of weeks of the tour. A week at home had been enough to feel more rested and less acutely pained, and I desperately wanted to believe that I was cured and ready to start performing again. But I knew inside that this was not a fix—not even close. I was going to will myself through the end of the tour, however, after which I would just have to pray that things would resolve themselves before I started another year of touring.

Strangely enough, the shows on the last leg of that tour gave me some of my best memories of performing. Even with the pain, even with the diminished coordination, I felt that we played some of the most inspired concerts we'd ever had. The week off had been just enough time for me to gather my energy for the push through the end of the year, and I settled into a somewhat contorted way of playing that was temporarily effective. "Harder to Breathe" was peaking on the radio charts, and our new fans were coming out in droves, so the energy of the crowds was reaching a fever pitch. After our huge show at the Roseland Ballroom in Midtown Manhattan, we received our first gold record, presented by the legendary Clive Davis himself, and we partied the night away in NYC like the rock stars we were becoming. One of the last shows of that tour was at the famed Fillmore in San Francisco, and that night stands out in my mind as perhaps our most epically beautiful concert. Maybe it's just because I got through the show at such a legendary venue without faltering, but I really thought it was a special show. Jesse was quite sick with a high fever that night, and he didn't even come out for the encore, so maybe, again, I'm judging it more by my own performance, rather than by the group's performance as a whole. When I came to center stage to finish the set with "Highway to Hell," however, it felt like the culmination of two long years of hard work, and a true moment of celebration.

We closed out 2003 on a high note, feeling pretty good about ourselves overall, and we had high hopes for what was to come in 2004, when the next phase of our career would play out on a massively larger scale in terms of global media exposure and record sales. I did my best to believe that a break for the holidays would rejuvenate my body and mind for what was to come, but I was still feeling worried and scared, and doubting my abilities. We were about to hit the big time, and I was just barely hanging on for dear life.

chapter 16

the big time

During our much-needed holiday break at the end of 2003, Shan and I moved into a one-bedroom apartment together in West Hollywood. The band had finally made a little money from the first headlining tour and the first publishing check, so I figured it was time to set up a home base with Shan again, even though I didn't know how much I would be there. We enjoyed a brief reprieve from the chaos of touring and a temporary moment of domestic bliss, and then 2004 began with a bang, and we were off to the races. First, we all had an amazing week in London, doing international promotion for our second single, "This Love," during which we made several TV and radio appearances, held interviews with reporters from countries spanning the globe, and were whisked around the city to glamorous hot spots and fancy dinners. It became very apparent that our music was going to be heard and played all over the world with great anticipation, and we were beginning to be treated like pop stars.

In the midst of all this, surreal experiences started piling up one after another. When we were shooting our performance on *Top of the Pops* at the BBC, our dressing room was right next door to that of U2, who would be filming a live concert outside that night. We ran into Bono and the Edge on our way back from one of the dress rehearsals, and Bono immediately flirted with Shan (who was traveling overseas with me for the first time), only he did so much more suavely than John Mayer had. As we were all walking in together, he scanned the lot of us, then looked directly at Shan and said, "You played the Telecaster, right? Love your guitar." He gave a wink with that gem, and I could see why he was one of the most charismatic rock stars in the world (as if we didn't know that already). Bono and Edge then gave us some sage advice, but it was a little ironic, given the context. They said that we should tour as much as possible and say yes to everything offered to us on our first album cycle. Given that we had adopted that mindset two years earlier and we hadn't been home for more than a few days at a time since, we had to chuckle to ourselves a little bit. We appreciated the kind gesture of advice anyway, and the validation for working so hard.

The reason for saying yes to everything involving your first successful album is that concert venues, tour promoters, late-night talk-show bookers, radio programmers, and so on have no reason to be loyal to your band . . . until you give them a reason. If you say yes to things that are offered to you, you build bridges that sustain themselves throughout your career as a performing artist. Every time you say no, however, you burn that bridge, and it most likely won't be offered again. The executives at our record label were smart enough to include this instruction in their grassroots strategy for building our career, and it was a message we received from established artists again and again. We got the same advice from Adam Duritz of Counting Crows (with whom we had toured). He told us that their band said no to touring the UK on their first album (because they were exhausted from touring the States for a couple of years), and as a result, their band still doesn't do well in England. So insisting on more days or weeks off was never really an option for us at that point in our career. Those dates would inevitably get filled with whatever was offered to us.

We returned to LA for our ten-year anniversary as a band, and we were informed that *Songs About Jane* had been certified platinum in the United States and it was set to ship all over the world with the release of our new single and video. Clive Davis invited us to play at his annual pre-Grammy party at the Beverly Hills Hotel, where we walked onstage to perform right after the Foo Fighters to an audience of Jay-Z, Missy Elliott, Janet Jackson, Prince, Carlos Santana, Jamie Foxx, Kanye West, P. Diddy, Alicia Keys, 50 Cent, and other amazing talents. Believe it or not, we had that crowd of icons standing and grooving along to "Harder to Breathe" (joined by Rob Thomas as our guest vocalist) and "This Love," which this audience was hearing for the very first time. I even remember seeing Magic Johnson dancing and clapping along in the front row.

Next, we went to New York to perform on MTV's *Total Request Live* and *Late Night with Conan O'Brien*, the former of which was our first live performance on national television. I was very anxious about that performance, but I pulled through it okay, feeding on the excitement of everything that was going on for us. But the big tamale was *Saturday Night Live*, which came soon thereafter. *SNL* was the grand prize in terms of late-night appearances. Most artists with a hit song get asked to do the talk-show circuit, but only iconic artists or ones with incredible buzz around them get asked to play on *SNL*, and it had the largest audience in live TV. So playing on that show, in front of millions of people, was the biggest and most nerve-racking thing we had done to date.

Unlike the host, the musical guest is not on set all week (other than for a couple of photo shoots and promos), but the day of the performance is a very long day of sound, lighting, and camera checks, all in Studio 8H of 30 Rockefeller Plaza. I have a very distinct memory of playing our first sound check of "Harder to Breathe" and seeing Jimmy Fallon (in his last season on the show) standing right in the middle of the empty audience floor, watching us and seemingly enjoying what he was hearing (Jimmy is a rather exuberant character, after all). I made the mistake of having a big cup of Starbucks that morning, knowing that it would be a long day on set, but not realizing that my nervous energy would have been enough to get me through. When we listened back to the recording of that sound check from the mixing board backstage, Adam complained that every take of "This Love" was too fast.

"It's too fast, Ryan! It doesn't groove when it's that fast!" he said.

"No, man, it's gotta be a little faster live! It's gotta have that live energy!"

"Not on TV, dude. It's gotta be just like the record on TV. It's gotta groove."

"I don't know, man . . . I like when a band plays with a bit more urgency for a live performance. I like when you can tell they're not just slogging through another performance exactly like the one on the record," I said.

"Can we split the difference maybe? It's way too fast right now."

He was right, but I was just too amped up. I was amped up all day. I was excited . . . and nervous . . . and cocky . . . and defensive . . . and terrified . . . It was an emotional day, to say the least. In between rehearsals, all we could really do was sit in our little dressing room and watch the last-minute run-throughs of "Weekend Update" and the other skits on our feed. It was actually one of the funnier episodes that year, which served to distract us for the moment, but you could feel the tension in the room the whole day. None of us wanted to talk about how much pressure we were under to be at our best, knowing that these performances would catapult our band to a whole other level of fame if they went well. So we mostly just sat there, chuckling at Tina Fey's and Jimmy Fallon's jokes on our TV screen.

We finally went onstage that night to an audience of millions at home, and a strange calm came over me. Somehow, in that moment it was clear to me that this was the mountaintop, and we had earned this day in the sun. This was the promised land, and all we had to do was go out there and do what we had done a thousand times before. The host, Christina Aguilera, came to the front of the stage, looked right into homes across the country, and said with her signature attitude, "Ladies and gentlemen . . . Maroon 5 . . ."

And we nailed it. We played with groove and feel. We played with poise and swagger. We played the best we had in two years of touring. Adam was a bit more reserved than usual, because he was as nervous as anyone about delivering his best performance, but he still had enough cockiness about him that he appeared like a true front man, stepping through the cameras into TV sets nationwide. *We're gonna be fucking rock stars!!!*

After playing both "Harder to Breathe" and "This Love" very well on the live show, we came to center stage with the whole cast, to stand with Aguilera as she said her thank-yous and goodbyes to the camera. I couldn't help but laugh as the producer was counting in that last curtain call, the same as I had when they'd pulled up the house lights during our first arena show with John Mayer. It all just felt so surreal, standing next to all these people we had been watching on TV, waving good night to the whole country, after having achieved something *very* few musicians and performers ever do. After hugging Christina Aguilera, shaking hands with Tina Fey, and meeting everyone else on that stage, we were all escorted to the downtown after-party, where we enjoyed the great humor of many of the new cast members, including Fred Armisen, Seth Meyers, and Will Forte. And finally, we felt like we had arrived.

As we watched "This Love" shoot up the charts and album sales jump exponentially each week, we did another arena tour with John Mayer in February, during which management booked us to shoot a popular MTV show called *Room Raiders* on one of our precious few days off. For those of you who don't remember this silly dating show, a cute girl on spring break would inspect a few guys' hotel rooms, and then she would pick one with whom to go on a date, based on what she found. The only catch for our episode was that the guys would not be random; they would be the members of a popular new band, Maroon 5. We were introduced to the video crew at our show in Sacramento the night before the shoot, and they requested that we get up before dawn to set up our rooms at the W hotel in West LA. This was our first foray into reality TV, but it already seemed pretty false in its premise. Besides the fact that it made no sense that we would be staying at a hotel in our hometown of Los Angeles, setting up our rooms at 6 AM for the express purpose of a girl rummaging through them seemed inherently ridiculous. But really, we just didn't want to get up so early on our day off. So, rather than set up the rooms ourselves, we opted to hand our bags to the crew the night before, instructing them on what our personalities were like and how to set up the rooms to illustrate them.

Of course, everyone insisted that my room be set up "obsessive-compulsively." I didn't object to this, because I took pride in being neat and tidy, and it would probably make for some funny dialogue. When we showed up to film our reaction shots, however, it became clear to me that the crew had accidentally mixed in one of their own bags, and someone else's stuff was set up with mine. So what already seemed like a silly premise became all the more ludicrous. The crew had taken our advice to make my room very neat and organized, but there were also a few items that were not of my choosing, like books on photography and socks with an NBA logo on them. My amused reactions to the girl inspecting these things were genuine, because they were news to me as well. It was actually pretty funny.

(*The girl, Harper, enters my hotel room . . .*)
ADAM: Oh, here we go, "Organized Johnson."
HARPER: Okay, this room looks . . . really clean . . . Looks like you have some drumsticks right here, which is pretty cool, 'cause this probably means you're a musician.
ME: Probably a drummer.
(*Everyone laughs.*)
HARPER: (*Entering the bedroom*) Wow . . . (*reacting to how tidy it is*)
EVERYONE: Ooooohhhhhh, my god!!!!!!!!
ADAM: Dusick!!!!! That, Ryan, that is a painting; that is a portrait of Ryan Dusick.
HARPER: You're obviously a very, very, very organized person . . . This almost seems like way too neat. I'm gonna have to, like, mess something up here.
ME: NOOOOOOO!!!!!!!!!!!!!!
(*Jesse tries to shield my eyes from the horror.*)
HARPER: But it looks like you're into sports, which is cool; I like athletes. You have some baseball caps . . .
ME: I used to play baseball.

HARPER: Your socks have an NBA logo on them, which is cool . . .
ME: I used to play in the NBA.
(*Everyone laughs.*)

In the delirium of the moment, the five of us were finally able to be our normal, silly selves, as if the camera weren't rolling, and the resulting footage captured a good representation of the kind of fun that we had on the road when it was just us. When we finished filming, we wondered if this had just been too juvenile for where we were in our career, but in the end, it turned out to be a great thing, because it showcased our sense of humor. People got a glimpse into the more casual charm of the band and how we relate to one another as friends, which is not always easy to do in interviews.

Jet lag became an issue for me again on our first headlining tour of Europe, but I was able to work through the exhaustion this time, drawing on the excitement and romance of it all. After a few days of adjustment to the time zone, we started playing some amazing shows in beautiful old venues across the continent. Because our career had jumped up to an exponentially larger scale and we were now feeling the love from our international fans, I was able to push the negative feelings out of my consciousness for a time, anchoring myself in the present moment of success, and enjoying the grandeur of the Old World. This tour was particularly romantic, because all of us brought our girlfriends overseas with us, and our travels had a wonderfully communal feeling to them.

The Amsterdam show was broadcast live on the internet, and it stands out in my mind as a high point of that tour. However, watching the recording of that set brings up mixed emotions for me now. The day of the concert had been as lovely as any day on tour that I can remember. Shan was with me, Adam brought Kelly, Mickey brought his girlfriend Z, and Jesse and James were with a couple of girls they were dating at the time as well. After doing some sightseeing, we all spent the afternoon by one of the canals, lounging on a patch of grass and acting like a bunch of careless hippies. I was never a big pot smoker (it makes me even more anxious), but the other guys were partaking of the local flavor, for sure. The feeling in the air was very relaxed and collective, and it really just seemed like we were on a lovely vacation with a big traveling entourage of friends. The show that night was an excellent one at a beautiful, old building called Paradiso, and the production of the video was stellar for a very casual shoot. However, the mechanics of my drumming had degraded so far by that point that watching it feels ominous now. Knowing that I was hiding so much pain by then, and knowing where my life would go after, makes it an uncomfortable viewing experience. I don't think that casual viewers would necessarily know that I was so pained, because I was in a particularly good mood for that concert, but if they knew anything about drumming, they would probably see clearly that my movements were rather contorted and strained.

Our girlfriends went back home after that show, and my momentary feelings of delight went with them, as the fatigue of three years of touring continued to wear on me more and more in the coming weeks. Every time we received a revised tour itinerary, I would brace myself to find that more of our precious days off had evaporated, as had been the case every month since the album was released. When this happened again at the end of that European tour, I really lost my shit. I had been clinging to the notion that we would get a couple of weeks off at some point, during which I could rest and recuperate once again, but it was not to be. As we were getting ready to leave Milan, we were handed a new schedule, on which I saw that our break had been filled with our first trip to Australia. My heart sank, and I just broke down emotionally. I knew I couldn't keep up with this pace much longer, and it all just hit me like a ton of bricks: I was going down, and I was going down hard. I remember sitting on the floor with my backpack on, slumped over in the middle of the Milan airport, not wanting to look another human being in the eye, while our tour manager Fred was checking us in at the counter. My bandmates and I hadn't really been talking about my condition since I came back from my break in the fall, but they could tell I was not in a good place, so they also knew not to talk to me in that moment. I'm sure they were concerned, but they just let me sit there in the middle of the international terminal, as travelers walked by with their luggage.

Australia was a mess for me. I barely slept at all the entire week that we were there. I could not get over the jet lag, and the performances *really* suffered. I was in full breakdown mode by our show in Sydney. My body had started to feel like a foreign machine that I just couldn't get working. When I came offstage, I slumped in the corner again, head down, and I began to cry. Jordi asked if I was okay, and for the first time I admitted that, no, I was not okay. I had never felt this level of exhaustion before. It was physical, it was mental, it was emotional, and it struck to my very core. This was not just "I need a good night's sleep." This was "I just want to curl up in a little ball for the rest of eternity." The difficulties with sleep I had suffered since high school and the arm problems I had dealt with since my pitching days were so exacerbated by the jet lag that my problem was becoming much more than just one joint or one arm—it was my entire constitution.

The next tour back in the States, performing mostly in college towns in the spring of 2004, would be my last behind the drums. We did *The Tonight Show with Jay Leno* before the start of the tour, and I barely got through that performance. And then every show after that just felt like I was going out there on a wing and a prayer. I had started icing my shoulder every day, trying to keep the inflammation at bay, but it was so far beyond "chronic tendinitis" at that point that there was really nothing that could be done. I had been playing through the pain for so long that my nerves were shot, along with my joints. With each passing show, it became more and more obvious to everyone that this was an untenable situation, moving forward. It would take an almost comic moment, however, in its sad absurdity, for me to finally go home.

After sound check at a venue in Illinois, I went back to the bus to ice my shoulder. The ice pack in the freezer had been sitting right on the coils, and within a minute of putting it on my skin, I could tell something was wrong. I pulled it away, and my skin was bubbling, crinkling, and sliding around like I was the Toxic Avenger. Normally I might have gotten really scared and panicked at the sight of a wound like that, but for some reason I just sort of accepted that this was the strange way my tour would end. The daily struggle to perform, growing more difficult with each passing week, had so beaten me down, and made me feel so helpless, that this pathetic injury seemed like an almost fitting end to the pain of it all. So, instead of descending into panic, I descended into oblivion. I suppose it was more comfortable to believe that none of this meant anything anymore than to feel just how soul crushing it really was.

I got a ride to the emergency room, where they examined me and diagnosed me with frostbite. They applied some ointment, wrapped my arm up in a sling, instructed me on how to continue to dress the wound, and sent me back to the venue. Sara Bareilles was finally opening for us on that tour, so we asked her drummer Josh Day to fill in for me for the time being. I had to spend the rest of the afternoon going over all our songs with him, in hopes that he could deliver a passable performance on a moment's notice, before I had to watch yet another drummer performing onstage with my band that night.

"Don't think of this as a setback, Ryan," Jesse said in our hotel-room meeting that night. "Think of this as an opportunity."

I tried my hardest not to roll my eyes. I sighed instead.

"Look, man," Adam said tenderly. "I know this is hard, but there's no rush this time, okay? Take some time . . . figure out what's going on with your body, and get better . . . even if it takes a month . . . three months . . . six months . . . a year . . . whatever it takes, just get better . . . We'll be here when you're back."

"I appreciate that, Adam, but I hope it doesn't take that long," I muttered.

"It doesn't matter how long it takes, because you're on a mission now," Jesse said. "You're on a hero's quest to recover from this . . . just like Lance Armstrong was with his cancer."

I flew home to LA the next day. As much as Jesse's grandiose evocation of an epic hero's quest was another eye roller for me, I had every intention to "Live Strong" when I got back home.

chapter 17

the small time

Returning home to spend my days and nights in our one-bedroom apartment, while my band was still out there on the rocket ship to fame and fortune, was very humbling and extremely depressing for me. To make matters worse, Maroon 5 was omnipresent at that moment in history. I couldn't turn on the TV, get in my car, go to a mall or a movie theater, or even walk down the street without seeing or hearing something related to the band I felt was leaving me behind. "This Love" was playing on every popular radio station twice an hour; the video was rolling on MTV and VH1 in heavy rotation; our songs were featured in movies, TV shows, and record and clothing stores; and there were advertisements for our album and concerts on every piece of media one's eyes would come across. As a result, people started recognizing me when I would go out into the world. I felt an unsettling contradiction of emotions when this would happen: I was flattered that people were expressing their love and appreciation for the music we had created, and I felt pride for what we had achieved in our career, but I also felt wounded and impotent, because these occurrences only made it more apparent what I was missing out on and what I had been incapable of maintaining.

On the home front, Shan and I were looking forward to spending more time together again, but we experienced a rather difficult transition to being around each other all the time. She had gotten used to me being gone for long stretches, and she had adapted to that lifestyle by retreating into her own space and becoming less dependent on my attention. And I had gotten used to the circus life of touring, with all the flashing lights, bells, and whistles of constant stimulation and adrenaline. So, as a result, we were like two planets colliding when I came home: Shan had to adapt to the added stimulation of my energy, while I had to adapt to the mundanity of normal life. My nervous system had become accustomed to the natural rise of anticipation that came with each night's performance, so my brain and body would naturally produce feelings of anxiety in the evening, regardless of what I was doing. And Shan was more habituated to enjoying quiet time to herself, reading and relaxing in the evening. So while she was coming down from her day, I was becoming restless, which caused agitation for both of us.

I started having panic attacks as I lay in bed each evening, trying to calm my overactive mind. Just the thought that the guys were out there in the world somewhere, playing a huge rock show for thousands of our fans, while I was trying to get to sleep at a sensible hour like a regular working stiff, was causing my heart and mind to race uncontrollably. My difficulties with sleep escalated to a literal dread of it, which resulted in a level of anxiety that often required a walk around the block in the cool night air to quell. I was becoming rather edgy on a nightly basis, but I realized pretty soon that drinking some wine in the evening helped relax my nerves. Drinking wine at night quickly became a ritual, regardless of whether we were out at dinner or just sitting in our apartment watching TV.

When I first came home, my dad went into full caretaker mode, taking charge of my medical care by booking appointments with every kind of doctor and specialist who might have some insight into what was ailing me and how to fix it. He took me to more orthopedists and radiologists, who conducted more invasive MRIs (including one in which dye was injected into my shoulder to determine if there was something surgically fixable in there), injected me with more cortisone, and prescribed heavy anti-inflammatory medications and physical therapy for the chronic tendinitis. My dad also took me to a neurologist, who ordered a specialist to conduct something called a nerve conduction study, which involved sticking needles all over me and then electrically stimulating the nerves to examine their functioning. After the test found slowing of the nerves going down my right arm, the neurologist diagnosed me with something called thoracic outlet syndrome (which is kind of like carpal tunnel syndrome of the whole arm) and prescribed a central nervous system (CNS) depressant called Neurontin, which was originally created to treat spastic nerves and nerve pain associated with seizure disorders and other neurological diseases. My dad then took me to a rheumatologist, who ordered a panel of blood tests to see if I had contracted some kind of inflammatory or autoimmune disease like lupus or rheumatoid arthritis. I was also sent to a psychiatrist, who prescribed antidepressants that might help with the physical pain and the emotional turmoil of what I was going through, and for sleep . . . more Neurontin. "More Neurontin" became a theme among my many doctors, and pretty soon I was taking as much of that shit as an epileptic. Doctors after doctors after more doctors . . . and none of them seemed to have a definitive answer as to what the problem was and how to solve it. They each had a theory, but none of them seemed to capture the whole picture, which felt much more global and debilitating to me than any of these individual diagnoses.

In some ways it felt good to have my dad take care of me in that way. I suppose when things are going poorly in your life, you yearn for the feeling of being very small, when your parents would take control and "make it all better." But at the same time, his hyperinvolvement in my life made it easier for me to retreat into myself, feeling like I was just being carted around to these appointments and being stuck with needles like a lab rat, and having no sense of control over the process or any sort of self-reliance. It all started to seem so totally futile to me, as each procedure and each medication yielded no improvement, causing me to sink further into my state of oblivion. I really started to lean into a nihilistic mindset, attempting to care less, instead of embracing the struggle to fight.

Rather than improve, I actually started feeling worse. The Neurontin, which had been increased to three heavy doses a day, made my coordination issues go from bad to confounding. The CNS depressant made me feel foggy and slow both mentally and physically, and I developed a very strange sensation of sluggishness in my right leg and foot, which often felt lifeless and slow to respond. Even walking felt strange and uncoordinated, and I actually developed a slight limp at times. The pain in my right shoulder and the functioning of that arm had deteriorated to such a degree that even nonstrenuous activities that barely involved my arms would cause soreness and dysfunction for days. My shoulder blade was winging out and causing my joint to slide around in strange ways, and coordinating simple things like brushing my teeth proved extremely difficult, leaving me with more pain and disability in the aftermath. I couldn't lift or carry anything heavy, and even trying to get some cardiovascular exercise by simply peddling on a stationary bike at the gym would put stress on my arm somehow, so I just kind of gave up. I let myself get totally out of shape because it just didn't seem like I was capable of doing anything productive. I had always been a very active and athletic person, so this diminished state of physicality just made me feel totally incapacitated.

At a certain point, Shan stepped into the role of caretaker that my dad had started, as she could sense that my motivation and general will to fight were declining. I was feeling increasingly defeated, growing more depressed with each seemingly pointless session of physical therapy, acupuncture, or further diagnosis, so Shan started booking my appointments for me and making sure that I would go to them. Taking care of me seemed to give her purpose, but it also allowed me to sink even deeper into my oblivion and nihilism. She fought the good fight in trying to save me from my own surrender to defeat, but I would push back against her the more she would try to encourage me. These arguments started to create resentments between us, and for the first time our quarrels could become more tempestuous, as

I lashed out in pain and self-loathing. I felt totally powerless, and having Shan mother me was only increasing that feeling.

A week or two after I left the tour, the band invited Matt Flynn to join them as my full-time replacement (until I might be able to return). Remembering how impressive his chops had been when he performed with Gavin DeGraw, I knew that Matt could deliver the bombastic rock show that we had developed over the years of touring, and I also knew he could bring it to an even higher level than I had been able to for some time. So, even sitting back home in LA, I couldn't help but feel jealous that the guys were enjoying the solid, heavy beats that Matt was surely providing onstage each night. Sometimes, the thought of how well the band was doing without me would depress me to such an extent that only a stiff drink could distract me from the feelings of inadequacy. I was retreating into a rather small life in the process of nursing a broken body (and a broken heart), lounging around my apartment and watching my band conquer the world from afar, and on some nights a good drunken buzz was the only thing that could fill the void that seemed to be growing in me like a sinkhole. I tried combining the meds with the wine for the first time, realizing that when I did so, I would melt into the couch with a level of relaxation and comfort that I had never felt, and my anxieties would subside for the moment.

The band came home to LA to shoot the video for our third single, "She Will Be Loved" (again directed by Sophie Muller), and despite my current state, I would have to somehow represent myself as the drummer in the band who had helped create and record that song and album. Sophie once again designed a beautiful video, this time featuring a mother-daughter love triangle, in which Adam would get to make out with one of our childhood crushes: Kelly Preston. Shooting the video had its fun moments of hanging out with the guys again, but as far as the performance element was concerned, I just had to fake my way through it, relying on very short, quick shots of me pretending to play, even though I really couldn't play at all anymore. It was humiliating to have the whole crew of the production watching me as I tried and failed to simply drum along to the track coming through the playback monitors. There he is . . . the drummer of the hottest band in the world . . . and he can barely even hold a beat.

The band's next big tour was a co-headlining bill with John Mayer, and I decided to join them on the road for that, as an attempt to stay connected with my bandmates and to the excitement of everything going on in our career. Jesse had the clever idea of bringing a trainer on the road as part of the crew, because he was having some mild wrist issues himself and he liked the idea of daily exercise regimens in the locker rooms of the arenas and amphitheaters the band would be playing. It didn't matter to me if I was doing physical therapy back home at a clinic or on the road with a professional fitness trainer, so I figured I might as well be out there with the guys as much as I could, to feel like I was a part of the process. At least that way I could sing my backing vocals from the side of the stage, come out to sing "Highway to Hell" for the encores, and participate in the meet-and-greets, interviews, and other promotional appearances.

I was only half there, however. I had descended into a depressed state that was transforming and degrading my very spirit, making me a shell of my former self. At that point in my life I had no real understanding of what was happening to me (other than that I was in pain and feeling sorry for myself), and for that reason, it became impossible for me to talk about it with anyone, even the band. The feelings were just too big and too agonizing to even allow myself to feel them fully, let alone share them or process them with my bandmates. So the topic of my condition became "that of which we cannot speak." It was just the big elephant in the room that none of us wanted to acknowledge.

As a result, I only got better at masking the pain, which was as much emotional as physical by that point. When we would do meet-and-greets with our fans, I got so tired of answering the same questions about my injury that I started making up ridiculous stories to answer them: "I was attacked by a bear," or "It was a boating accident." I would smile and joke about it, trying to make the other guys laugh at the silliness of my responses—anything to avoid the reality. And on some nights of intentional escape, I began to step into an alter ego of sorts: a freewheeling party guy, who was hell-bent on enjoying himself at all costs. This Mr. Hyde character would go out into the night to "party like a rock star," until it was time for him to turn back into the sad, pathetic Dr. Jekyll in the solitude of his hotel room.

Also, right away, the vibe of the band on that tour felt somewhat different to me than it had when I was last out there with the guys. The magnitude of the stage on which the band was performing had grown both literally and figuratively, and the relationships between the members had evolved in some ways I couldn't yet understand. It was clear to me that the four of them had made a connection with Matt, both musically and personally. His metronomic consistency and driving intensity had brought the rhythmic "perfection" of the band to a new level, and his personality was also funny and charming, making them laugh to a degree I hadn't seen in a while. Perhaps it was just the newness of his energy, but it all just felt very unfamiliar to me. I don't say these things in any derogatory way, because Matt was extremely gracious and deferential to me and my place in the band, but it was impossible for me to not be jealous. These guys had been my best friends and musical soul mates since they were fourteen years old, and they were now having an exciting love affair with a new drummer.

We went to South America and Asia for the first time, which was sad for me, going to new continents but only as a spectator. I tried to enjoy myself, but more and more that meant putting on that mask of escapism. In Tokyo, the six of us shared a night that was as close to a portrait of pop stardom as I had ever experienced. We were joined by a couple of British journalists, who were in town to document our first trip to Japan, and they arranged with our local reps to take us out on the town for an interview. They began by taking us to a site down in the depths below the city: a themed restaurant called the Lockup, in which scantily clad female dungeon keepers shackled us, escorted us through a torchlit cavern, and threw us into a dingy cell, where we ate sushi on the floor. We were interrupted by occasional strobe lights, death metal, and invasions by a knife-wielding attacker in a *Scream* mask. It started out as awesomely bizarre, but I suppose it ended up a bit kitschy. But next, they took us to a famed nightclub known as the hang site for many a notorious rock star over the decades. As we entered, we walked past photos on the wall of Freddie Mercury, David Bowie, Mick Jagger, Rod Stewart, Elton John, and other rockers partying the night away in that club. I don't know if it was a slow night or if our reps arranged it this way, but the total population of the club was our band's entourage and about fifteen young ladies, who were all in town on modeling jobs. There were girls there from every corner of the globe, with whom we enjoyed a few drinks, and then we rallied the entire group to go to our final destination: a karaoke bar, where our bevy of rock stars and models continued to party the night away, singing until our throats were raw. James even found "This Love" on the machine and sang it an octave below Adam's normal key, which had us all in stitches.

I was in full character that night, freewheeling and over-the-top, pretending to be a man without a care and without any restraint. I could tell that the other guys were kind of looking at me like I was a little crazy, but I didn't care. I was putting on a performance for them as much as for myself. The charade of decadence was so convincing that we decided the theme of our next video should be "a crazy night in Tokyo, where we sing our own song in a karaoke bar with a bunch of beautiful models." We wished that we had just documented that actual evening when it had taken place and turned that into the video, but instead we scheduled a time to re-create it on a set when we got to the UK on the next tour.

In London, we shot the performance part of the video for "Sunday Morning" at none other than the legendary Abbey Road Studios, the mecca of pop/rock recording and the creative home of our personal heroes: the Beatles. It was an honor to be playing in those hallowed grounds. The performance aspect was once again extremely difficult for me, though, as I again had to fake my way through it the best I could, taking breaks between takes for our trainer to release the muscle spasms and stretch my shoulder. I slipped right back into the party guy character for the next day's shoot, however, when we re-created the Tokyo karaoke bar scene. The drinks on the set were fake (according to the laws), but I snuck some booze into our trailer, and I made sure that I could fully embody the carefree attitude I was adopting in my attempts at distraction (and overcompensation). The video looked great visually and delivered exactly what we had imagined, but I couldn't help but feel like a bit of a phony in the process.

Back home in LA after that, I ran into an old friend of mine at a bar near our apartment, who told me that she was actually moving to the UK soon. Realizing that London was becoming like a second home to me (or third, if you count New York City), and recognizing that I would be returning to Europe with the band in the fall, I made plans to spend some time with her when I would be there next. I had another depressing stretch at home between those tours, making no progress on recovering from my ailments, before I jumped on a plane to Zurich, Switzerland, to join the band midtour. I did my best to put on a happy, smiling face again, as I was becoming so accustomed to doing. I slipped back into the Mr. Hyde role on the plane ride over the pond, sucking down the complimentary wine in business class, as if I hadn't a care in the world. After a few dates on the continent, we rode back to the UK once again, and that was where things started to get even darker for me.

The band was playing three sold-out nights at a big theater in Central London, and the local label reps threw us a party on the second night. I stayed up all night drinking, assuming the "rock star" role to escape my inner turmoil. The old friend I had run into in LA, who had just moved to London, was my partner in crime that night, and we stayed up most of the night partying together. I was so hungover the next day that I couldn't eat a thing, and I showed up to the venue for the last show feeling quite ill. We had already performed our usual closer, "Highway to Hell," the previous two nights, so the band wanted to play a new cover to end the last set. They demanded that I learn the lyrics to the White Stripes's "Seven Nation Army" on the spot and perform it later that night. Memorizing a song's worth of lyrics would normally take me days, but I had to do it in a few hours while feeling as hungover as I'd ever felt in my life. I told the guys that I felt like absolute shit, but they had little compassion. So I spent the rest of the evening going over the lyrics, as I nursed a beer and tried to pull myself together.

With my regimen of Neurontin, antidepressants, and whatever else the doctors were prescribing me at that point (on top of the increasing booze), I was more than a little unsteady on my feet. The nausea and frayed nerves from a night of heavy drinking were making not only my hands shaky but my legs and feet, too. When Adam introduced me for the last song, walking out to center stage felt like an eternity. That feeling of jelly leg hit me full force as I became very aware of five thousand people watching me walk, only this time it was coupled with an almost spastic reaction of my feet trying to catch up with each other. I played it off the best I could, pretending I was just kind of strutting up to the mic, but it was agonizing and embarrassing to imagine what it must have looked like to the crowd. I have no idea if anyone could tell that I was actually limping, but it felt very obvious to me in my state of total anxiety. The band kicked into the song, I sang the first two lines, then all the lyrics went right out of my head. Adam said afterward that it sounded like this: "I'm gonna fight 'em off . . . a seven-nation army couldn't hold me back . . . (*grunt*) aaaahhhh, fuck . . ."

All the previous times I had experienced the feeling of drowning onstage couldn't hold a candle to that moment. I felt like I was engulfed by a sea of eyes watching me flailing and grasping at nothing. That four minutes of torture felt like an eternity in hell. As we were about to come off the stage, Adam insisted that we redeem ourselves by finishing the set with a reprise of "Highway to Hell," even though we had performed it the previous night to perhaps many of the same fans. Fortunately, the muscle memory of having sung that song a hundred times kicked in, and I slipped into autopilot mode to finish the show with a somewhat passable performance. Afterward, I did my absolute best to block that experience out of my mind with another night of heavy drinking and revelry. However, the unfortunate memory of it left a lasting sense of trauma in my mind, to add to the list of other wounds. I would begin to have flashbacks to it in some of my later panic attacks . . .

On top of all these failures and disappointments in myself, around this time the band started making some not-so-subtle comments, letting me know that they were growing resentful of my coming and going, partying on the road, and then returning home to LA whenever I felt like it.

Adam made a remark to the effect of "I wish I could just go out on tour and party without having to worry about performing, then go home and relax whenever I want."

To which James added, "It must be nice to just lie back and collect a paycheck."

All I could say in response was "Do you really think I'm enjoying this? Don't you know that I would kill to be in your shoes right now?"

I didn't blame them for being tired of touring after three years on the road (or even for being jealous and resentful of the fact that I was making money without maintaining the same schedule of performances as they were), but I was dumbfounded that they actually thought I was relishing my incapacity. I guess my carefully crafted disguise of debauchery was working better than I had intended—they didn't know how much this was killing me and that I would do anything to be able to return to what we had worked so hard to do, rather than suffering this degradation. I guess that just shows how much you really don't know what's going on inside someone's heart and mind, unless they open up and talk about it.

To make matters much worse, during those three days in London, I cheated on Shan with the old friend I had arranged to see while I was there. I guess I was just feeling so completely wounded and emasculated that I wanted some kind of ego boost to let me know that I was still desirable in some way. The escapist, nihilistic party-guy alter ego took over completely, allowing me to do things I never would have done before in my life. This girl was at a transitional point in her life as well, so it was easy for both of us to rationalize the idea that we were just two lost souls (swimming in a fishbowl) sharing a couple of fleeting nights in a far-off, romantic locale on another continent.

When I came home from that trip, it became apparent immediately that I hadn't been fooling anyone with my entirely self-absorbed plan to hook up with this girl in London. Given the state of our increasingly tumultuous relationship, Shan had been losing the trust we had been building up since our last break from commitment. She was becoming increasingly suspicious of me, especially when I started making plans to see old female friends in foreign countries. It wasn't something that happened overnight, and it wasn't something she did lightly, but she began going through my computer to read my emails, where she found a correspondence between me and this girl, and she confronted me with it.

Whereas she had been very hurt the last time we took a break in our relationship, this time she was downright mad—and rightfully so. And I had no excuse. The reality was that my physical and psychological breakdown was making me feel totally defective as a human being for the first time in my life, and I just didn't know how to deal with it. I thought that if I just started doing whatever felt good to me in the moment, pushing any responsibility or care for others out of my mind, that I could at least feel some pleasure for an instant, and perhaps feel a little bit more potent in the process. But it was all just another lie and another mask that I was wearing to disguise myself from the worthlessness I was really feeling. There was no excuse for it. Shan didn't deserve that. So all I could do was apologize and try to explain that it was done out of sheer weakness, not out of malice, and out of pathetic ego compensation, not out of any real feelings.

But it didn't matter. Her heart was broken.

She did forgive me, however. And she didn't break up with me. We stayed together and tried to work through it this time. But I had wounded her so deeply that she had very little trust in me, moving forward. And I don't blame her. I had very little trust in myself at that point.

chapter 18

fame & fortune, part one

The next year was the most schizophrenic year of my life. So much good and so much bad were packed into that one year that I thought my head would spin. Maroon 5 was the hottest "new" band in the world when awards season began in late 2004, and one after another, the gatekeepers to the most exclusive corners of the entertainment industry were handing us the keys to their kingdom. And our arrival into the world of the Hollywood elite ushered in some of the most memorable and exciting moments of my life, ranging from the comedic to the surreal. Winning accolades at highly visible ceremonies brought yet another level of success and exposure to the band, and the events to which we were getting invited became even glitzier and more coveted. The MTV Video Music Awards came first, but we had been so sure that we wouldn't win the Best New Artist award that we didn't carve out time from our busy tour schedule to attend. Along with everyone else, we were convinced that the hands-down favorite to win was Kanye West. We were absolutely shocked to find out that we had in fact won Best New Artist at that year's ceremony. Soon thereafter, we were informed that we had been bestowed the same honor from the Latin

American version of the show. When it came time for the MTV Europe Music Awards, the band agreed to fly back to the continent to perform at the big event held in Rome, where Duran Duran handed us our third Best New Artist award on live television, making it a clean sweep of three continents.

The two days we stayed at the swanky Excelsior hotel in Rome felt like the intersection of every facet of mainstream pop culture. We partied at a very exclusive nightclub the night before the event, alongside hip-hop and R&B luminaries like Outkast, Usher, and Kanye, as well as many other pop fixtures of the day, such as Gwen Stefani, the Black Eyed Peas, and the Backstreet Boys. After the show, we all returned to the hotel, the most glamorous in all of Rome, where we continued the festivities, mingling among the stars. At one point, Adam and I found ourselves in a conversation with one of our heroes: Pharrell Williams of the Neptunes. His beats and hooks had been a major inspiration for many of the tracks on *Songs About Jane*, so we just had to express our admiration and ask him to work with us.

"We need to work with you sometime, dude," Adam said. "You have no idea how much we've been influenced by your tracks."

Pharrell made a funny smirk and said, "Y'all don't need me. I make beats for rappers and pop stars who need hot tracks. Y'all got all of that in your band already."

I was deeply flattered that he thought our recordings were on a level where we didn't really need the help of his talent. I considered it a huge personal compliment coming from him (if not so much for my drumming abilities, then certainly for our taste and style as artists).

Next, we performed at the VH1 Big in '04 event held at the famous Shrine Auditorium in downtown Los Angeles, where our dressing room was situated right next to that of veteran rock band Velvet Revolver. With three-fifths of that band having come from Guns N' Roses originally, it was as if the whole backstage area of the venue had been transported in time to a *Headbangers Ball* video from 1988.

Returning from sound check, I walked up the steep theater stairs into the smoke-filled hallway, lined with scantily clad, bleached-blonde women showcasing big, fake boobs and even bigger hair. I turned into our dressing room, where I found bassist Duff McKagan sitting on our couch, strumming an acoustic guitar rather earnestly. It sounded like he was playing the song "Patience," and it looked like an image straight out of the 1989 video. Duff continued to strum our acoustic like he was stuck in time, while I just stood in the middle of the room watching him. He was so wrapped up in the dulcet, suspended chords he was playing that he hadn't noticed me walk in. Also in our dressing room, however, was Mötley Crüe drummer Tommy Lee, sloppily thumping a beat against the bathroom door with his closed fist and booted foot. He seemed pretty drunk, judging from the loose, out-of-time rhythm he was pounding out. I stood there for another moment, dumbfounded by these two massive rock stars jamming like a couple of teenagers who had just learned to play the guitar and drums.

When the other guys started filing in, Tommy and Duff finally noticed that we had entered the room, and Tommy opened his eyes, turning to see who was there. Looking a little dazed, he apologized, "Oh, is this your dressing room, bro? I'm sorry."

Duff followed suit. "Oh, is this your acoustic? Sorry, man."

Adam and I were giddy. I couldn't help but think of him and Jesse Nicita playing their competing versions of "Wild Side" on my Pearl Export Series drum kit in my parents' garage.

On our previous trip to Europe, we had all gotten a glimpse of the life Adam was entering as the face of a very successful pop act when he was no longer able to walk around the city of Milan without getting swarmed by fans. However, I got my first image of just how isolating that kind of fame can be when we attended the Billboard Music Awards in Las Vegas that December. After receiving the Digital Media Award (handed to us this time by Tommy Lee and the rest of Mötley Crüe), we ventured to the after-party for more revelry with our pop compatriots. For some reason, the enormously famous million-heiress Paris Hilton decided that Shan and I would be her best friends for the night, and she wanted to escort us to her own after-after-party in her personal limo. We needed to get from the club to the street through the lobby of the MGM Grand, but a huge crowd of onlookers and media stood in our way.

Paris gave us very specific instructions: Shan was to hold her hand as they walked ahead of me, I was to stay a few paces behind them, and we were all to walk very briskly, straight through the lobby and out the front doors to her waiting limousine. We walked out of the club and into the lobby, and immediately tons of paparazzi and fans came streaming toward us from all sides, yelling Paris's name. We bolted for the doors, just narrowly avoiding the onslaught. It was amazing, surreal, and kind of terrifying.

When we made it into Paris's limo, I got the feeling that being in the eye of that hurricane is not all that it's cracked up to be. It actually seemed pretty lonely to me. She had just met us and was telling us all about the things she was doing in her career; she was excited to play us a song that was to be her first foray into music. However, it struck me that she had no one close to her with whom to share these things in her life. It seemed that maybe she was yearning for some kind of real connection beneath all the surface attention she was getting from the public.

After eating a late dinner at Nobu, we went to Paris's huge suite at the Hard Rock Hotel, complete with a bowling alley in the living room, which was filled with a bunch of people whom she didn't even seem to know. She talked about some of her friends in LA, but she didn't speak very fondly of them, and the "partying" that we did felt almost routine rather than festive. She then wanted to leave her own party, so we gambled for a bit down-stairs, then headed back to her other hotel suite at the MGM. We left her there alone in her room, as we had to go jump on a private jet to New York in the morning. As we were leaving, she asked if she could come with us on the plane. The band was on its way to perform on *The Today Show*, however, so we were told by Adam and our management that she was not allowed. I guess there really are some things that money can't buy.

During that holiday season, the band played some radio festivals alongside a number of pop stars, including Jessica Simpson. Having taken a liking to

the band, she invited all of us to Prince's concert after-party at the House
of Blues in LA in early 2005. Adam, James, and I arrived to meet her in the
Foundation Room upstairs, and she looked amazing. This was right around
the time she was shooting *The Dukes of Hazzard*, for which she had gotten
in really great shape to put on the Daisy Dukes. I introduced myself to her,
and she said, "Oh, I know who you are." I was a little taken aback by this,
but then she said with a smile, "My sister talks about you a lot."

Jessica was very friendly, and we got to talking for a while. She introduced us to Justin Timberlake, and he was an affable guy as well. I told
him how much I had enjoyed seeing him perform with Fishbone drummer
Phillip "Fish" Fisher, who was another one of my heroes in the '90s, and he
regaled me with the pleasures of playing with such an awesome beat maker.
The big prize of the night, however, was to be invited into the Parish Room,
where Prince was jamming with his band the New Power Generation, as he
would famously do well into the morning hours after one of his concerts.
Just think about how exclusive that room must have been: big pop stars of
the moment like Justin Timberlake, Jessica Simpson, and Maroon 5 were
sitting in the staging area, just waiting to be invited into the VIP. From time
to time, Prince would stick his head out into the room, whispering into the
ear of his bodyguard, who would then escort his chosen guests into the jam
session.

The guard eventually escorted Jessica inside, and she promised she'd
work on getting us in as well. A few minutes later, one of the guards came
and fetched us, bringing us around the long way to the front entrance.
When we walked into the Parish Room, it was quite a scene. The venue was
about the size of my living room, but there were probably about fifty people crammed in there, all sitting up against the walls and around the floor
like it was a 1960s sit-in. Prince's backing band was onstage jamming, and I
could hear his voice coming from somewhere, calling out instructions like
"Drum break on the one!" and "Hit it, Maceo!" (referring to James Brown's
saxophonist Maceo Parker, who was playing stage left with the three-piece
horn section). I looked down to my side, and there was his purple majesty,
all five foot two of him, his head at about the level of my chest, standing

right next to me in the back-left corner of the room. He had a wireless mic in his hand, and he was playing the role of emcee from across the audience.

The guard escorted us right down to the front of the crowd, and my head was positioned directly next to Maceo's horn. I took a gander back around the room, and it looked like a wax museum had come to life. Every face in that room was famous: there were Justin Timberlake and Cameron Diaz, John Stamos and Rebecca Romijn, Elijah Wood and the other hobbits, and on and on around the room. Prince finally made his way to the stage to play the keyboards with the band, and then he encouraged everyone to get up and dance, which was when the party really started. We were all moving in a sea of sweat, pushing up closely to Prince and the New Power Generation, as if it was their own house party. Jessica and I were dancing closely against each other, and I couldn't have been more thrilled!

Jessica and her friend Cacee Cobb wanted to continue the party with our crew, so we invited them back to Adam and James's apartment, which was nearby in Hollywood. We all jumped in their driver's SUV and rode over to the spot. When we got there, we cracked open a bottle of champagne, and everyone was getting a little tipsy. Adam was excited to play us some demos he had just recorded, including the song "Makes Me Wonder" (which would end up on the next album). In her slightly inebriated state, Jessica started ribbing Adam a little, saying, "Oh, Adam, don't try to be cool. You're not Justin Timberlake. Don't try to be like Justin." I could see steam coming out of Adam's ears when she said that. I have to admit, he had a pretty good comeback, though, "Sorry, I don't do Berlin covers."

Adam seemed genuinely peeved after that exchange, and he retired to his bedroom for a while, which left James and me in the living room with Jessica and Cacee. After laughing a bit at how pissed Adam had gotten, the two of them started reminiscing about their life together growing up in Texas, and somewhere along the line, Jessica started talking about Jesus. I knew that her dad was a pastor or a minister of some kind, but her whole demeanor took on a much more serious tone when she began professing her love for the Lord. As she was giving her sermon, the top of her form-fitting dress kept inching down, until her breasts were just hanging out of the top of it. Cacee was laughing and trying to pull her dress up for her, saying, "Her boobs are always falling out all over the place." It didn't seem to bother Jessica at all, though, or maybe she didn't even notice. She just kept on talking about Jesus.

I eventually walked the two of them to their car at the end of the night, and the next day one of Adam and James's neighbors wrote a very aggressive letter, complaining about the "two blonde bimbos making all that noise in the courtyard last night." If whoever wrote that note only knew about whom they were complaining! We all hung out with Jessica and Cacee a few more times after that (and Jessica's sister, Ashlee, a couple of times as well), and they seemed like very sweet and genuine girls; they were very easy to like.

In the weeks following that night, Prince invited us to two very exclusive parties at his house in Bel-Air, where we finally formally met him in his own home, shaking his hand and "kissing the ring," so to speak. We also got to watch him rip a shredding guitar solo right there in the middle of his own living room, which was an awe-inspiring moment for me. He truly was the most impressive guitarist I've ever seen play, and he played with such ease and flair, even in a casual setting like that. The first party was a milder affair, but he had an astounding group of musicians playing all night for the select crowd in attendance. Prince never disappointed with the level of talent around him. However, the second party we attended was that incredibly A-list post-Oscars party, at which I finally met Leonardo DiCaprio. Talk about a room full of famous faces! Samuel L. Jackson, Renée Zellweger, Salma Hayek, Laurence Fishburne, Matthew McConaughey, Justin Timberlake, Usher, Penélope Cruz, Joni Mitchell . . . the list goes on and on. I know I'm just name-dropping now, but it truly was extraordinary to be in one room with all these epically talented artists, who are all so incredibly gifted in their respective fields.

We showed up early, and the house band started playing to welcome the first arrivals. I, of course, wanted to see the talent onstage as much as the celebrities coming through the front door. But all of a sudden, I found myself standing in the middle of the dance floor alone with Justin

Timberlake. We had met that one time before at the House of Blues, so we acknowledged each other with a smile and a wave, both enjoying the rhythms coming from the drums and amps. I was a huge fan of Justin's first album, *Justified*, which featured some awesome tracks produced by the Neptunes and Timbaland, so I stood there quietly at first, feeling a little starstruck. I was just hoping he didn't challenge me to a dance-off.

He leaned his head over to mine at one point and commented, "The drummer hits the snare just a little late in the pocket, doesn't he?"

I must have just been in a really sensitive state, given everything going on for me at that time in my life, because I heard this innocuous comment as an insult toward the drummer, and I couldn't help but internalize it as an insult toward me and my drumming.

One of two things was definitely true: (1) Justin was just making some small talk with another musician, being social at a social event; or (2) he was trying to connect with me, because he was actually a fan of my laid-back drum groove on the album. And I should have taken it as such . . . but I didn't.

"I don't think so, man. He sounds pretty right on the beat to me," I said somewhat defensively.

Justin looked a little confused at my dismissal, and I'm sure he thought I was a sourpuss for not just agreeing with him like any normal person making pleasantries at a party would. Either that, or I was just reading way too much into absolutely everything. Which was probably the case, because my head was a mess in those days.

No matter, though, because the party picked up shortly thereafter, and before I knew it, the whole place was jumping, with all of these massive stars drinking and dancing together in Prince's living room. And it was a real party! I guess stars really are "just like us," as *Us Weekly* magazine has been saying all this time. You couldn't get McConaughey off the conga drums, except to take more tequila shots and do a little mock tango with Penélope Cruz. And Usher just looked like a fanboy, enjoying himself and soaking up the excitement of a celebration at his hero's house. At a break in the action, I sat down behind the drummer's kit just to see how he had things set up, but Justin decided to sit down at the keyboard right at that moment, wanting to partake in the jam session. He started playing the electric piano riff to his song "Señorita," looking at me to follow along. There was no way I could play for that crowd at that moment (I could barely even hold a beat at that point), so I just stood up and walked away. Again, I'm sure he thought I was a total weirdo. Sorry, Justin, if you're reading this! If you only knew what was going on in my body and mind at that time . . . However, it wasn't long before James and Jesse got onstage and jammed with Justin, Herbie Hancock, and Prince. What???!!!!!

Early in that year as well, the band played Clive Davis's pre-Grammy party once again, just after receiving our first two Grammy nominations for Best Pop Group Performance and Best New Artist (which was obviously a very big deal). After performing for Clive and his many iconic guests, we got to watch another star-studded list of artists onstage that night, as well as mingle with the many faces of music history. At a quiet moment between sets, sitting all together at our table in the ballroom of the Beverly Hills Hotel, we noticed a very refined-looking English gentleman coming over to us. He stopped in front of our table and asked, "Would you fellows mind if Mr. Jimmy Page says hello to you?"

Would we mind? Are you kidding?

This nice man escorted us over to Jimmy's table, where the founder of Led Zeppelin immediately greeted us by saying, "Hello mates! I'm a big fan of your record!"

Think of that. Jimmy Page. The rock god. The guitarist, songwriter, and bandleader who had inspired every heavy band that came after Zeppelin . . . told us he was a fan of *our band*! That's not supposed to happen. We're supposed to be stumbling over ourselves, effusively telling him what an honor it was to meet *him*. Not the other way around! Talk about surreal.

That was the glamorous life that was emerging for us in 2005, as I was still struggling personally. These inconceivable stories illustrate just how much difference there was between my outward life and my inward life at that moment in time. And the discrepancy between the two was a total mind fuck. There we were, being escorted to the most glamorous places and doing the most glamorous things, being honored and recognized by our heroes of yesteryear and the biggest names of the pop-culture moment. We were selling millions of records and concert tickets all around the world, and the riches from the many royalties and tour profits were finally funneling into our bank accounts. We were on top of the world. We were living the dream. And I was in the depths of despair at the very same time.

I was still trying my hardest to put on a happy face, enjoying the amazingly decadent fruits of our labor, while my self-worth was deteriorating more and more each day. I started to believe that I didn't deserve any of this: that I was just some impostor along for the ride with my very talented bandmates, as if I hadn't put a decade-plus of hard work into getting to this place. I almost felt guilty for being showered with so many blessings, when I didn't feel worthy of any of them. Outwardly, I would soak up the entitlement by indulging in the parties and the lavish trappings of success (as I imagine any pop star in my position would), but more and more that meant pushing down the real feelings of self-contempt, trying to pretend that everything would get better soon, when inside I didn't believe that it would. One can only shove down the real emotions for so long before they start to bubble to the surface one way or another.

The band had the honor of being asked to perform as part of the big opening medley to kick off the Grammy's ceremony of 2005, along with the Black Eyed Peas, Franz Ferdinand, Los Lonely Boys, and Gwen Stefani. Although it seemed unlikely that I would be able to return to playing onstage with them for that event, I figured I at least had to try. Having allowed months and months for my arms to recover from the inflammation, and for the nerves to "reinnervate," as the neurologist had put it, I decided it was finally time to try my darndest to start playing the drums again. I rented a 24/7 lockout in my very own rehearsal space in North Hollywood, set up all my gear for daily jamming and practicing, and sought out the best drum teacher in Los Angeles, to see if he could possibly get my arms moving and playing properly.

I made a little bit of progress, finding myself able to hold the sticks in the way that the teacher was instructing me, and finally beginning to learn some of the basic rudiments of drum technique on a practice pad in his garage. But coordinating playing the full drum kit was a whole other beast to conquer, because the problem was no longer just the nerves in my right arm—my whole body felt totally out of whack at that point, and my brain just seemed entirely out of sync with what my limbs were trying to synchronize. I could visualize what I wanted to play, and I could even envision the way I would have played it before, but the connection between my mind and my body was frayed, if not cut off completely. I tried and I tried, imagining what it used to feel like to play the drums when it seemed so easy, and attempting to incorporate the new and proper hand techniques that the teacher was trying to impart. But it just wasn't happening. The band came to my rehearsal space at one point to play with me, just to see if maybe I could swing the couple of minutes of "This Love" that would be necessary to perform in the Grammy's opening medley, but it became clear very quickly that it just wasn't possible.

After a short break from that failed attempt at playing together again, the guys all returned to my rehearsal room to break the news.

"I'm sorry, man," James said. "I really wish that you could play with us for this, but it just doesn't seem like you're ready yet."

"I know I'm not," I said testily. ". . . It shouldn't be that hard though . . . I mean, all I have to do is *this* like ten times." As I said that, I hit the hi-hat stiffly, doing a simplified version of the chorus of "This Love" (which was actually better than how I'd just played it a few minutes earlier). "I should be able to do *that*, right?"

"We just feel that the musical deficiencies are too great right now," Jesse said. "We just can't afford for this big a performance to not be great."

All I could do was shake my head. Musical *deficiencies*, he'd said. Might as well drop the word *musical* off that statement, because that's how I felt:

totally *deficient*. Whatever hope I'd had of playing on the Grammys was dashed, and I quickly spiraled back down into self-hatred.

The other guys apologized and wished me well, leaving as quickly as they had come in, but Jesse hung back for a minute.

"How are you doing, Ryan? Are you okay?" he said.

"Honestly, not really, man."

"Is there anything I can do right now? Do you want to talk about this some more?"

"There's nothing you can really do, Jesse, but thanks . . . It seems that all that helps me feel better at this point is having enough drinks to forget about it for a few hours."

"Do you want to go get a drink somewhere?"

"No, no . . . you can go, Jesse . . . I'll be all right. Thanks, though."

I probably should have taken Jesse up on his offer. Drinking to escape your problems doesn't lead to anything good, but drinking with a friend to unload your feelings can actually be productive. I just didn't think that he could possibly understand what I was going through.

I was devastated not to be able to perform with the band for the Grammys, but the day of the ceremony was still a pretty exciting series of events for me. My live-TV, awards-show moment behind the drums was not to be, and I would again have to watch my band performing without me (this time on one of the biggest stages in the world), but I still got to dress up in a fancy designer suit, walk the red carpet to be interviewed by Joan Rivers and the other mainstays of the entertainment media, and sit with the band down low on the Staples Center floor for the main event. However, even though we had won several Best New Artist awards by that point, everyone was still expecting Kanye to win it at the Grammys.

The very first award presented that night was for our other category, Best Pop Group Performance, and we lost it to Los Lonely Boys, so right away we were convinced that there was no way we could pull out the most coveted prize. But the moment came, the presenters called our name, and funny enough, we had to walk right past Kanye on our way up to the stage. He graciously hugged Adam first, and then we all ended up hugging him kind of awkwardly on our way by, before Adam acknowledged him to start our acceptance speech. I guess we all felt a little guilty, because Kanye's first album had been such a big breakthrough in the world of hip-hop and pop culture, but it was still *our* moment in the sun, and it felt like an absolute dream. Standing on that Grammy stage, with the entire industry (and the entire country) watching us being honored in that way was an epic signal of arrival in our career. Of course, the irony of being named the best "new" artist, after working toward that moment for eleven years, was not lost on any of the original four members. But no matter, we were happy to be considered the fresh-faced ingénues of the music world. And this was just a few years before Kanye's Taylor Swift moment at the 2009 MTV Video Music Awards, so I guess we should consider it a compliment that he didn't bum-rush the microphone.

chapter 19

fame & fortune, part two

The band continued to tour throughout most of 2005, as the campaign in support of *Songs About Jane* reached four full years of promotion. I joined the guys on the road for stretches throughout the year, staying physically close to them at times but feeling more and more distanced emotionally. I kept up with the physical therapy, continued to practice my rudiments, and tried in vain to regain my coordination. The band did its first full-scale, solo-headlining amphitheater tour, sponsored by Honda Civic and featuring opening acts like the Donnas, Simon Dawes, and Phantom Planet, in the middle of which I sang "Highway to Hell" at the Houston Rodeo, following a military parade that included fireworks and assault rifles, which was just bizarre. We also released our fifth and final single from the album, "Must Get Out," which didn't do as well on the charts as the first four had, so it was becoming apparent that we were rounding the corner toward the completion of the album cycle.

Right in the middle of that year, we all flew back to Europe to perform at Germany's two biggest summer festivals: Rock am Ring and Rock im Park. The *ring* in that first name refers to a massive Formula One racetrack, filled with about 75,000 music fans. We performed in a lineup that included Incubus, My Chemical Romance, Weezer, and Green Day. We even had a dressing room right next to our *Fourth World*–era heroes, and we could hear Rivers Cuomo doing his vocal warm-ups through a thin dividing wall. The members of Green Day were very friendly and kind to us, remembering us from our Rob Cavallo connection, and the whole event was a rather enjoyable experience. However, I was a little preoccupied, pondering some looming eventualities. We weren't talking about it explicitly yet, but I think everyone was thinking that pretty soon we would be heading home to start working on the next album.

We had started writing songs for the follow-up to *Songs About Jane* pretty early in the touring in 2002. Adam was still on a roll from the inspired renaissance in our band and sound, so we had been working out arrangements for songs like "Can't Stop," "Won't Go Home Without You," "Miss You, Love You," "Wasted Years," and "Makes Me Wonder," practicing them in sound checks around the country and world. We even played a couple of them in our set a few times, after which "Wasted Years" became a staple of our set list for a couple of years. As we were winding down toward the eventual end of the long four years of touring, I couldn't help but wonder what the other guys were thinking in regard to writing and recording our sophomore album, given my current state of disability. So I decided to have a heart-to-heart with Adam in our hotel room in Germany that night.

"Adam, I'm worried that the band is going to be in a rush to make another album soon," I said. "I think we need to take our time and make sure we do it right."

"Well, we do have to start thinking about it," he said. "The fans are waiting at this point . . . We need to keep up the momentum."

"I know . . . but I'm afraid that you're thinking about doing it . . . whether or not I can play yet," I said, trying to sound calm and objective about the situation.

"I really don't want to do that, Ryan . . . but we do have to make a record sooner or later."

"I'm aware of that . . . and I don't want to hold the band back from that . . . but I just want to be a part of it . . . We've been working toward this for a long time . . . and I want to believe that I am an important part of the process."

"You are important," he said firmly. "We're not going to make this album without you, Ryan . . . I promise you . . . we can't make this album without you . . . we need you . . . Whatever happens . . . whatever that means . . . even if someone else has to play for you, your involvement is definitely going to be important, and you'll be there . . . as always."

The distinct possibility that Matt or someone else might be playing on the follow-up to *Songs About Jane* hit me like a slap in the face in that moment, and I began to well up.

"I appreciate that, Adam," I said, sniffling. "And I want the album to be as good as it can be . . . I really do."

Adam did his best to alleviate my worries. I knew that it was mostly just a pep talk, an attempt to make me feel better and encourage me to maintain hope, but I held on to that statement as a promise, wanting so badly for it to be true.

The next day we headed to Nuremberg to play the second festival, Rock im Park. This one was held in the old Zeppelin Field, where we noticed a rather jarring sight as we approached the performance stage. On one side of the long corridor of fans stood a rather ominous relic of German history: the military grandstand made famous by black-and-white Nazi propaganda films of Hitler rallying his troops. I knew that the structure still stood on this site to remind tourists of what had happened (and what should never happen again), but at the same time it felt just totally wrong that it hadn't been torn down, and that we were now being asked to entertain people right in front of it. Growing up as a Jew, I had received implorations at every Passover Seder to "never forget" the Holocaust, so the dissonance between the past and the present was a confusing thing to wrap my head around. But sure enough, I went to center stage at the end of our set, and I sang "Highway to Hell" to 75,000 Germans in view of Hitler's podium. To say I had mixed feelings about that would be an understatement.

Next up, to cap the success of an album that was approaching ten mil-lion records sold worldwide, it was time to shoot a concert DVD, and again, it would be Matt performing in my stead. As I had been doing at venues all around the world, I sang my harmonies from the side of the stage at the Santa Barbara Bowl for that recorded performance. As depressing as it was to watch someone else now contributing to a product that would end up in stores for sale, shooting the interviews and other material for the DVD was actually a somewhat positive and cathartic experience. The label put us up at the beautiful Four Seasons Biltmore Resort in Santa Barbara, and we filmed some candid dialogue over a game of poker, as well as conducting some individual interviews. I tried my best to be honest about everything that was going on for me, while maintaining a more optimistic and upbeat attitude about the future, and it felt good to express my pain, framed in the context of hope. The other guys and the video crew seemed to like my contributions to the DVD, and I think the end result avoided pulling the attention from where it needed to be at that time: on the success of *Songs About Jane.*

In August, the band was asked to open a few shows for the frigging Rolling Stones . . . and again I could only sing my harmonies from the side of the stage. But at least I got to watch the Stones in sound check, playing "Ruby Tuesday" to an empty stadium, which was quite a trippy thing to behold. They sounded just like the Rolling Stones! I found it kind of funny and fitting that those guys had made a whole career in the '70s of emulating the soulful, weathered bluesmen who had inspired their style and passion, but now they had really grown into the role, looking the parts of the griz-zled, old veterans. Once again, this was something that very few artists get asked to do, so it was both an honor to be there and a disappointment not to be onstage behind the drums.

In the fall, my family, Shan, and I took a trip to New York City (sep-arately from the band) to see my aunt Michele perform her one-woman show at Feinstein's/54 Below club, and my uncle Fred escorted us all to the famous Elaine's restaurant after the show. There were a few famous faces in there as usual, but we were able to secure the prime table, in the corner facing into the room. Michele is Broadway royalty, having starred in the original casts of *Seesaw* and *How to Succeed in Business Without Really Trying*, so the staff treated her as such. Partway into our dinner, a few familiar-looking men walked in and sat at a table by the door, and I instantly recognized them as Neal Schon, Jonathan Cain, and Ross Valory of the band Journey. They must have been in town on tour. I leaned over to my family and told them who they were, to which my aunt said, "Oh, I know them! I met them at the Kennedy Center Honors!" She then instructed Fred to go bring them over to say hi.

Neal Schon looked exactly as I imagined him, still sporting the cut-off jean jacket and tight pants from the band's 1980s heyday, and he had the swagger of the guitar hero that he was. I don't know how Shan never got a big head with all these huge rock stars hitting on her, but sure enough, Neal came over, sat down next to her, and started flirting directly with her, as if I weren't sitting right next to them. At one point, my uncle Fred asked him, "Do you know my nephew's band, Maroon 5? They've sold ten million records." Without missing a beat, Schon responded, "We've sold seventy million." He then informed us that he was in fact *not* a fan of Maroon 5, explaining, "I like a little more *cock* in my rock." I was dying.

From September on, the band was mostly back home in LA, starting to take its first steps toward the next album. We were meeting with a bunch of producers, including the famous guru of Def Jam Recordings, Rick Rubin, who offered to put us up in his residence-style recording studio the Houdini Mansion, where we could write and record demos. I still had my separate rehearsal space to keep working on my drumming, but the band was rolling right along and starting to churn out new songs, coming mostly from Adam alone this time around. I think he realized that the big money was in publishing, so he figured he could write a whole album on his own. By this point Matt was pretty well involved in the process of the band and was becoming a part of the creative team, so I would often show up to the Mansion to find that he and the guys had already recorded a demo for a song that Adam had written, without my input, which was upsetting, to say the least.

Around this time as well, I finally invested some of the money I had been making in my first dream of a house, located in the Los Feliz area adjacent to Hollywood. It was a charming 1921 Spanish-style home, situated right below the Griffith Observatory, with a view of downtown LA from the master bedroom. I had always thought romantically of owning my own old-Hollywood charmer, and now I could finally afford it. However, in my tortured emotional state, I sought out a rather dark, closed-in, moody house, more as a comfortable place to drink wine and brood than as a healthy place to settle down. Before my breakdown in 2004, drinking had always been a way to enhance the good times and to add to the pleasure of life, but now it had become a way to escape the pain: to feel nothing other than shallow indulgence for an evening. Sipping a fine bottle of wine behind the heavy curtains of a beautiful home sounded like a pleasant departure from the agonizing thoughts and feelings that were plaguing me. I had also purchased my first fine automobile that year, a black Mercedes-Benz E 350. Decay wears luxury well.

My days were filled with more failed attempts at playing the drums, then shopping sprees for furniture to fill my empty house, then decadent nights either at the Houdini Mansion or out at swanky nightclubs and parties with the guys. Every twenty-four hours that came and went were a reminder of what I had achieved and what was slipping away. Amid this constant dichotomy of splendor and rot, I ran into another girl from my past . . . this time one whom I had built up in my mind as "the one that got away." She was somebody I had become friends with back when I was in a relationship with Taryn, and I had always wondered what could have been if I had pursued her romantically. So, in my state of confusion and despair, I decided that I wasn't going to make the same mistake again. I started communicating with this girl every day via text, until once again, Shan figured out what was going on.

Shan confronted me about this new flirtation, of course having no trust that it was just an old friend. I didn't try to deny it this time. I admitted that this was a girl for whom I had feelings that I wanted to pursue. Because I had downgraded my consciousness to total nihilism in coping with the magnitude of my sorrow, I decided to break up with Shan, just to see what could be with this girl whom I had barely known for years. Although Shan had already lost trust in me after the last time this sort of thing happened, she was still devastated again. She couldn't even look at me. When I was out at my rehearsal space the next day, she packed up her things and left the house we had just moved into, to stay at a friend's apartment.

I dated this other girl for a total of about a week, maybe less, before I realized that I had only built up what was between us into something more than it actually was. "The one that got away" had worked as a powerful force in my psyche, especially at a time when I had lost faith in myself and in my purpose for being. Believing that a relationship with this person could act as some kind of elixir for my soul was just another fool's errand—an attempt at diversion from what was truly ailing me. But that didn't matter. Shan was so upset that she got on a plane and headed to North Carolina to stay with her mom and brother for a month.

I decided at that point that I would just be "married to my drums" for a while, hoping and praying that dedicating my entire attention to my relationship with my craft would somehow be the cure to my problems. I spent the next few weeks just trying to find any state into which I could slip to play the drums well, practicing at my rehearsal space in North Hollywood, jamming in the basement of my new, empty house, and then trying to play with the band at the Mansion. It seemed, however, that every time I took two steps forward, I would take three steps back. I tried to distract myself from the failure by spending time with other girls I would meet at parties and clubs, but again, these were just momentary indulgences that left me feeling even more nihilistic when they were over. It seemed the only thing that could save my spirit would be to regain my position in the band . . . but I sensed that the moment when such a possibility would be gone forever was approaching.

After about a month alone in my new house, the band called me to the Mansion for one last attempt at drumming well enough to perform on the upcoming album. I drove up Laurel Canyon in my Mercedes, pulled up the long driveway to that beautiful, dilapidated estate, and made one last valiant effort to will my body into playing with the guys, and then they called me into the formal dining room for that fateful, mournful meeting. I suppose their decision to move on was really just a formality at that point, after a year and a half of playing with Matt and waiting patiently for my condition to improve. It wasn't like I didn't see it coming. No, it actually felt more like I had willed it to come.

I suppose it would have been easier if I could have just believed that I was getting fucked over or screwed out of my place in the band by a bunch of selfish guys who didn't care about me at all. But the reality was much harder to swallow: I'd done this to myself. The band had waited as long as they possibly could for me to recover, and I just couldn't do it. The damage I had done to my body, my mind, and the nervous system that connected them was just too great to overcome. My own inadequacies had led to that moment, and I had no one else to blame. That didn't stop me from holding on to some misdirected anger toward the band, however. I needed a direction at which to aim my resentment other than solely at myself, and they were the most logical choice for deflection.

My parents hadn't been aware of the level of my suffering until that moment came. I knew I had to tell them what had happened, but I didn't know how I was going to say it. It's interesting to think that in that instance I was most concerned with how my parents were going to take the news. I remembered how nervous I had been to tell my dad that I wanted to quit playing baseball in high school; I had feared that his disappointment would be even more profound than mine. And I had been right; he was really upset, even angry at first. So I decided that I needed to cushion the blow by telling my parents that it was actually okay that I would no longer be in the band, because now I could go on to be what I really wanted to be: a record producer. I had always enjoyed the creative process more than the touring, so it seemed like a perfect fit for my talents and personality. My dad's first reaction was as dramatic as when I had told him I didn't want to play baseball anymore; both times it was a loud "OH NO!!! RYAN!!!" But this time was a little different, because instead of trying to talk me into keeping up the fight, he very quickly shifted into damage-control, caretaker mode.

"Ryan, I'm sure you'll make a great producer, and I look forward to that, but that is an unknown right now. Maroon 5 is a known entity. We have to make sure you retain your stake in that company," he said, becoming my lawyer in that instant.

"I don't even really care, Dad . . . I just want to move on," I said meekly.

"You worked too hard for too long to not get what you deserve from that band. They're going to make another record and they're going to tour the world, making millions of dollars. You deserve your share of those profits for what you contributed to the band's success."

"Yeah, I guess . . ."

My desire for oblivion included a total disregard for practical concerns, like how I was going to continue to pay this new mortgage I'd just signed. So my dad went about representing me for the negotiation of my termination from the band agreement, while I just twiddled my thumbs, trying to occupy my mind with what kind of records I might produce in the future. After some debate, he and the band's attorney were able to come to a reasonable agreement on what my share of the future profits would be, they finalized the documents, and like that, I was officially out of the band. Part of the contract stipulated that I would be involved in making the next album in a production capacity, however, so I had to shift gears almost immediately and start wrapping my head around the idea of working in the studio with the guys, trying to contribute to the quality of the follow-up album as only an "additional producer." The word *additional* was just too demeaning for me to accept, as I'd been a founding member of the band, so we settled on the term "musical director" instead. I suppose the title was kind of meaningless.

Realizing that I had just lost my band of twelve years, right after losing my relationship of five years, I felt a huge hole right in the middle of my being, as if a huge chunk of me had just been torn out, leaving me hollow and wounded. Shan had just gotten back in town from North Carolina, so I asked her to come to the house to talk things through.

"I've been an idiot, Shan, I'm so sorry," I said. "I've been going through hell personally, but the fact that I have made you suffer as a result makes it even worse."

"What is this?" she said, a tear rolling down her cheek already.

"It took losing the band to realize that you are more important to me than anything. I need you in my life. I've been an absolute fool for taking you for granted."

"I don't know . . ."

"I do know . . . We belong together . . . I can move on from this . . . but I need you . . ."

"Is that really what you want? Or are you just feeling sorry for yourself now . . . and you don't want to be alone?" she said.

"Well . . . I am feeling sorry for myself . . . and no, I don't want to be alone . . . but I also just realized that you're the only person who I can imagine being with and getting through this with. You've been there for me through everything, and I've never been able to appreciate it fully until right now . . . I need you . . . and I love you more than anything."

A glimmer of joy and satisfaction shone on her face when I said that, and even though she was still crying, I knew that it wasn't too late for us. I still had my partner in life, despite having done everything in my power to push her away. She hugged me, and I could feel that she was shaking.

"This is not going to be easy, Ryan . . . you have a lot of work to do to earn back my trust."

"I know that . . . and I'll do whatever it takes to get it back, I promise . . . I'll go to couples therapy with you if you'd like . . . I'll show you how much I love you and how much I appreciate you. I promise."

When she finally smiled and kissed me through the tears, I felt a sense of relief. I felt that we had each other no matter what, and that was enough for both of us to go on. I still had my family, who loved and supported me unconditionally, I still had some income as a part owner of the growing Maroon 5 corporation, and I still had my loving partner, with whom I could try to move on . . .

Now I just needed to figure out what the hell I was going to do with the rest of my life.

chapter 20

the lost weekend

As much as I would have preferred to slip into a state of denial about what had happened and just move on, my best intentions required me to immediately swallow my pride and embrace a subjugated role with the band I helped create. On top of that, my departure from the group's lineup hadn't yet been announced to the world, so for all intents and purposes I was still being treated as a band member ... by everyone except the members of the band, who now expected me to show up at the studio hat in hand, sit on the sidelines until someone asked for my opinion, and then try to add my two cents to the process as some kind of third-party adviser, or more like a fifth wheel. And as much as I wanted to pretend that my relationship with Shan was back on track, my erratic behavior in the previous year had created so much distrust and resentment that the tension between us was palpable, and it would stay that way for some time. We both tried to settle into a new life, nesting in our beautiful bungalow below the observatory, adopting a cat, and attempting to create a comfortable, domestic life together, but the memories of the recent past were just too fresh in our minds. As I had agreed to do, I found a good couples therapist, we started attending weekly sessions, and I did my best to pick up the pieces of my life and relationship, while simultaneously attempting to contribute to the new Maroon 5 album on which I wouldn't be playing the drums.

In negotiating my release from the band agreement, Adam had reaffirmed his assertion that "we can't make this record without you, Ryan," which I chose to believe, grasping at the last straws of my remaining self-esteem. Although I wasn't entirely happy with the settlement we reached at the time (due to misdirected anger toward the band), I truly believed that I could keep my ego out of the equation and show up to contribute to the quality of the music. This was too big. This was the album we had been working toward our whole lives. This was going to be our *Blood Sugar Sex Magik*. *Songs About Jane* had only been a warm-up to what was supposed to come next. And the fact that I wouldn't be able to play the drums was unfortunate, but I'd be damned if I wasn't going to contribute in whatever way I could, to make that record everything it could be, everything it should be.

Although two top-flight producers were now working on the project and I was just the third guy sitting off to the side of the control room in studio A of Conway Studios, I felt that my involvement in the first week of recording was pretty productive. Perhaps I couldn't see how I must have appeared to everyone else in the room, however. In my mind, I was focusing on the task at hand, intending only to aid in the process, and hiding my pain and resentment. But I'm sure it was more than obvious that I was depressed, angry, and self-destructing. I was drinking more heavily at that point. I was acting out and behaving in ways I never had before; I blamed my friends for not making more of an effort with me, but in retrospect, I can't blame any of them. I was a mess. I'm sure that nobody could even figure out how to be around me, let alone do anything to make me feel better.

Hanging on to the idea that I was truly enhancing the band's creativity, I showed up to the studio every day, poured myself a drink, and offered my suggestions on whatever the band and the new producers were working on. My perception was very skewed, however. I still needed to feel important. I needed to think that I had something to offer, as small as it might be. The magic and chemistry that had created *Songs About Jane* needed to be maintained at all costs, if we were going to achieve greatness. To hell if I was causing more tension in the room.

One night about a week or two into the recording, the whole band ventured out from the studio to attend a private show that Prince was hosting in the ballroom of the Hollywood Roosevelt Hotel, and for some reason Jesse asked me to ride alone with him in his car. I found this a little strange at the time, but I didn't really think much of it, until we were riding down Melrose Avenue in his very practical Volvo station wagon.

"Ryan, I think it's pretty clear that your presence in the studio is affecting the vibe in a negative way," Jesse said bluntly.

I tried to hide the steam that was wafting from my ears. "You and your 'vibes,' Jesse . . . Dude, we're working on a highly anticipated album right now . . . I'm just trying to do my part," I said.

"I know you are . . . but I think it's just too much sometimes . . . I think you're trying to be too involved and put your stamp on everything . . . it's making us . . . it's making me uncomfortable."

"Jesus, get over it, Jesse! It doesn't have to be all 'good vibes' all the time! We're working on something that's pretty fucking important! Not everything can be a hippie commune all the time!"

"You're not hearing me, Ryan . . . I think it would be better if you just came into the studio at the end of the week to provide your feedback. You can listen to what we've done and give us your notes . . . and I promise we'll take them to heart."

Now I was really steaming. I tried to contain myself the best I could. "You've got to be fucking kidding me, Jesse. You and I both know that giving 'notes' on something you guys have already finished would have no effect on the final product. That would be entirely pointless. I might as well not come at all."

"I don't think that it would be . . . I think you would get to have your say," he said calmly.

"I really don't think that I'm imposing myself, Jesse. Quite the contrary! In fact, I feel that I've been restraining myself *a lot* and only speaking up if I have something important to add to the conversation. I've been sitting off to the side, letting you guys do your thing most of the time."

"Well, it's not coming off that way, Ryan . . . I'm sorry, I know you want to be involved, but we need to think about what's best for the process and what's best for the album . . . and I think it would be best if you just came in once a week to give us your comments on the recordings."

There was nothing I could say at that point. The guys were mostly just humoring me by allowing me in the studio at all. It all came crashing down on me that I had become a charity case to them. They felt so badly about what had happened that they were just trying to do me a favor by inviting me to participate and giving me a title of some kind. That reality was entirely demoralizing to me. I could no longer convince myself that I was in fact essential to the formula, and I instead had to face the fact that the band would rather just move on without me. I couldn't handle the full impact of this crushing blow just yet, however, so again I held onto misdirected anger. Jesse was just the messenger of what I'm sure was a universally agreed-upon decision by everyone in that studio, including the producers, but I blamed him personally for that for a long time.

Things weren't much better on the home front. Shan was still very angry at me, and she didn't trust me at all at that point. She was going through my cell phone and emails daily, worried that I was still carrying on an affair with "the one that got away." This felt like an invasion of privacy to me, as well as seeming like an exclamation point to illustrate how dysfunctional our relationship had become, so my defense was to blame her for being a snoop, holding on to resentment toward her for that (a convenient deflection from the blame that rested solely on my shoulders). We were going to couples therapy every week, and I was putting my best foot forward on all fronts, trying to tell her and show her, in any way I could, that I loved her and wanted to make our relationship work again, but I just couldn't seem to find anything I could say or do to fix the situation. It just seemed like too much water had passed under the bridge.

We made a tactical decision to stop arguing outside the therapy room and to save disagreements for when they could be mediated by the therapist, but this just meant that both of us were holding on to grievances and anger for most of the week. Our communication, which had been excellent earlier in our relationship, was actually devolving as a result of this avoidance, and we could only pretend to read each other's minds as to what was up. I was convinced that she truly hated me and was just trying to punish me for what I had put her through, but she would then tell me in our sessions that she really did want to forgive me, but she was just too hurt by what I had done. This went on for months.

In addition to the turmoil between the two of us, I was suffering from some new symptoms in my personal struggle with mental health. The anxiety attacks that had started when I first came home from touring were now escalating to full-scale panic attacks at times, resulting in a total loss of functioning for twenty to thirty minutes. The worst episodes were triggered by reminders of what I had gone through or what I had lost, and would be followed by an almost dissociative state, in which I would end up curled up on the floor in a fetal position. A couple of highly triggering movies had made their way to cable at the time: the first was Martin Scorsese's gripping Howard Hughes biopic, *The Aviator* (starring Leonardo DiCaprio), which very realistically depicted Hughes's intense obsessive-compulsive disorder and eventual descent into madness; and the second was James Mangold's *Walk the Line* (starring Joaquin Phoenix), which portrayed Johnny Cash's personal shame and self-loathing, leading to drug addiction and a nightmarish onstage meltdown. Both of these performances hit a little too close to home for me, leading to flashbacks of my trying desperately to control what I could not in my performing career, and the overwhelming feeling of drowning onstage.

Tired of all the doctors and the medicines that didn't seem to help at all, I decided to get my own hands on some Xanax, thinking that I knew best how to medicate my own symptoms. But what I ended up with was a much worse situation, when I started combining the Xanax with the alcohol. *Do not try this at home.* Alcohol and benzodiazepines together are a *very* dangerous combination because both of these drugs are central nervous system depressants that have a synergistic effect on each other. So you might feel like you're fine one minute on a little Xanax and a couple of glasses of wine, but the next minute you're in a full-on blackout, unaware of what you're saying or doing. And just a little too much of that combination can shut down your nervous system completely, leading to respiratory failure and even death, especially if you're taking any other kind of medication, like a painkiller or a sleeping pill, as well. We all remember Heath Ledger's tragic death from relatively small amounts of these drugs in combination around that time.

And as my relationship with Shan continued to degrade, therapy was becoming less and less productive. Finally, after about six months of trying to overcome our issues together, we needed to have a really honest conversation about what was still between us at that point.

"It feels like you hate me," I said directly to Shan, as the therapist had instructed me.

"I don't hate you. I'm just hurt," Shan said, more sad than angry.

"Well, that's the way it feels . . . Do you know what it feels like to live with someone every day, feeling that they just hate you? It's not a great feeling."

Shan just nodded her head, tears in her eyes. "I don't know what it's going to take for me to get past it . . . it's just still in my mind . . . all the time."

"I really have been trying, though, Shan . . ."

"I know you have . . . It's just that you really destroyed me last year . . . twice . . . I don't know what it's going to take to get over that."

"Maybe there's just too much water under the bridge between us . . ."

"Maybe you're right."

We agreed that it wasn't working and that it was probably time to try to move on with our lives. Neither of us was happy about any of it, but we were both just tired of walking on eggshells, feeling disrespected, and feeling wounded. I arranged to rent an apartment for Shan, she packed up all her stuff for real this time, and she moved out completely.

In the fall of 2006, the band asked me to write a letter to post on their official website, stating that I was leaving the band, just as they were getting ready to announce the 2007 release of their new album and subsequent world tour. This is what I wrote:

> *Due to the rigors of touring, I have sustained joint and nerve injuries that have made me unable to continue performing as a drummer in a touring rock band. I am therefore leaving Maroon 5 to pursue songwriting and producing on my own, a process I have already begun with much enthusiasm.*
>
> *The split is amicable, and I have made my peace with this unfortunate reality, because I feel that I have a lot of music still to make. I worked in the creative process and production of the new M5 album with the title "Musical Director," and I hope to collaborate with the band again in the future. I am still close friends with the guys, including my replacement, Matt Flynn, to whom I wish good luck and much success.*
>
> *I would also like to thank all of you who have supported me for many years, and I hope to create music for you in the near future. It's been an incredible twelve years since Adam, Jesse, Mickey, and I started this band. Now I begin a new phase in my life, to which I look forward graciously. Thank you, and I love you all.*
>
> *Ryan Dusick*

And that was it: I was officially a free agent, with no prospects for future employment of which to speak. I was also now completely alone with my thoughts, with a whole lot of free time to fill, no responsibilities of any kind, and enough money to do whatever I damn pleased. Sounds like a pretty privileged situation, right? Well, from a practical standpoint, it was. I even had the band's management team taking care of all my personal bills, doing my taxes, and basically arranging for whatever I needed at any moment. But from a mental health and addiction standpoint, it was a disaster waiting to happen. What little shreds of consistency and structure

I had left in my life were now gone. I had no accountability for anything, and I now had no one close to me, physically or spiritually, to help me fill the gaping hole in my soul.

My entire identity had been wrapped up in being a member of the band, so I really had no idea who I even was at that point. I held on to vague notions of becoming a record producer, a songwriter, or a music manager, but I had no real sense of the person I wanted to be underneath it all. Many of the things in which I had found purpose were now gone, so everything I did just seemed void of meaning. And anything I chose to pursue with any seriousness paled in comparison with what I had already done. So, consciously or unconsciously, I chose to embrace a lifestyle of total decadence as my new plan for getting through the rest of what was sure to be a disappointing letdown of a life.

I was very isolated at that time in 2006–7 (alone in my house with a couple of cats), but even when I would go out to see my friends on occasion, the experience was largely triggering for me. Most of my social circle spent their free time at Adam's glamorous new bachelor pad in the Hollywood Hills, and I couldn't help but feel jealous and resentful every time I would go to his parties. His life looked a lot like the HBO show *Entourage* at that point (or rather the show looked a lot like his life): we played poker with all the bros some evenings; had pool parties with models, actresses, and *Playboy* Playmates; and spent wild nights in the VIP of the hottest clubs in town. I would attempt to enjoy these occasions, seeing how happy all my friends looked to be partaking of Adam's new life of fame and fortune, but all I could think to myself was "Why them and not me? Why can't I just be happy for everyone around me and happy for myself that I'm getting to live this lifestyle of leisure and luxury?"

It wasn't just the dual losses of my band and my relationship that were weighing so heavily on me. My entire social world centered around the band. All my college buddies from UCLA had coalesced with my Hollywood friends to form this very large circle of compatriots, situated around the band and its scene. By losing my position in the middle of that circle, and by descending into a breakdown that I hadn't even begun to process (let alone work through), I was alienating myself not only from the band but from my entire social sphere. I would still show up to these events at times, and I would put on a good show, pretending that I was a rock star and that I was still enjoying the fruits of our success. But just seeing all those people, partying and having fun like they were living their best lives together (almost like a glorified and glamorous version of our life in college), would send me into a spiral of regret and self-contempt. I truly felt alone and disconnected from everything that had once defined me. So hard liquor became my escape more and more, as I now fully embraced my nihilistic attitude about life and everything in it . . . because if I didn't care about anything, then nothing could hurt me like this again.

With each passing week, it became more and more difficult to pretend that I wasn't suffering when I was around all these painful triggers, so eventually I just stopped showing up to these events, for the most part. I spent the following months just indulging whatever form of escape came to mind, staying separate from anyone who ever mattered to me. I would go out by myself some nights in search of a distraction from the loneliness of my self-imposed isolation, but I don't even remember how some of those nights ended, due to the amount that I was drinking in combination with the pills.

As the saying goes, however, great art comes from great pain, so I wrote a few of my best songs during this period. Sara Bareilles (who was now working on her first real major-label album) was kind enough to lend her beautiful voice to some of the demos of these compositions. The songs were something of a cross between Kara's Flowers's earlier rock style and the Maroon 5 ballads, but punctuated with much darker lyrics about disconnection, loss, and loneliness. The first song I wrote, titled "Time," contained the sad refrain "Time takes away the things you love / Time leaves you with the pain of your regret / I couldn't understand it then enough / You have to learn some things the hard way." Jordi actually found some genuine interest from a few artists wanting to record a couple of these new songs, in particular the catchy ballad "Feeling So Gray" (which sounded like a more depressing version of "She Will Be Loved" or "Won't Go Home

Without You"); however, that dream of hearing my own songs recorded and performed by major pop stars never came to fruition, and I was left with another feeling of failure. I really could have used a win right about then, but it wasn't to be.

I think I need to take a moment to emphasize that I was also very fortunate and blessed, even at that terrible point in my life. I have always had a family that loves and supports me unconditionally, for which I am eternally grateful. Plus, the success of *Songs About Jane* and subsequent touring had provided me with a financial comfort and security that most people never enjoy, and I didn't even have to work a day job to pay the bills. The discrepancy between these amazing blessings and the existential agony I was experiencing, however, was a difficult paradox with which to grapple, as I struggled to find a new identity. Whether I was sitting in my beautiful home, driving my new Mercedes, eating at fancy restaurants, or partying with all the beautiful and fabulous people . . . inside, I still felt hollow. I also felt guilty for not being able to appreciate my good fortune, mostly because I felt unworthy of it.

I should also admit that it wasn't all bad all the time. I went to a lot of glamorous events, to which most people would kill to be invited. I dated some very appealing young women, whom most men would kill to date. I had no real responsibilities, so there was no particular stress or worry, other than the stress of avoiding reality at all costs. And I had enough money to do whatever fanciful thing that would keep my mind on worldly delights, rather than on my growing spiritual bankruptcy. But in a lot of ways this made my descent into the insanity of addiction even worse, because I didn't experience the kinds of consequences that usually go hand in hand with self-destruction. I had no boss to tell me that I was a mess, that I needed to clean up my act or I'd be fired. And I would do my best to alleviate my family's worries by showing up to our family events and putting on a happy face, so for a time no one was really questioning my well-being, at least not outwardly.

Nonetheless, despite all my valiant efforts to hide my suffering from the world, I eventually did get the message from several friends and family members that they could tell I was really drowning. I had a couple of instances in which people took me aside and asked me how I was doing, encouraging me to take better care of myself. So, in the spring of 2007, about a year and a half into my new reality as the former drummer of Maroon 5, I finally decided to try to "get my shit together." After having been overly medicated for the better part of two years, I made a concerted effort to return to some modicum of health. I quit the medications cold turkey, curbed my drinking to some extent (I went back to only drinking wine), started exercising again to work my way back to a certain level of physical fitness, and, at least on the surface, was able to project an image of having straightened out my act. In my mind, I was finally moving on with my life. I tried my hardest to accept the reality that an awful thing had happened but overall I was a blessed human being with many things for which to be grateful. I just needed to turn the page and start enjoying life again, hopefully in a slightly healthier way. I was convinced that all I had to do was relearn some moderation and embrace the freedom to pursue whatever my heart desired from that day forth. But in actuality, this was just the beginning of what I refer to as the illusion of control.

chapter 21

the illusion of control

When the dust from my career meltdown had finally settled, and I made my first real attempts to turn the page and start anew, I settled into a new mode of domesticity that felt mundane by comparison but allowed for a little bit of normalcy. Shan and I had started seeing each other again from time to time, when one or both of us were feeling particularly lonely and, strangely enough, we got along just fine on those occasions, without any hint of animosity or resentment. Shan was clearly having a hard time with the separation, however. Even after everything I had gone through myself, I was actually worried about her for the first time. She had lost a lot of weight since we broke up, and she seemed to be having a hard time balancing medications and alcohol in the same way that I had. I knew she was depressed, and I still cared about her too much to let her suffer like that alone. The self-indulgent bachelor lifestyle I was living had already grown old, so I also began yearning for the kind of connection that had always been there between us. Toward the end of 2007, we started spending a lot more time together, even to the point of her staying with me at the house for stretches. In 2008, when those stretches started outnumbering the ones she was spending at her apartment, we decided it was time to move her back into the house with me for good.

Shan and I had weathered quite a storm in our relationship; however, she was finally able to forgive me for my transgressions, and I really felt that she was probably the only person on the planet who could understand what I had gone through. Neither of us was in a particularly good place in our life at that point, but we now had each other to lean on, so we tried to have a real go at domestic bliss in our thirties. Enough time had passed since the height of the tumult between us that our home life actually started looking pretty romantic. We tried to do a lot of the things that "normal" couples do, like staying in and cooking dinner or going for long walks around the neighborhood. Our general lifestyle started to seem more consistent with our status as a couple who had settled into mature adulthood. On top of that, we started taking frequent trips, traveling to Europe to see some of the most beautiful places on the planet, and basically just trying to live the good life with the comfortable income that success had provided. On the surface, things looked pretty wholesome. We would show up to family functions looking relatively healthy and happy, the outwardly erratic behavior was no longer apparent, and it appeared that we were finally moving on with our lives.

Having convinced myself that I was stable and only indulging to a degree that was appropriate for my position in life, I tried my hand at producing as my next venture back into the world of music. I started by working on some demos with an unknown rock band from the UK, and I eventually went on to record a few independent albums with groups that were either old friends or new friends of friends. Being in the studio again felt right to me, and it gave me a sense that I had something to offer, having worked in that creative process for so much of my young life. Also, being involved with other people's music allowed me to move out of my self-criticism and perfectionism for the time being. I started having fantasies about developing, producing, and managing new bands and becoming my own man in the music business. Nothing I did could possibly compare to my previous experience, however, or to the heights of success that my old band was still achieving. Kara's Flowers/Maroon 5 had been a journey for me that most artists never get to enjoy, from the evolution of our creative chemistry to the ultimate success, so nothing I worked on afterward could hold a candle to that.

During this time, I also continued to frustrate myself by trying to relearn to play the drums. We had a basement big enough to set up a jam room downstairs (an anomaly for Los Angeles), but my sessions down there would play out the same frustrating cycle of "two steps forward, three steps back" every few weeks. Whatever progress I would make in starting to improve my coordination would get wrecked every time I would drink too much and fry my nerves, and my poor mechanics just continued to reinforce bad habits and chronic injury. Shan would often ask me why I would torture myself with it, when I didn't need to perform to make a living, and my only response was "It's just something I have to do." Playing the drums had been such a big part of my identity for so long that giving up and retiring from playing altogether just seemed like an impossibility; I needed to continue to feel some connection to that part of myself, and I needed to hold on to the idea that someday I might be able to play well again. Due to the constant frustration of frequent failed attempts, however, I felt more and more that I needed alcohol to be creative, or really to enjoy playing music at all.

Going to Maroon 5 concerts when the band was in town was particularly triggering for me. Seeing how well the band was doing without me would result in a flood of emotions from envy and regret to self-anger. To compensate, I would try to treat the evening as just one big party in order to mask the pain and resentment. I would drink before the show straight through to the after-party, pretending to still be a rock star along with the band members. Also, as the band moved on to its third album, I was growing more critical of the direction and production of the music. As brilliant a pop songwriter as Adam had become, I felt that the albums were getting more and more slick and overproduced, and losing the soulful vibe of *Songs*

About Jane. Adam started appearing on the TV show *The Voice* at a certain point, which ended up being a net positive for the band and exposing it to an even larger audience, but I was a little wary of the band leaving its roots behind and embracing full-on pop status. Upon hearing that album for the first time, I had a conversation with Jordi, who was curious to hear my feedback on it, and I expressed my frustration with this reality. He offered some kind words that changed my perspective.

"So, what do you think of the new record?" Jordi said.

"I don't know, Jordi . . ." I said. "Don't get me wrong, it sounds amazing, the songs are really catchy, and the recording is top-notch, but it just seems like they're going further and further away from the vibe that made us great in the first place."

"Yes, that's true . . . but moving more to the mainstream is a natural progression for an artist like Maroon . . . they can't really go backwards and try to re-create the past."

"I understand that, and I agree . . . but it's just a shame that we never got to make our *Blood Sugar Sex Magik*. The band and I always looked at that album as a really magical moment for the Chili Peppers, when the chemistry of a really eclectic group of guys created the perfect intersection of genuine, organic funk and mainstream pop hits. I guess I had always thought that after the success of *Songs About Jane*, we would have a chance to make a record that accomplished the same things."

"You know, I hate to break it to you, Ryan, but I think *Songs About Jane* *was* that album for Maroon. I think it did all the things you just described, and it *was* that magical moment when everything came together for the band in all those ways. You should be proud of having been a big part of that."

Jordi's incredible kindness in framing it that way left me speechless. I like to believe that he was absolutely correct. Not to diminish all the truly wonderful hit songs that the group has created since, but *Songs About Jane* really was a uniquely special moment, not just in our lives but also in the career of the band. I have known since early in our career that Adam would never be one to go backwards or to try to re-create something from the past. He's always looking forward—always wanting to do something new and better. After that conversation with Jordi, I fully understood that Adam was correct both personally and professionally for not wanting to try to re-create *Songs About Jane*. Clinging to the thing that made an artist famous in the first place is the mistake that desperate artists make in fear of alienating their audience. Adam somehow understood innately that it's boring and irrelevant to continue to rehash what has already been done. So I finally got on board with Adam's never-ending quest to remain relevant and to stay at the top of the charts. And I am supremely impressed by his ability to continue to do so.

As much as I was trying to move on, create a new identity for myself, and embrace my new life, the pain that I had stuffed down for so long started bubbling up from underneath in new and frustrating ways. My OCD behaviors were becoming more pronounced over time. I would spend hours tuning and retuning my drums, even though I had no reason to do it. I would organize and reorganize things in my house like the books on the shelves, the CDs in their folders, and whatever else I could exert some control over. I would count while doing household chores, making sure that the numbers rounded evenly, and I would check things over and over, like the parking brake in my car, the locks on the doors, or the temperature on the thermostat. Enacting these rituals never did alleviate my anxiety, however. Quite the contrary, my tensions got worse over time, and my drinking ramped up again to the point that I needed to have cocktails before going to have cocktails, in order to stem the nerves.

As the years of drinking dragged on, my attempts at moderation turned into a repetitive cycle of alcoholic binges followed by periods of abstinence. To me, the fact that I could abstain for a time proved that I didn't have a problem, and I had it all under my control. I would even take off the entire month of February (the shortest month) from drinking, just to prove to myself that I could. When I would inevitably start again, however, the benders would get longer and more intense, and the withdrawal periods would get more painful as a result. Somehow, I convinced myself that drinking to this degree of dysfunction was acceptable for me, because if anyone knew what I went through on a daily basis, they wouldn't begrudge my using alcohol to self-medicate.

Every alcoholic is familiar with these common phrases: "I can stop any time I want; I just don't want to"; "I'll only drink beer (or wine) from now on"; "I'll only drink on the weekends"; and "I'll drink during the week, but only after five o'clock." I went through my phases with all of these clichés of denial (and even a few new ones of my own invention), but I always ended up back at the same place. I refer to this pattern as the illusion of control, because that's what the disease of addiction is all about for me: the belief that I can exert control over what is uncomfortable about my reality. I really believed that I had control over my drinking, and so, in turn, I had power over the pain. And that worked for me for some time. Or better yet, it maintained that pattern of escape.

My anxiety level was also escalating over those years. The windows during which I felt calm and relaxed were becoming smaller, and I was having more periods of intense nerves and panic. These incidents were most pronounced when I was trying to get through the days of withdrawal after an alcoholic bender. One such event, when I was about thirty-three, scared the shit out of me. My binge and withdrawal cycle had gotten so bad that one particular hangover convinced me I was having a seizure or a verifiable case of delirium tremens. I lay in bed, trying to sober up the way I had a hundred times before, but this time was different. I was having auditory hallucinations, hearing the hum of the cable box growing louder and louder in my ears. I started to hyperventilate, my toes and fingers started to tingle and go rigid, and I was sure that this was it: I was having a full-blown, withdrawal-induced seizure. Shan called the paramedics, but when they showed up, they told me I was just having a really bad panic attack. They suggested I try to breathe slowly, take some Benadryl, and get some rest.

This incident was scary enough for me that I checked myself into rehab the next day. I will admit that my choice of venue was largely influenced by watching *Celebrity Rehab with Dr. Drew* while drunk; however, the Pasadena

Recovery Center was not as glamorous as it looked on TV. The intake person on the phone had told me that doctors on-site could prescribe me something for the detox period, but when I showed up, there was only one doctor, who had a very large caseload. On top of that, it would take about three days for insurance to clear any medications. I was shaking like a leaf from alcohol withdrawal, but I was basically left to my own devices. And it was scary. A lot of the people I saw seemed more fucked up than any drunk or high person I had ever seen. I didn't know if it was mental illness, brain damage, or heavy medication, but I found it strange that these people came into this place to get off drugs, yet a lot of them seemed more fucked up than anyone I'd ever seen.

I really didn't feel like I fit in with these people. Some of them were hard-drug users; some had been to jail multiple times; some had had multiple overdoses, heart attacks, and seizures; some were facing consequences for DUIs and other felonies; and then there was me . . . a depressed has-been rock star with a little drinking problem. As the sun went down, I was crying to Shan on the phone: "This isn't the right place for me! They're not helping me! I feel worse here than at home!" Shan rightfully persuaded me to give it a couple of days and reassured me that my fear was totally normal. This gave me the strength to at least see it through, but when the lights went out and I was lying in my bed that first night, my reality became terrifying again very quickly.

The panic of the previous night hit me like a tidal wave. Fearing that the total seizure was coming on for real this time, I got up and wobbled toward the front office, feeling almost unable to hold up the weight of my body. The night receptionist didn't know how to help me, so I just sat in that office, trying desperately to control my breathing, looking pale as a ghost, while this lady tried to figure out what to do with me. Finally, a security guard drove me to the emergency room, where I spent the next few hours in full panic, waiting for someone to help me. When I finally got into a bed and the IV of Ativan hit my bloodstream, a calm came over me in a matter of seconds. Suddenly, everything was okay again, and I drifted off to sleep shortly thereafter. When I came to, the doctor sent me back to the recovery center, but now I had a prescription for Ativan to get me through the week. Everything got a lot easier to deal with after that!

Although that facility was not the right place for me (nor was I yet ready to fully accept the nature of my illness), that first experience of three weeks in rehab ended up being good in a lot of ways. I had been very isolated and had avoided responsibility for the previous few years, so the structure and pace of living in an inpatient facility allowed me to awaken to life to some extent. Having to follow a strict schedule and interact with my fellow patients every day made me realize how important structure and connection were to my sanity. Being cooped up in my house with a bunch of booze and no real commitments had been killing my spirit, but being in that clinic forced me to rejoin the living for a moment. I didn't invite my parents to visit me while I was staying there; in fact, I didn't even inform them of where I was exactly, because I was still protecting them from the reality of my condition. Shan came to family hour a couple of times, however, and we discussed the present and the future. She was worried that sobriety would mean a big change for our relationship; she even feared that I would meet someone in recovery with whom I'd be happier. She had good reason to be distrustful of my commitment to her, so I couldn't blame her for having those fears. I did my best to alleviate her concern, and she was less worried about the state of our relationship after that conversation. So I felt pretty good about where I was in my life and where we were as a couple. By the time I checked out, I was feeling optimistic about the future, and I was making a lot of resolutions to implement the lessons I had learned from my time there. I was still in the rationalization phase of my addiction, however. I found every reason to believe that what I was taught didn't really apply to me: "I wasn't as far gone as a lot of the people in there"; "Their stories about stealing cars or prostituting themselves for drugs—they don't represent me"; "I just need to learn some moderation and drink like a gentleman." But perhaps most dangerously, I now had a familiar formula for avoiding alcohol withdrawal symptoms in the future: benzodiazepines.

The next phase of my addiction was all about psychopharmacology. I was convinced that there was some chemical equation that would set me

free from all the anxiety and panic. My psychiatrist tried out every antide-
pressant, antianxiety medication, and sleeping pill in the book. I even tried
some mood stabilizers and antipsychotics. But what do you think was the
one thing that really seemed to work for me? What was the one thing that
seemed to scratch that itch that only alcohol had seemed to scratch before?
Benzos. Why? Because I'm an addict. If it wasn't alcohol, it had to be the
good stuff.

Benzodiazepines are like pharmaceutical-grade alcohol. They go right
to that same part of your brain and knock out the anxiety and all the physical symptoms that go with it. They are very effective and "clean" chemicals, without all the toxic effects of alcohol. But that's also the problem
with them: they're too effective. In a relatively short period of time, your
brain stops doing the work of self-soothing that the benzos will do for it,
and now you're dependent on the pills. I honestly never took a benzo to
"party." I never thought to myself, "I want to get high on benzos tonight."
Alcohol was still my drug of choice. The benzos just became something
that could stand in for booze when I could drink no more, or something
to alleviate that feeling of doom that had become so familiar. But in time
they became something that was a necessity and a dependence more than
a desire.

Klonopin (and to a lesser extent Xanax) became a new maintenance
program for my alcoholism. And so, an even more destructive cycle began:
I would go on my usual drinking sprees, but now I could detox myself from
them as if I were in the hospital, using the Klonopin that I had been prescribed by my doctor. It seemed like a stroke of genius at the time: "I won't
stay on either chemical long enough for it to become a problem. I'll drink
for a few days, then I'll take Klonopin for a few days." This is the kind
of thinking that many refer to as the "insanity of addiction." Somehow,
this seemed like a manageable lifestyle to me. Meanwhile, my anxiety and
panic continued to get worse and worse, and the problem was beginning
to border on agoraphobia. I couldn't go anywhere without having a pill or a
drink to calm my nerves, even to the store to get more vodka. I had to have
a drink to go see the doctor, so that I could calmly tell her that I needed a

refill on my benzos. Believe it or not, I lived this way for a few more years, with my grip on sanity slipping with each passing day.

Around my midthirties it became clear to me that my mental health issues had become completely unmanageable, but I just didn't see what could be done about them. I was anxious to an unreasonable degree all day, every day, and even the alcohol or benzos wouldn't alleviate this completely until I was so intoxicated that I was bordering on passing out. Deep down, I knew the only real answer was to quit completely and to start over with a lifestyle of recovery. As most addicts do, however, I clung to my denial for a while longer. The periods when the drink or the pill helped me feel some peace became shorter and fewer as time went on, but I still believed that those moments were my only salvation from the misery. As obvious as it might seem to an objective person that the chemicals were perpetuating and maintaining the problem (if not causing the problem completely at that point), I still chose to believe that the only serenity I could achieve was through some kind of chemical intervention. So it took a few truly humbling moments at the end of my drinking to finally come to a place of acceptance.

Shan and I moved to the San Fernando Valley in 2013, having found a bigger, more private property with enough usable land to build a home studio, and my intent had been to live a healthier lifestyle in this quieter, more open, and brighter home out in the suburbs. I don't do very well with change, however. The first year in the new house was very difficult for me, and my addiction patterns worsened. On top of that, my attempts to build the studio hit some roadblocks, and when those best-laid plans went awry, I found myself commuting to a little workspace in Van Nuys, then coming home and drinking until I passed out on the couch most nights. I no longer had a basement with a drum set in it, so my regular obsessive-compulsive routines were often unavailable to me, which meant I wasn't receiving that regular escape or relief. So I drank so much on some nights that I couldn't even remember what I had watched on TV the next day. Even when I was conscious of what I was doing, my cognition was diminished, and I had a hard time staying focused on anything for very long. Making music became harder and harder, and what I did manage to create was absolute crap.

Somewhere in the middle of all this, I was able to have one really nice moment of reunion with my old bandmates, which served to heal some old wounds for me. Adam got married to his lovely bride, Behati, in a big, beautiful, outdoor ceremony in Cabo San Lucas, Mexico, in the summer of 2014, and he invited me to come play a song with the original members of the band as the newlyweds walked down the aisle. I sobered myself up for a couple of weeks leading up to the trip, knowing that was the only way I would be physically able to participate. I practiced playing the bongos until I could hold down a solid groove, so that I could join Jesse, Mickey, and James in playing Paul Simon's "Me and Julio Down by the Schoolyard" just after the couple said "I do." I had to pound a couple of drinks right beforehand to steady my nerves (even though I had abstained for the weeks leading up to the event), but I was able to perform in this lovely moment with my old buddies, and it helped me work toward eventual closure.

I was back to my usual patterns in the two years after that, however, going back and forth between drinking heavily and "detoxing" myself with benzos. I tried my hand at abstinence a few more times, but these periods were so much more difficult now. I lived in a constant state of anxiety, not wanting to be around other human beings at all. I was now convinced that even if I could abstain from drinking, benzos were something I would need for the rest of my life, due to the intense pain of this constant anxiety. I knew that the alcohol was killing me slowly, but the benzos just seemed like a necessary maintenance plan to avoid total psychological breakdown.

In the last months of it, my using became even scarier and more dangerous. I was hiding alcohol from Shan now, something I had never done before. I had a little bottle of vodka in one of my shoes in the closet. I would take my snare drum case to and from the studio so that I could transport liquor undetected, and I would take a swig before I had to interact with any human being because the agoraphobic response was so strong.

The back-and-forth between booze and benzos had become so treacherous that often I couldn't stop drinking all night due to the benzo withdrawal, yet I didn't want to take the benzo for fear of mixing it with so much alcohol. So I would enter these paranoid manic states, in which I thought my cats were looking at me funny. I became fearful even of the gardener or the UPS guy walking up the driveway, and I would hide so I didn't have to talk to anyone in that state of insanity. And when I did take the Klonopin with the alcohol, I would pass out in strange places, such as on the floor of the guest room or even on the toilet.

Only in the last few months of my addiction did I finally hit a place I had only heard about, however: literally having no control over it anymore, whatsoever. I would leave the house with no intention of buying or drinking booze, yet there I would find myself, at the liquor store, buying more vodka. And after years of feeling like I could gauge my level of intoxication to maintain some control over it, I no longer could. I would go from sober to totally wasted in a short period of time, and I would have no recourse for how to manage it. So my only option at that point was to try to white-knuckle abstinence as much as I could.

It got really scary after that. A few times I found myself unintentionally drunk at my studio in Van Nuys, and I didn't know how I was going to get home. I had to take an Uber, then go get my car the next day. Even when I was "sober," I was at greatly diminished capacity. I was shaky and extremely nervous. My reflexes were shot. I was increasingly paranoid and detached from reality. I had serious cognitive issues—I had difficulty focusing on anything well enough to understand it fully and had problems with memory—and even started having pain in my abdomen, itchy skin, and gray eyes during and after a particularly bad bender. I had reached another and more lethal stage of alcoholism.

One day, I went to the studio with no intention of getting drunk and with every intention of coming back home by dinnertime. But of course, I did get drunk, and I continued to drink until I passed out at my desk. When I came to, I looked up at the time and realized it was well past when I was supposed to be home. I checked my phone and found a bunch of missed calls and texts from Shan. I felt terrible, and the shock of the situation jolted me "sober" for a minute. So, rather than wait for an Uber (or wait until I sobered up for real), I jumped in my car, feeling very awake for the moment, and drove home. When I got there, Shan was extremely upset. But more than anything, she was just really worried about me, rightfully so. But this time, I finally had no rationalizations. Nothing I could say, or even think to say, could make this behavior seem acceptable or anything short of downright deadly.

Shan wanted me to go back to rehab, this time *for real*, meaning that I would see it through completely, even if it meant that our lifestyle would have to change completely . . . and even though we didn't know what it would mean for our relationship. I fought her a little, but I finally submitted to the idea. And when I say "submitted," I mean I fully committed to the idea of recovery once and for all. I had gone as far as this thing could take me, and I finally realized that there were only two directions I could go from where I was: toward the light of recovery or toward darkness and death. The illusion of control had finally been lifted from my eyes, and it was clear to me that I was powerless over my addiction and that my life had become totally unmanageable. When Shan helped me come to this realization (or moment of clarity, as they call it), it was actually a relief. I was just so tired of living this way: hiding the pain, constantly working to maintain this totally unsustainable lifestyle, and feeling the control slip through my fingers more and more each day. It was all just so exhausting. So when I finally agreed to check into rehab again in May of 2016, I actually looked forward to telling the world that I was an alcoholic and finally being able to live openly and honestly for the first time in a decade.

My therapist recommended I go to the Betty Ford Center this time, and that sounded comfortable to me, but it didn't have an opening for a few days. So I did what any good alcoholic would do with a couple of days to kill before starting rehab: I drank more. If I had learned anything from my first experience, it was this: drink up until the moment you get there, and make sure there is an actual medical detox facility on-site. I promised Shan I would just stick to wine rather than hard liquor, until she could drive me out to the desert that weekend. I took my last drink in the parking lot of the Betty Ford Center in Rancho Mirage, California, and I knew that I was done. Somehow, I had managed to drink enough wine in those last forty-eight hours, however, to show up with a .39 blood alcohol content on intake. I was incoherent and unable to finish the interview process, as my BAC was still going up and would probably peak somewhere over .40 before I passed out. So staff members took me into the detox wing and put me in a bed in one of the rooms, and Shan went back home to LA.

That was May 29, 2016, Memorial Day weekend, the day I took my last drink.

My lost weekend had lasted nine years, seven months, and fourteen days.

chapter 22

connection and purpose

I woke up in the middle of the night confused and terrified. Of course, I had no pills or alcohol on the nightstand to ease the onslaught of nerves, so I was desperate to summon a nurse or a doctor to give me something for the withdrawal. I remembered that I had checked myself into the Betty Ford Center, but I had no memory of being placed in a room. Because I couldn't remember being walked in, I didn't really know where I was situated or where to go for help. I was a few days off my benzos and hungover from a long alcoholic binge, so the panic came on immediately. I was shaking and sweating already, smelling the wine and dysfunction coming from my pores.

I poked my head out into the hallway, but I couldn't even remember the direction from which I had come. After negotiating with myself for a while over whether I could brave a journey out into the unknown, I finally ventured around the corner and found the nurse's station. A nice older lady responded to my stress with calm, as if nothing was wrong, which immediately set my nerves a little more at ease. She took my vitals, and my blood pressure was through the roof, so she gave me some BP medication and fluids, let my blood alcohol come down some more, then finally offered me some Valium. I was more than happy for the drugs, because I had no intention of quitting benzos at the same time as the alcohol. I knew the drink was the major problem that was killing me, but I was convinced that the benzos were a medical necessity, upon which I would probably be dependent for the rest of my life.

My first full day in the hospital consisted mostly of sweating and shaking, feeling weak and nauseated, and worrying intensely that the doctors would send me into the general population of the facility before I had overcome the intense withdrawal. Adding social anxiety on top of those symptoms sounded like a cruel and unusual punishment. The fact that I had nurses tending to my needs allowed me to accept the position into which I had put myself, but of course I was still looking for any excuse to go home (like "they're mistreating me" or "I'm not being given what I need," but neither of those things were true this time). I was also able to talk to Shan on the phone in the evening, and she sounded very calm and encouraging, which helped me a lot.

By the second night, the nurses were telling me that if I wanted to eat dinner, I would have to walk myself over to the cafeteria, grab a tray, and make myself a plate. This sounded like an impossible undertaking in my condition. Not only was I going through withdrawal, but my blood sugar was very low, my blood pressure was very high, and I was basically living in a 24/7 panic attack. I had been largely agoraphobic for the months leading up to this detox, so venturing into a brand-new place and trying to acclimate with a bunch of strangers milling about was an absolutely terrifying proposition. I was finally getting hungry for solid food, however, so I shivered over to the cafeteria across the quad, hesitantly grabbed a tray, shakily served myself a chicken drumstick and some white rice, then slowly made my way to one of the tables to feed myself. I was extremely self-conscious as I walked, feeling those who had been there longer than me quietly judging just how fucked up I was compared to everyone else they saw coming through the door. My tray was shaking visibly as I hobbled like a ninety-eight-year-old convalescent, and when I finally sat down to eat, I found that bringing a forkful of rice to my mouth was almost impossible without a lot of it ending up back on the plate. I realized in that moment that I had become one of those supremely wasted people who had alarmed me my first day at the Pasadena Recovery Center—that's how far my addiction had come in the intervening years.

I only spent the weekend in the detox wing before they moved me over to one of the men's dormitory halls. I was still wobbly, and meeting new people was making me very nervous, but the nurses felt that I was ready to join the actual rehab program. One of my new dorm mates escorted me over to my new digs and handed me the master schedule, to which I needed to get acclimated almost immediately. I was required to attend a yoga class the very first day, and just twisting from side to side had me feeling like I was going to keel over. I had to do what was asked of me and get with the program quickly, however, because the schedule didn't provide much time to question it.

After breakfast and exercise, all the men and women from the various halls would congregate in the main auditorium for a mandatory lecture, educating us about the nature of addiction and recovery. I remember sitting in one of the seats toward the back-left corner of the auditorium that first day, my eyes darting back and forth between the windows to the outside world and the large panels inscribed with the Twelve Steps of Alcoholics Anonymous on either side of the stage. Although the steps still seemed so daunting and foreign to me, I could finally relate to Step 1: "We admitted that we were powerless over alcohol—that our lives had become unmanageable." I could finally accept that premise. I was already lost when I got to Step 2, however. I didn't fancy myself a particularly religious or spiritual person, and the step was demanding that I believe in God or a "higher power," so I wasn't sure how I was going to handle that principle. Given my state of desperation, however, I decided to drop my usual disdain for dogma and just try to sit with the reality of Step 1 for the moment.

After the lecture, we reconvened in the men's hall for a meditation session with a "spiritual adviser," and this was extremely difficult for me. Just closing my eyes and being present in the moment made me very uncomfortable. Focusing on my breath actually had the opposite effect than intended, causing me to hyperventilate and panic. It brought me all the way back to those times as a teenager when I would focus on my breathing so intensely that I would become light-headed, feeling anxiously detached from my surroundings. I was also amazed that some of the guys in our meditation circle could fall asleep and snore in the midst of my anxiety. How could they possibly be that relaxed, going through what we were all going through? I just had to pray that maybe I could achieve that level of serenity by the time I was done with my stay at the Betty Ford Center.

Thankfully, I was scheduled for my first session with my therapist/ counselor right after the meditation, so I was able to process all the nervous feelings immediately. I decided on my way into his office that I was just going to let all of my emotions come out, telling him exactly how I was feeling and hoping that maybe he could understand . . . or at least have some compassion for me. I had spent so much time hiding my inner turmoil from the world, taking care not to let others worry about me or see how I was suffering, so now I thought to myself, "Here I am. I'm at the Betty Ford Center to give this a real go, right? Why not just lay it all on the line and see if it helps?"

I told my shaggy-faced, middle-aged counselor Michael that my anxiety was at a 10 . . . all the time, and that I basically had been in a never-ending panic attack for months, except for when I was drunk or on Klonopin, and that I didn't think I could handle "reality." He responded by telling me he knew exactly how I felt. He had been extremely anxious as a young man, feeling that he was different from everyone around him and that no one understood him, which was why he escaped into the bottle for years. But it only got worse during that time, until he finally got sober and accepted recovery. When he did this, he went through what I was going through, but it got easier in time, and now he didn't feel that kind of anxiety anymore.

I did actually feel a little less anxious after Michael related his own experience with me. For the first time in years, maybe ever, I felt that I wasn't alone in my unique discomfort with living and that someone could really understand what I was going through. So I decided right then that processing my feelings as they arose was my best approach to dealing with the anxiety. I was processing feelings *constantly* that first week or two. I was experiencing a flood of emotions every few minutes, but fortunately, I now had people around me with whom I could share these overwhelming experiences.

After that first day, my counseling sessions with Michael became a process group with four or five of my peers, and the group dynamic allowed me to see the ways in which my issues had been similar to those of other men in the unit. I would pour my heart out to them the way I did alone with Michael, allowing my raw nerves to be exposed to this assemblage of fellow sufferers, and just having their understanding ears around to hear my concerns was a very liberating feeling. It even allowed me to begin to talk about some of the deeper feelings I held beneath the anxiety: the trauma of what I had gone through in breaking down onstage in front of the world, the pressure I put on myself to be perfect, the obsessive thoughts about controlling every outcome, and the compulsive behaviors that failed to alleviate those feelings. I would get choked up if I started to delve more deeply into my past, but many of my peers were people who could understand (if not the literal circumstances I had lived through, then at least my *feelings* about what I had endured), and this gave me some peace. And then there were others who were still in total denial or were even more entrenched in their addiction than I was, which allowed me to realize that my condition wasn't quite as bad as it could have been and there was still hope for me in my path toward recovery.

I was impressed that our hall ran its own nighttime process group, and from the first night, I felt like I was a part of something—like I had assumed a new identity that was connected to something larger than myself, probably for the first time since I had left the band. I didn't realize just how much I had been missing that feeling of camaraderie and connectedness that the band had provided for me. I was also astonished by some of the "old-timers" in the hall: these men had only been there for a few weeks, yet they had achieved a sense of calm that seemed impossible to me, given what I was going through. They were talking about their life of addiction as if it were something in their distant past, speaking with the confidence and glow of men in their prime, and looking forward to everything they were going to do once they finished their stay at the BFC. The idea of struggling through a whole month of anxiety during this time of transition was still terrifying to me, but seeing these guys looking almost as if they were thriving already, less than a month out from where I was sitting, gave me even more hope. I wanted what they had. I wanted to do whatever they had been doing to get to that place of confidence. Just a few weeks earlier, these guys had been as deep in their illness as I currently was, and they already seemed to have it all figured out. I was in awe, and I was inspired.

It only took a few days to get acclimated, and then I became one of the guys who was introducing the newcomers to the routine. And within that first week, I was already experiencing the power of service. Having been sober only a few days, I was now able to help someone who was suffering to a greater degree than me, and it made me feel purposeful and proud. I felt that I had something meaningful to offer another human being, which hadn't been the case since before my breakdown a decade earlier. This experience led to what I would reluctantly call a "spiritual awakening." Spirituality was a concept I had never really related to before, and the pre-scripted notions of religiosity had always been somewhat off-putting to me, because I associated them with either heavy-handed dogma or new-age, self-help nonsense. All the "logical thinking" of my addiction, however, had gotten me to a place that was totally disconnected from life, so even this small amount of helpfulness to another person made me feel more alive and more connected to the world than I had even thought possible. And it was powerful. It was tangible. I felt I had awoken in some way. I had a *long* way to go, but for the first time in years, I felt optimistic and hopeful. And it was all because of this feeling of connection and purpose.

During that first week, I was still under the impression that I would not be quitting benzos amid all this transition. The drugs were still a medical necessity to prevent seizures, so the doctors had me on a Valium taper that lasted the first seven days. However, when that week ended, the nurses informed me that the doctors were switching me to a three-week barbiturate regimen, to wean me off the benzos completely. This scared the living hell out of me. I was just getting comfortable, feeling that my anxiety and agoraphobia were finally somewhat manageable, and now they wanted to pull the rug out from under me again? I called Shan to discuss what I was going to tell the doctors: that I couldn't yet handle being taken off a drug that I had been dependent on for years. She was calmly encouraging again, reminding me that the doctors wouldn't recommend anything I couldn't handle, and that I'd be able to adjust to this transition once again. I didn't put up much of a fight because I knew she was right. I just needed to hear her say it—that's why I'd called her. The inspiration of recovery had already worked its way into my spirit, and I would be submitting once again to this better plan. I realized that my way of doing things had not been working, clearly. I had been stuck in my ways for years, and look where it had gotten me! As defeated as I had been feeling, I decided to give someone else's plan a chance and see where that could get me. And in that way, I now had some understanding of Step 2 for the first time. I didn't believe in God or a "higher power" in the religious sense, but this program of recovery was bigger than me. It offered me something better than I could offer myself. And it was clearly working for a lot of the people around me. So I just looked at the program itself as my higher power for the time being, surrendering to its wisdom.

It seemed that everywhere I went, the Serenity Prayer was inscribed on almost every surface: "God, grant me the serenity to accept the things I cannot change, the courage to change the things I can, and the wisdom to know the difference." Believe it or not, I had never seen or heard these insightful words before my time at the BFC. So I must have read those three lines about twenty different times before I started to grasp any notion of what they meant and how they applied to me. Not only was the idea of giving up control an extremely difficult proposition for an obsessive-compulsive perfectionist like me but I also couldn't even wrap my head around what that would look like or what it meant practically. I had heard about the idea of "giving up control, to gain control," but that meant nothing to me when applied to real life. It just sounded like some new-age nonsense again, created for self-help books. It also sounded like a total paradox or a catch-22. The best I could figure was that it had something to do with the AA notion of "giving it up to God," which had always bothered me. Why can't I take control of my own life? What good does it do to "turn it over to God" when I don't even believe in God? Am I not the one who is ultimately responsible for my own life?

I again remembered, however, that all my best thinking—all my attempts to control things I could not—had led me to this extreme point of powerlessness, so who was I to say that I had any control over anything? All my attempts to change uncomfortable realities had failed, yet somehow I had avoided the real changes I could have been making during that time. Now there's the real paradox! I still couldn't understand what reversing these behaviors would even look like, but again, I ultimately decided to surrender to this new plan, realizing that my way had not worked and it was now time to try another way. The wisdom part would have to come later.

About a week or two into my stay, I was walking into the lecture hall for our regular morning routine when one of the counselors asked if I would like to read a passage from the Big Book of Alcoholics Anonymous to begin the lecture. Agreeing to this request would mean going up to the podium in front of a hundred or so people and reading a few pages over the loudspeaker. I immediately said, "No, I can't do that right now. My anxiety is still too bad."

Of course, three or four of my fellow patients were in earshot when I said that, and they all turned to me and said, "Well, then you have to do it! Get up there and do it! You'll feel better." I was very reluctant, but they kept twisting my arm (out of love and support), so I finally got up from my chair and sort of staggered up to the lectern.

As I began reading the passage, the anxiety first went straight to my throat, and then it made its way down to my legs. I felt my vocal chords start to waver and my knees start to shake. About halfway into it, I could tell that my voice was warbling and giving out, and my legs felt like they were going to buckle, so I just stopped, looked up from the book, and said to the full auditorium, "I'm sorry, guys . . . I have really bad anxiety . . . this is really hard for me."

This large crowd of enthusiastic men and women in early recovery cheered and yelled to me, "You've got this, Ryan! We love you! You can do this!"

I'd be lying if I said my nerves went away completely after that, but I was able to get through the rest of the reading and wobble back to my seat. And that experience helped me realize that my path through the anxiety would have to be just that . . . through it. By facing and staring down the panic, with the support of my comrades in sobriety, I was able to regain a little bit more confidence. And I knew that each time I did something like that, I would be taking one more step toward feeling "normal" again.

Shan came to visit me after two weeks, to participate in Betty Ford's acclaimed family program. We had been together for the better part of fifteen years at that point, but it was really the first time in a while that I had been truly sober with her, so it took a little bit of an adjustment just to feel comfortable in this odd setting. But pretty soon, we began the program, and we got an insight into the different forms of dysfunction that occur within addicted and codependent families—and we actually felt pretty healthy by comparison! Some of the couples in our group were arguing in what seemed like total contempt for each other, and we couldn't relate to that at all. We realized from that experience that we had a lot of work to do to function as a healthy couple again, but we still had a connection that was much stronger than most.

My parents came the following week to join me in the very same program; however, I had to explain a lot more to them about the nature of addiction and recovery. I had spent so much time in the previous years hiding my lifestyle from them that it actually felt good to be totally honest. My mom was concerned about what to tell our family and friends, and I told her they didn't have to tell anyone anything—or do anything at all. This was my journey, and I only needed their love, support, and understanding. I also had to introduce the idea of codependency to my dad, as well as inform them both that I would be setting some healthier boundaries regarding their involvement in my life. I told them that they didn't have to worry about me anymore. I was going to take care of myself now.

As the three-week barbiturate taper came to an end, I was terrified that I would no longer have a medical crutch to deal with the feelings of anxiety and panic—that I would just have to cope the best I could on my own, the organic way. And finally getting off all the meds was definitely scary, but it wasn't as bad as I had imagined it would be. The panic had decreased to manageable anxiety, and while I wasn't out of the woods completely yet, at least I knew that I wasn't having a meltdown every three seconds. I was also now feeling that I was one of the guys who was "in charge" of the dorm, so I felt a sense of comfort and control in taking on new and larger responsibilities. I was the one graduating the old-timers, handing out welcome pins, and offering help and encouragement to the new guys who were still going through withdrawal. And it felt amazing. I felt like I had scaled a mountain and I was offering a rope down to those still climbing. I had a sense of purpose in offering others what had been offered me, and this helped me understand the Twelfth Step (the one about being of service to your fellows), even while I was still working on the first three. So it was time to move on to the next level of recovery. I moved out of the inpatient hospital and into a sober living house, commuting onto campus each morning to do day treatment.

I was feeling pretty good about myself, having finished the first and hardest month of sobriety, and my work with my counselors was yielding a lot of growth. One day, however, my psychiatrist asked me a question that threw me for a loop. He had seemed like a wizard to me up until that point, asking questions that pulled insights out of me like some kind of witchcraft, but this one stumped me.

"Ryan, what do you think your purpose is?" he said.

I was still just acclimating myself to the notion of living without alcohol and drugs, and now I had to figure out the meaning of life?

"What do you mean?" I said. "Like . . . what was I put on this earth to do?"

"You can answer the question for whatever it means to you. I just wonder if you have a sense as to what gives your life purpose."

He was very persistent, but I couldn't come up with a definitive answer. "Well . . . I suppose music was my purpose at one point . . . at least for a while . . . but to be honest, I haven't really seen much meaning in my life ever since I had to retire from that career."

He asked again, "So what do you think is going to give your life purpose and meaning going forward from here?"

"Jeez, I don't know . . . Can't I just focus on the fact that I'm sober right now? Isn't that good enough?"

"That's great! And you should be very proud of yourself for that. But you're going to be back home sometime soon, and I wonder if you have something to go home to . . . something you feel connected to in some way."

"Well, I have my girlfriend . . . and my cats . . . and my house . . . and I'm building a little studio . . ."

"What are you going to do with the studio?"

"Honestly . . . I don't really know . . ."

"You have a lot of freedom that most people don't have, Ryan . . . and that's really great for you . . . But I'll ask you again . . . Is there anything you can see yourself doing that provides a sense of purpose in your life?"

Answering that question would be difficult for me for some time.

chapter 23

the impossible has happened

That first month of living inpatient at the Betty Ford Center was basically like learning to walk again, or maybe like going back to the first grade to relearn how to read and write. So, by comparison, commuting onto campus for the day treatment program felt like I was attending a graduate school for addicts in recovery. Everyone in my new counseling group had a month or more of sobriety, and their level of awareness was staggering to me. We were no longer just dealing with the day-to-day business of abstinence; we were now delving into deep-seated pain and trauma, addressing the issues that drove our addictions. This level of psychological discovery was exciting and illuminating for me. I received an education in not only how I ended up with my problem but also how these issues develop and manifest in other people in similar or dissimilar ways. The common theme was that we were all trying to fill a void created by some kind of pain from our past. For me, I'd always had some issues with anxiety, perfectionism, obsessive-compulsiveness, and so on, but it was the

272

excruciating loss of my identity within the band and my circle of friends that had sent me over the edge into alcoholism. For others, their addictions had started much earlier in life, because they just were not given any coping skills for managing uncomfortable feelings in their younger life, or because they had suffered such terrible abuse and trauma in childhood that the emotional toll was just unbearable. Learning about how each of us came to be the people we were now was beyond intriguing to me, and it felt deeply meaningful for me to be a part of it.

When Shan came to visit me during that second month, the rules of the sober house allowed me to go out into the world for a few hours with my guest, before I was required to be back on the property for curfew. After a month of living within the walls of the clinic, even just riding in a car on the quiet streets of Palm Springs was scary for me. I had been under the effects of various kinds of sedation for many years, so just the sights and sounds of normal traffic were overwhelming to my senses. And when we went to eat at a restaurant for the first time (at the California Pizza Kitchen in Palm Desert), the sight of people drinking alcohol was an immediate challenge to my internal psychology. I hadn't yet learned exactly what cognitive behavioral therapy (CBT) was, but for some reason I took it upon myself to devise my own method for changing the thoughts that surrounded these triggers. Rather than allow my mind to go straight to that old place of craving when I saw a martini or a glass of wine, I forced myself to "play the tape forward" to the inevitable hangover, withdrawal, anxiety, paranoia, pain, and suffering that would accompany it. Each time I'd see a new glass being served, I would condition my mind to picture it more and more for the poison that it truly was for me. I needed to view the alcohol as entirely toxic, because that's what it had become in my life. Sure, drinking it might make me feel good for an instant, or maybe even for a night, but then I would be right back where I always ended up: isolated and suffering. As I reprogrammed my mind in this way, taking a sip of that deadly venom became entirely unappealing.

We were seated by the window as the sun was going down, and I ordered my new favorite cocktail, a Sprite on the rocks, while Shan ordered an iced tea in place of her usual glass of wine with dinner. I could tell that there was something on her mind, however. She told me that she was planning on abstaining from drinking for a while as well, so that the temptation wasn't right in my face, but she was wondering if this meant that she was basically going to have to be sober forever, too. I could tell that she really wanted to do whatever was necessary for me to stay sober, but I could also see that she was a little nervous about what it was going to mean for us—for our lifestyle and for our relationship. I realized right then that this was going to be just as big an adjustment for her as it was for me. We agreed upon six months of total abstinence and decided that once that period ended, we would discuss the topic of what would be appropriate at the next stage.

After I had survived my first venture out into the real world, my day treatment counselor suggested that I go home for a weekend as a test run, so that I could come back and discuss the experience with the group before I would be going home for good. I thought that was a pretty interesting way of allowing us to dip our toes back in the water for the first time, but also have that safety net to process it back at BFC. It wasn't particularly hard not to drink over that weekend, but I realized pretty quickly that almost everything back home was a trigger, in a house and a neighborhood where I had been drinking alcoholically for the previous three years. Just driving down the roads around our house reminded me of going out to buy more alcohol or coming home to drink it. And just sitting on the L of the couch where I used to drink until I passed out at night felt like I was in danger of slipping right back into that state of mind I had been avoiding for a month and a half of rehab. Again, I had no real desire to drink, because I knew how poisonous it was for me, but I could see that I would need to be extremely vigilant about my program of recovery, even after two months of living at the BFC, in order not to let these reminders of a toxic lifestyle become triggers for alcoholic cravings.

I also played the drums sober for the first time in a while that weekend, and it felt as if someone had lifted weights off my limbs for the first time in years. Just sitting down behind the drum kit in the living room, I could *see* the drums again. It was like I had taken off a pair of fogged-up sunglasses, and the drum set looked brand-new to me again. For the longest time, the drums were my enemy as much as they were my friend, but now I could see them for what they were again. They were just drums. Not a burden or a cross to bear. Just a bunch of skins and cymbals and hardware and wood. What I did when I sat behind them was entirely up to me, my state of mind, and the health of my body. And the condition of my being was so drastically improved from what it had been for a decade that I could play with a freedom and comfort that had eluded me that entire time. I still didn't quite have the command of the instrument that I hoped to someday regain, but this small sense of progress filled me with optimism about my ability to achieve mastery of my instrument at some point in the future.

After two full months at the Betty Ford Center, I finally graduated from its program completely, and the pride of that accomplishment was as significant as when I'd graduated from college at UCLA. Turning that page in the book of my life felt like the end of another era and the beginning of something new and exciting—as if I had accomplished something profoundly momentous but my whole life was still on the horizon. When I was leaving, however, my counselors recommended that I *not* go back to normal life quite yet. They suggested an outpatient program back in Los Angeles, and as with everything else in this process, I said yes, jumping at the chance to maintain structure in my recovery. I scheduled a meeting at the Matrix Institute on Addictions before I even got home, and within that first week I joined its intensive outpatient program, which would last for four months.

The Matrix is a cognitive behavioral program that teaches its clients about the brain biochemistry of addiction and how to use "thought stopping" to preempt the addiction process. I realized that my newly self-imposed, reconditioned response to alcoholic triggers was the product of exactly that CBT principle. Of course, the idea of stopping one's thoughts had seemed like another paradox to me when I first heard the term. If I could stop my thoughts, I wouldn't have a problem, would I? When I realized I had already been doing it, however, by "playing the tape forward" from the sight and smell of alcohol to the noxious end result, it became a much more understandable concept to me. By stopping or, better yet, changing the thought associated with the trigger (before it becomes a craving), I could prevent my addictive compulsion from taking hold. Believe it or not, this new psychology took the reins in my mind very quickly, and I had zero cravings for alcohol as a result. As they sometimes say in AA meetings, "The obsession to drink had been lifted." I felt free and light as a result, no longer enslaved by the tedious mental energy I had expended in the past, when I would obsess about my drinking and attempt to control it with sheer willpower. Beginning a life of total abstinence was actually a relief, because I just didn't have to think about it anymore. Alcohol was a lethal idea to me now, and I wanted nothing to do with it.

Along with the relapse prevention program, the Matrix offered a loosely affiliated twelve-step group, which took a much more progressive approach to AA than I had experienced in any other meeting. A group of Matrix graduates had started this weekly group to incorporate the CBT program into the spiritual program of AA or NA. Still thinking of myself as an intellectual, I found the mission statement of this meeting very appealing, so I quickly ingratiated myself into their ranks. My feeling was that there are many roads that lead to recovery, and what works best for one person is sometimes different from what works for another. The goal is ultimately the same for every path (total physical, emotional, psychological, and behavioral sobriety), and the same conditions of living are required to establish and maintain that sobriety (radical acceptance and self-honesty), but we're all a little different in terms of our specific, unique needs and our understanding of our illness. For some, the hard-core twelve-step, AA, or NA approach is just what the doctor ordered, so to speak. Surrendering to such a group and its traditions provides the structure and path to find a better way of living in sobriety. For others, the psychological CBT approach is more appropriate and works equally well. For still others, it may be a church group or some other form of purposeful life that drives their recovery. Personally, I needed a little of everything. I wanted to pursue any concept of sobriety I could wrap my head around to overcome this affliction because, for the first time, I saw the disease for what it truly is: an all-encompassing mental obsession, physical allergy, and spiritual malady—affecting the mind, body, and spirit.

I was firing on all cylinders at this point, embracing recovery for everything it could offer. If the abuse of a substance affected all these elements of my being, then the solution needed to be entirely holistic. It was daunting, but I needed to change everything about the way I had been living my life. Obviously, for starters I needed to do away with the influence of the substances themselves. Some brave souls can do that on their own, but I'd really needed that month in a hospital to do it properly. I also needed to treat my body better in other ways, eating well and exercising daily. Rehab was a good jump start for this drastic change in lifestyle, but it was up to me to maintain that routine once I got home. Lack of consistent structure had been a big problem for me, so staying on the schedule that rehab created for me was very helpful. I continued to go to bed early and wake up with the sun, filling my day with productive pursuits like attending morning meetings, connecting with my sober friends, going out on hikes and other ventures with them, exercising in the gym, playing and writing music, and so on. I also needed to work on the psychology that created and drove my addiction, however. That meant psychotherapy for me, which I attended weekly. And lastly, it was important to reconnect with the world in a way that embraced being part of something larger than myself. Being of service to the community at the Matrix provided me with that greater purpose for the moment.

After I had been home for a few weeks, when Shan had seen just how much this new path of sobriety was affecting my spirit, she and I had an interesting conversation—one that I had not anticipated. I was carrying on again one day, offering yet another one of my highly impassioned speeches on the beauty and profundity of my new lifestyle of recovery, but instead of rolling her eyes at my ridiculous level of enthusiasm or worrying that I was changing into someone to whom she couldn't relate, she actually started tearing up as I was reaching the crescendo of my sermon. I didn't understand what this meant at first.

"What's wrong? Are you worried about something?" I said.

"No, no . . . It's amazing . . . really. I guess I . . . I'm actually just jealous," she said.

"Jealous?" I was stunned.

"Yeah . . . I mean it's ridiculous . . . You have this glow . . . this energy coming off you . . . it's like you're ten years younger."

I chuckled, realizing I was probably sounding kind of "born again" in my passion.

"Yeah . . . but that's what it feels like! This stuff really works, I'm telling you!"

"I know . . . and it's amazing . . . I just wish I could have what you have."

"You can! You just need to embrace it like I have."

"But I'm not an alcoholic. I stopped drinking on a dime, and I don't have any problem with not drinking. I don't know what I would go into recovery for, exactly . . . I would love to do what you're doing and take from it what you are obviously taking from it . . . I just think it would be dishonest for me to go to a meeting and identify as an alcoholic or an addict."

"Well, you don't need to identify in any way you don't want to, Shan . . . you just need to embrace the principles of recovery the way that I have."

"Yeah, but you have this whole community around you . . . this fellowship of people who you feel connected to, and who support you, and who make you feel like you have something valuable to offer them . . . I just don't have that . . . I don't know where I would find that."

"Do you want to join me in my meetings?" I said.

"No, no . . . that's your thing . . . and I want you to have that to yourself . . . I just wish that I could find something like that for myself."

"I see . . . Well, we can figure it out one way or another . . . You really can have, and deserve to have, everything that I have found in sobriety . . . This feeling is there for anyone who pursues it."

"I guess . . ."

She was still reluctant, but she was actually feeling inspired by me and my new life. Given our previous conversations back when I was at the Pasadena Recovery Center, I had expected her to feel scared and sad that I was changing so drastically; I thought she might be worried that we would no longer feel connected in the ways that we had felt before. But instead, she was actually happy for me and jealous of my feeling of connection, and she wanted to experience that for herself as well. As much as I didn't like to see her crying again, I could see that it came from a good place, and I was happy that the spirit that had awoken in me was beginning to rejuvenate her as well.

I also had an interesting conversation with my personal therapist around this time, in which he told me that if I kept working on myself the way that I was, within five years my life would look entirely different than I could have possibly imagined. This was a guy who had gotten sober in midlife, and it had resulted in an entire career shift to helping others. After living the life of addiction and despair for decades, he finally got clean, went back to school, and eventually became a licensed marriage and family therapist and addiction counselor. He said to me, "You know how different you feel now than you did three months ago? Well, at your first sober birthday you'll barely even recognize the person you were before you started this. You'll be in such a different headspace than you could have possibly imagined when you were drinking. And at two years, you'll be that much more removed from the old ways of thinking and the old patterns of living as an addict. By five years, you'll be living a life you can't even picture right now. You'll be doing things you never would have expected or even dreamed of before. If you stay on this path that you're on right now, it's inevitable: you'll continue to grow and flourish, finding new and inspiring paths for your life and future."

I just kind of shrugged my shoulders and chuckled, thinking it sounded like a nice sentiment, but unable to picture what that would even look like. I couldn't really wrap my head around the concept that I would be doing something I couldn't currently imagine, but we began talking about things I might consider doing with my time, like writing and producing more music, going back to school to understand the engineering side of production, embracing my journalistic roots, writing more poetry and prose again, or becoming an author of some kind. He really just wanted me to open my mind to the possibilities, but it all seemed a little daunting to me still. I wasn't quite yet ready to envision all the ways that my life could change and the new identities that might define me, so I decided to just stay in the present, continuing to focus on what recovery looked like for me in the moment. The outcome of that path would just have to unfold in time.

Part of engaging in a twelve-step group meant telling my story several times over and attempting to relate it to a point or message about addiction and recovery. So I had many opportunities to verbalize, in storytelling form, the way I perceived my journey up until that point in life. Having to perform this exercise was like narrative therapy—reimagining the story of my life, from the disappointing loss of my performing career to the reawakening I was now enjoying. I talked about the things that I treasured from my childhood: my family life, my passion for baseball, and my academic pursuits. I talked about what starting the band had meant to me and how challenging that lifestyle ultimately became. I talked about how defeated and destroyed I felt in losing my identity attached to the band and how hard it had been to overcome the grief of that profound loss. And I also talked about how I was rediscovering my worth as a sober person, each day focusing mostly on what was going to keep me clearheaded and moving forward, but also finding new and inspiring paths for the future.

Each time I spoke, I would feel significant anxiety about getting up in front of the whole group and running the show for twenty to thirty minutes, but now I was able to overcome the nerves, calm myself with meditation or the Serenity Prayer, and settle into an unexpected new level of comfort with public speaking. So the twelve-step process also doubled as a form of exposure therapy, inducing a flood of emotions I might have previously experienced as panic but now just registered as excitement to tell my story and maybe help someone else in the process. Overcoming my fears in that way was extremely empowering. Along with that personal accomplishment, I received a lot of compliments from my fellow addicts on my ability to express my thoughts in an articulate way, which contributed to my feeling of self-worth—because I had something of value to offer those still suffering. Who was this new guy, speaking eloquently in front of a group of twenty people, as if he had been doing it for years? Where had this confidence been, and how did it arise again so quickly? It felt so electrifying to be living this new life that I started craving more of that positive energy wherever I could find it. I wanted to do everything I could to continue to grow and experience this "natural high" as much and as often as possible.

As I approached graduation from the Matrix program, the counselors allowed me to start attending the site's Wednesday-night "social support" meeting, which was created for graduates who wanted to stay connected and continue to talk about relapse prevention. I jumped at this opportunity as well, more so to be of service to my peers than to alleviate my own fears of relapse. My ability to offer useful words of encouragement both within the classes of the Matrix and within this support group led the counselors to offer me a position as a "co-leader" or "peer support" within the Matrix classes. This was only a volunteer position, but I considered it a great honor to be asked, and it was yet another wonderful opportunity to be of service. Being a mentor to those just starting recovery, by offering my own experience and hope, was just about the most fulfilling thing I'd ever done in my life, including playing on live television in front of millions of people and winning Grammy awards.

My anxiety began to creep up again upon graduating, as I recognized that the structure and consistency of my program would be ending. So I took that moment to delve more seriously into the Twelve Steps of AA again. I found a sponsor, who quickly reacclimated me to the process, and we were off to the races. He actually said that I worked the steps faster than anyone he had ever known. In some ways this was a wonderful by-product of how enthusiastically I had embraced recovery, but it was also a remnant of my perfectionistic mind—if I was going to be a sober person working the steps, I was going to be the best sober person, working the steps better and faster than anyone has before! So I guess I still had some work to do in that regard . . .

As I approached my first sober birthday, I had a new lease on life. I was enjoying a freedom and connectedness that had evaded me since before

I started having problems on the road with the band. I felt inspired and hopeful, wanting to help other people as much as I was helping myself. My relationships were improving, not only because I was more present in my experience of them but also because I could communicate my feelings in an honest and productive way, and I could allow myself to be invested in something greater than myself and my own needs all the time. I didn't have specific definitions for higher power or spirituality yet, but I knew that they required humility and acceptance—rejoining the flow of life, on life's terms. At a certain point I started looking at nature as my higher power, understanding that my folly had been in trying to control nature, by putting chemicals in my body to change or restrict the uncomfortable feelings. This attempt at playing God had inevitably failed and led to more painful feelings. So I didn't need to believe in "God" with a capital G in order to recognize that *I am not him.*

It didn't take a massive leap of religious faith to understand that *nature* has a better way. Nature prefers health, and there is an inherent *balance* to nature, something that my addictive lifestyle had greatly lacked. By submitting to what is natural and healthy, I can get out of my own way, allowing for my physical, mental, and spiritual growth. And I realized that spirituality is just all about *connection* to me. I can't describe what the spirit is exactly, but I can definitely describe what spiritual dysfunction looks like—passing out from drinking on my couch every night, waking up to a flood of panic, and feeling totally disconnected from the world. So the solution to that problem was just to do the opposite . . . By staying connected to the world and by doing whatever was necessary to get me out of that isolated space, I was living life again. And it felt good.

This understanding led to a profound realization about the role that spirituality had played in my younger life, without my even recognizing it as such. As cynical and disaffected as I had been as a teenager, I was kept sane by my spiritual connections. My love of music had been my first real spirituality, in my relationship with the artists who inspired me and in the collective of our band. The feeling of power I felt onstage at the Whisky, Roxy, and Troubadour had been more than just excitement to make a lot of noise for a captive audience—it was the expression of the very real connection I enjoyed with my bandmates and the music that we loved. That is the power of music or any art: to connect humans in a way that goes beyond mere words or surface experience. That power exists between the artists who collaborate with one another as well as between the artists and their audience. There's something amazing that happens when a group of musicians play with a sense of chemistry together. When the groove locks in and you can all feel it, you're communicating on a higher level. Those who aren't particularly musical by nature may not know what I'm talking about, but if you've ever had really good sex, I'm sure you can relate.

In that way, young love can be another spiritual experience. The excitement you feel when you find your counterpart in another human in a romantic way—that's another form of connection that goes beyond anything that you can experience alone. I was lucky enough to find that feeling in my early relationships. And even in my great friendships—like at UCLA, where I was surrounded by a big circle of friends with whom I was connected on many different levels—that was a massive spiritual experience as well. What I'm getting at is that spirituality doesn't necessarily need to be a moment when the clouds part and "God" speaks emphatically; it's just something that happens in the moments of joy in our lives, when we move outside ourselves and connect with something larger. Human connection is the simplest and greatest form of spirituality, at least it has been for me.

It was only in the grief of losing the band and connectedness to my close friends that I suffered a detachment from the spirituality that had buoyed me as a young man. As I sank deeper into depression and despair, the ultimate spiritual malady of addiction kept me separate from those things and pulled me further away as time went on. Through my awareness of this in recovery, I came to understand what constitutes a "spiritual awakening." Whereas I had thought it meant being "born again" in a religious sense, for me it just meant being born back into a way of living that had brought meaning, purpose, and happiness into my life.

In the last few years of my alcoholism, I was lucky enough to see my favorite rock band, Soundgarden, reunite for one last album and a series of concert tours. I went to several live shows during that time, but unfortunately, I was too intoxicated to remember any of them all that well. I was truly blessed in my first year of sobriety, however, to be able to attend the first and only Temple of the Dog (the Pearl Jam and Soundgarden supergroup) reunion tour at the LA Forum, as my first sober concert in over a decade. The band sounded amazing, playing for almost three hours, and I was clearheaded enough to enjoy and remember every drumbeat and every guitar stroke played by Stone Gossard, Mike McCready, Jeff Ament, Matt Cameron, and Chris Cornell. I was convinced at the time that both Soundgarden and Temple of the Dog were still capable of recording some of their best work, going back into the studio in middle age. Less than two weeks before my first sober birthday, however, I learned sadly that my greatest teenage hero, Chris Cornell, had succumbed to his battle with depression and substance abuse, dying by suicide while on tour with his original band. Reflecting on what he had meant to me in life, in art, and now in death allowed me to put into perspective the legacy of the artists of his generation who had moved me and inspired my passion for music in the 1990s, and how tragic it was that so many of them were already dead from drugs or suicide: Andrew Wood of Mother Love Bone, Kurt Cobain of Nirvana, Shannon Hoon of Blind Melon, Bradley Nowell of Sublime, Layne Staley and Mike Starr of Alice in Chains, Scott Weiland of Stone Temple Pilots and Velvet Revolver, and now Chris Cornell of Soundgarden, Temple of the Dog, and Audioslave . . . they're all gone. As if that hadn't been enough, just a couple of months later, my old friends in the band Linkin Park also lost their lead singer, Chester Bennington, to suicide.

I remember a lot of people from my parents' baby boomer generation, who had grown up watching the Beatles on *Ed Sullivan* and who had grown very passionate about music with more of a sociopolitical message in the 1960s, asking me in the '90s, "Why does this music have to be so heavy and depressing?" Sure, it was a time when it was very trendy and cool to be rather dark and introspective, expressing self-reflection about your own demons in your art. Most of those artists, however, were not putting on an act in the name of shoegazing or grunge glory, or simply playing the character of a depressed, drug-addled rock star. Their art was the product of their pain, and it was their sometimes agonizing attempt to process the heavy emotions they were feeling. When I think about how *real* Kurt Cobain's musical expressions of despair were, how devastating Layne Staley's addiction was in his life, and how tortured Chris Cornell clearly was by his own mental health struggles, I consider myself very lucky to have had artists like them to help me feel understood as a young man. These were musicians who used their art as therapy, right up until the point when they couldn't cope with living anymore. As much as I was already done with alcohol and drugs by the time Cornell died, his death evoked one more moment of solemn reflection, which helped me see just how lucky I had been to get help when I did, and made me wish that he and my other heroes had been so lucky.

Recognizing just how fortunate and grateful I was to be alive and healthy made the occasion of my first sober birthday that much more of a celebration of life in recovery for me. I invited Shan, my parents, my cousin David, my therapist, and my sponsor to come support me as I spoke and accepted a birthday cake at my Saturday-morning AA meeting, and it really felt like the culmination of something deeply significant in my life. David gave me a big hug and told me he was proud of me; my parents cried, of course; Shan had a smile on her face as big as I had seen in years; and I felt extremely proud and grateful for all of it. My dad came over to hug me as the meeting ended, and suddenly I felt like I was twelve years old again. It was as if I had just won the championship, having uncovered a strength and resilience in myself I didn't know existed, and just like the '88 Dodgers, I had overcome incredible odds to achieve something wonderful and transcendent. I could almost hear Vin Scully's voice echoing in my ears: "In a year that has been so improbable, the *impossible* has happened!"

I turned forty just a few months after that celebration, and the profound realizations of my early sobriety got me thinking about the rest of my life. A sense of my own mortality started to creep in as I entered "middle age," and I again thought about my psychiatrist's difficult question, "What do you think is your purpose?" I knew that working a diligent recovery program would only go so far in defining me, before I would yearn for more out of life, so I began to ponder the concept of my identity again. Having enjoyed a very significant one as a musician in a successful band at one point of my life, I had really struggled to find a new identity after that career ended so painfully. I was now in a place, however, where I had the fortitude to consider taking on new challenges, so I started doing some real soul-searching as to what the next phase of my life would bring . . .

chapter 24

there's no time like the present

When my therapist said that my life in five years would look entirely different than I could have imagined when I was in my addiction, I just kind of shrugged my shoulders and chuckled, thinking it sounded like a nice sentiment, but unable to picture what that would even look like. But boy, was he right! Actually, after only about two years of sobriety, I began to figure out what I wanted to do in the next phase of my life. I was noticing that several people in my sphere had gone back (or were in the process of going back) to school in midlife to become therapists or counselors, and so I got to thinking: "Should I consider becoming a professional in this field?" My peers had been so complimentary about my work as a co-leader/peer support in classes at the Matrix, and I had so enjoyed the process of being of service to them, that I started seriously considering the idea of seeking a degree and license to become a therapist or addiction counselor myself.

Ever since I left the band, I had been comparing myself and everything in my life to what I did back then, but now I finally had something to offer that was totally unrelated to that former life, and it was centered on my newly discovered strengths and passions. And my acceptance and embrace of this reality mirrored that time in my early twenties when I put the band aside for a while to go back to UCLA and earn my degree in English. This time, however, there was an added altruistic element, which made it all the more fulfilling and meaningful to me. After doing a little research, I discovered that I was qualified to apply for Pepperdine University's master's program in clinical psychology, which would put me on track to become a licensed marriage and family therapist, a title that I could use to work at addiction-recovery centers as a counselor, or even to start my own practice as a general psychotherapist. And I didn't hesitate to pursue it. How far I had come! After a decade of avoiding responsibility and keeping my distance from the world, I quickly jumped at the chance to take on this new challenge and to reengage with life in this new and exciting way.

When I told Shan about my intent to apply to the program at Pepperdine's Graduate School of Education and Psychology, again, her response was different than I expected, but also again, it was an interesting and welcome development.

"I think I want to go back to school and become a therapist," I told her.

After pausing for a few seconds to allow this idea to register, Shan responded, "How would you feel if I wanted to do that, too? To get my master's in social work?"

Shan had intended to go to grad school after UCLA, but she had put it off to take care of her dying father at the time. Life went on after that, and she had never seriously considered going back to that previous dream. Now that my life was on a road back to academia and into a career of mental health service, however, she wanted to do the very same thing.

"Really? You want to do this with me?"

"Well, I always wanted to get my master's . . . and I always liked the idea of helping young people who are going through some of the things that I did . . . and social workers do the majority of counseling in this country . . .

And I was cum laude at UCLA, so I could probably get into a really good school!"

I was blown away. All she needed was to see me turning the corner in my own life, venturing out into my new horizons, and she was already there as well. She didn't need to go into a program like I did to get to that place. She was ready to do it on her own, without hesitation.

I applied and was accepted to Pepperdine's program within a month. At the same time, Shan sought a position at one of the top social work programs in the country at the University of Southern California, and of course, she got in because she's brilliant. It was going to be an expensive couple of years, with both of us attending prestigious private schools, but it was well worth the investment in ourselves, our education, and our future. Without missing a beat, Shan and I both started school the following semester.

Just overcoming the anxiety that had plagued me was an accomplishment unto itself, but once I started school, I realized that my personal mental health struggles actually provided a unique perspective to bring into my future work as a therapist. The majority of the students in the program were younger than me (some having come straight from undergrad), so I found that I also had a bit more to offer in terms of general life experience. I still did what most grad students do when studying mental disorders for the first time, however: I diagnosed myself and everyone else around me, including my cats. I was convinced that I met the criteria for about half the disorders in the *DSM-5* at various points in my life, and I was probably accurate on a few, but I'm sure I was exaggerating on a few others. I also just started having fun looking at the world through the lens of psychology. Art, literature, and media became interesting to me again in this new context. I started analyzing the characters in movies and TV shows, applying what I was learning about personality and mood disorders. I began pondering the ego defense mechanisms that influence the different ways we communicate with each other, especially in a time of such sociopolitical strife. The study of psychology became my new passion, and it felt wonderful to have one again.

At the same time, music became more inspirational to me once again. Ironically, the studio construction on my property in the San Fernando Valley (which took three years to get going) had finally broken ground the week I checked into Betty Ford, so by my first sober birthday it was complete. As I moved forward into the next stage of my life's passions, I now had my own beautiful space to play and make music again. What I had once intended to be a professional endeavor in music recording now became a glorified man cave of sorts: somewhere private that I could work, play, and explore my new identity as a sober artist, student, and future clinician. I also continued to foster my greater appreciation for nature, venturing out on lovely hikes up into the hills around me; I kept close contact with my sober friends in the Matrix community; and I made many new ones in grad school. It was as if the world had opened itself up to me again and I was embracing it with open arms.

Grad school quickly became an opportunity to overcome a series of fears in rapid succession. From where I had been as an addict, just getting myself up in front of a classroom to give a presentation on mindfulness-based stress reduction seemed like an impossible about-face. But I did it. And each time I did something like that, it got a little easier. Also, the amount of study time that school required gave me less time to focus on my OCD rituals and other forms of self-obsession. As a result, I started to find that I was becoming more present and more able to live in the moment, rather than trying to control my reality or change it to something different. The therapeutic technique of mindfulness became my new form of acceptance, offering an alternative to the illusion of control. Meditation finally started to make sense to me, in a way I couldn't grasp when I first tried in rehab, but it was totally consistent with what I had learned from the Serenity Prayer.

As much as I had rejected the idea of God for most of my life, I found myself reciting that prayer as a mantra. The present moment is unfolding, whether I like it or not, and it's usually not as scary as I make it out to be. Once I let go of past regrets and worries about the future, I begin to live more fully in the present moment, which alleviates my stress and anxiety in turn. I started applying this principle to everything I was doing, including playing the drums. I realized that I carried so much baggage every time I sat down at my drum kit. Playing the drums was perhaps my biggest passion, bringing me the joy of self-expression, but it had also brought me more pain and suffering than any other thing in my life, before my addiction. I had played through that pain and dysfunction for so long that the bad habits were hard to shake off, but with a healthier nervous system and a more rational mind, I started allowing myself to just sit behind the drum kit, center myself before playing, then allow the session to unfold, rather than trying to make something happen.

I start with mindful stretching: calming my breathing and simply focusing on the feeling of my muscles relaxing and loosening. Then I sit at the drum set, scanning my body for lingering tensions and noticing any thoughts or feelings that arise from my past difficulties playing the instrument. I acknowledge these passing thoughts and feelings, but I allow them to float by like clouds, as I refocus my mind on the mechanics of playing simple strokes, sometimes just with one limb at a time. When my mind begins to wander back to unproductive desires to do more than what feels comfortable and natural, I gently bring my mind back to a visualization of calm execution, without tension or strain. As I begin to strike the drums and cymbals, it's rare that I'm able to play exactly as I would like to, but forcing something that is painful or unnatural will get me nowhere. Just by submitting to the flow of the process again, I have been able to recover and grow as a player, in the same way that I have grown as a person in general. I still have my baggage, but I've made a lot of progress, and I'm beginning to understand the idea of "progress, not perfection." Mind-blowing.

I actually start almost every day with a morning mindful stretching session, to carry this outlook into the new day. I'm not exactly floating on a cloud all week, because I'm still an imperfect human being, susceptible to stress and frustration just like any other person on this planet. But I just have a little more leeway to let life come to me, rather than force it so hard like I used to. I have also become inspired to write again, as my school assignments offered new opportunities to express myself the way I did when I was younger. Now I find, however, that I have so much more to say, and so much more insight to offer in what I'm saying. I was in grad school when I started writing this book, but I could wait no longer: I wanted to tell my story, not only as an exercise in narrative therapy but also as a way to potentially help someone still suffering.

Most importantly, I am finally beginning to figure out how to answer my psychiatrist's lingering question about purpose. The existential angst that emerged in my teenage years made me no stranger to the fact that finding meaning in life is often challenging. My new interests have provided me with a reinvigorated sense of purpose, however, and I am finally able to recognize that meaning is something that one defines for oneself. My purpose is whatever I want it to be. It is whatever I care about, feel passionately about, and make important to me. Whether as a psychotherapist, a writer, or whatever else my passions lead me to, I will find my purpose by investing myself fully in my role. I had been sitting around in my drinking haze, waiting for a new identity to define me, when all I had to do was choose one and pursue it. I don't know if I could have learned this lesson any earlier or if it was necessary for me to hit the spiritual bottom that I did before I could start anew. Of course, I would love to live that lost decade over again knowing what I know now, but we learn our lessons in our own time. I'm just grateful that I am where I am now and that I still have so much of my life to live with a healthier approach to living. I still have my challenges; I can still be perfectionistic, obsessive-compulsive, anxious, depressed, and so on. But my journey of recovery has offered me so many tools to cope with these challenges that I wouldn't have had otherwise. And for that reason, I am grateful for the struggles and for the things I learned in having to overcome them.

I can also now see that the ways in which I struggled for a decade were all part of a somewhat inevitable grieving process—I was grieving the loss of my former life and identity. If you're not familiar with the stages of grief, the ultimate goal is "acceptance," and the very idea of that used to perplex me. You go through all these horrible stages of pain and suffering, and all you get at the end of it is "acceptance"?! That's the big payoff? However, having achieved a certain amount of it by way of addiction recovery,

I finally get what that means. The reality of the past hasn't changed; however, my ability to function in the present has because I'm not holding on to things I cannot control.

In my drinking years, I had a perception that all my old friends were still living the same life I had been living in my twenties, just without me there. I would only see them at Maroon 5 shows, bachelor parties, weddings, birthdays, and other events, and through the haze of my addiction, I got the sense that their lives were still as exciting and playful as mine had been before the loss of my performing career. It didn't occur to me until I had been sober for a while that these moments were only brief reminders of the past: opportunities to get back together and reminisce. Most of my friends have moved on long ago to their own lives, careers, marriages, children, and so on. And the band is no different. Going to my first sober Maroon 5 concert was eye-opening. There was no big, wild party going on backstage. Instead, there were children and nannies. A few of the people in that circle had been sober for a while too. My skewed perception that I was missing out on some big party was replaced by the reality that everyone had grown up a bit. I cherish the times when I get to reconnect with my old friends, but I no longer torture myself with regrets or wishes from yesteryear. I am where I am supposed to be now, and I'm grateful for having had all these people in my life.

Adam and I text or call each other from time and time, just to catch up or joke around, and it's exactly like it was when we were sixteen: random, ridiculous, and hilarious. We just say the stupidest things to try to make each other laugh. Only now, we have moments of seriousness, as we share the important things in our adult lives. Adam has a beautiful family of his own now, on top of the amazing career he has continued to foster, and I get to share with him all that I have discovered in these new avenues and possibilities for the future as well. We had a wonderful conversation a couple of years ago, in which we talked about how special *Songs About Jane* was and is—how it's something that cannot be re-created, because it came from an extraordinary time in our lives and in the life of the band. It's only in retrospect that we have been able to appreciate what a truly special experience the creation of that album was. The synergy of the band, the inspiration occurring in both our personal and creative lives, the intersection of our complicated relationships with a moment that was a decade in the making: they all led to that record. And it was impossible to understand at the time that it would never be like that again. It was a once-in-a-lifetime endeavor, in which all the members of our group came together in a uniquely special way. And despite our struggles and frustrations, that juncture of our lives created something truly unrepeatable. It was only after years had passed that we started to see how fleeting and extraordinary that time in our lives really was—nobody tells you it's the good old days when you're living them. I am grateful, however, for the times I get to catch up with the guys now, even if I don't get to see them as much as I wish I could. It's as if we're a bunch of old army buddies, sharing a bond akin to brotherhood but connected by a uniquely intense common experience.

In early 2019, Adam invited me to a memorial concert at the LA Forum, this time to watch him and Jesse perform the Chris Cornell song "Seasons" (accompanied by Pearl Jam's Stone Gossard) as a tribute to the late singer. My being there to witness that performance was very important to Adam, because he knew how much Cornell had meant to me and how much I would appreciate the fact that they were honoring our teenage heroes, while playing with one of their biggest. Remembering the pictures and posters of Stone, Jeff, Mike, Dave, and Eddie on the walls of Adam's and Jesse's teenage bedrooms put a smile on my face, even as the twenty thousand people in attendance were celebrating our fallen hero. At first, the macho rock guys around me in the audience scoffed at the announcement that this "pop star" would be attempting to sing an untouchable song by one of their rock gods, but by the time Adam, Jesse, and Stone finished that beautiful performance, I'm quite sure that every person in that arena had chills and goose bumps just as I did. Jesse did an incredible job replicating the bluesy acoustic guitar parts with Stone, and Adam gave an impassioned rendering of just how important these artists had been in our musical and personal lives. I think a lot of people who might have passed off Maroon 5 as a lightweight pop act got a sense not just of the ability and range of my brothers, but also of how deeply our band's musical roots run. Knowing what that moment meant for Adam and Jesse, and being able to take in that moment for myself and see it all come full circle, left me with a sense of pride in my band's history and legacy, and in where they still are in their career today.

I was also more than thrilled to watch the band get to play the biggest show of their lives, the Super Bowl halftime show in Atlanta in 2019, feeling nothing but pride and joy for them. Gone are the days of any jealousy or resentment, having been replaced by a feeling of honor for having been a part of what we accomplished and what they continue to achieve. I even got to play basketball with Adam and his crew at the Atlanta Hawks training facility, and I felt like I was just one of the guys again. A few months later, I was also able to attend Adam's enormous fortieth birthday bash back down in Cabo San Lucas, and it was pretty amusing to observe such an over-the-top, outrageously decadent celebration, as one of the few sober people there. Watching everyone struggle to overcome their hangovers each morning, after I had already gotten up with the sun, worked out in the gym, and eaten a delicious breakfast buffet, made me realize just how far I had come. I honestly didn't miss the "partying" at all. I was happy to be there in exactly the way I was. I even helped Adam win his big softball tournament with a bunch of hits; an opposite-field, inside-the-park home run; and a good play on a screamer down the third-base line to throw out Ray Romano at first. Whaaaaat?

Oh yeah, that reminds me . . . I even started playing baseball with my dad again (well, softball, but who's counting?), and I'm actually hitting and throwing the ball better than I have since high school. My dad is still out there, playing the outfield at age seventy-five, coaching everyone on the field, and positioning all our players like the control freak he always has been and always will be, but everyone loves his enthusiasm! He's still an athlete and a competitor, even as his body is finally beginning to slow down a bit, and it really is a lot of fun just to be out there with him, trying to win a ball game together again. And I've been using my mindfulness techniques in my approach to the sport I've always loved so much. I've been able to rework my swing to hit the ball consistently harder and farther than I ever did before, and I've even started playing shortstop at times as well! The teenage "yips" of throwing the ball across the diamond still recur from time to time, but I don't let that stop me from continuing to work at it.

In general, I actually find myself moving toward the things that make me anxious, rather than running away from them, as I had for so many years. I have learned that the only way to overcome the anxiety is to walk through it, so I now look at every nervous moment in life as an opportunity for growth. Public speaking was scary for me at first, but I've done it enough times now that it has become more comfortable for me. Playing music sober with other people again was also scary, because I'll always feel an expectation to be "the original drummer of Maroon 5," playing in a way that people will recognize as "the guy who played on *Songs About Jane*," but I can only be what I am today, and that has to be good enough. Slowly but surely, I'm starting to be kinder to myself, accepting that I am not perfect and knowing that if I try to be, I will only frustrate myself.

I have thoughts about the future, and I have memories from the past, but I can only live in the present. So I try not to have too many expectations or too many regrets. Life will be what it will be, and I can only live it the best I can, one day at a time. That no longer means escaping it with alcohol or drugs. And it also no longer means letting my fear or anxiety get in the way of exploring new connections to the world around me. My tendencies toward perfectionism are part of my reality as a somewhat neurotic person, so I accept them as things I cannot fully change, but I try not to let them dominate my being. And again, my background and my experience with this part of myself allow me to better understand the people I will be working with as a therapist. I also have tools now, which provide me relief from the obsessive thoughts. When all else fails, I find that lying in warm water and reciting the Serenity Prayer centers me. Whenever I start to get frustrated, whether it be by expecting too much of myself as a student, as a drummer, as an athlete, as a sober person, or just as a person living life, I'm now able to catch myself, realizing that I'm not helping anyone or anything by driving myself crazy!

In December of 2017, I learned another meaningful lesson along with everyone else in the Maroon 5 family, with the sad passing of our great champion, Jordan Feldstein. He had been the architect of our young professional lives, and he created an impressive business for himself and others with Career Artist Management, but most importantly, he was a good son and brother to his family and a good father to his own two children. He died suddenly at the age of forty, and it has been very hard to make sense of something that seems so senseless. If nothing else has come from this tragic loss, however, it serves to remind me and everyone else who cared about him just how precious and short life is. I don't know how many years I'll have on this planet, but I know I won't take any one of them for granted ever again.

In the spring of 2020, the entire world faced a terrifying and overwhelming challenge with the onset of the Covid-19 pandemic and the ensuing quarantine, isolation, and economic shutdown. There are very few people who haven't been affected by this long and trying ordeal; millions of people have died and millions more have suffered greatly with sickness, grief, anxiety, depression, financial uncertainty . . . you name it. Personally, I have been incredibly privileged to have the securities and freedoms that I do, but it has still been the most trying time in my six years of sobriety. Isolation is not a good thing for an addict, for a survivor of mental health struggles, or for anyone really. Fortunately, I was able to keep myself occupied by attending school online, writing this book, and finally working with clients as a professional mental health counselor. Yes, believe it or not, I earned my degree in clinical psychology, and I am now working as an associate marriage and family therapist, en route to my license. My job involves collaborating with my clients (which is what we call our patients) and offering what I have learned and gained from all the different forms of education I have received. The heavy weight of the world has affected me just as much as it has the people I have been charged with helping, but I have been sustained by the fact that I have overcome so much, and that I have taken so many lessons with me. All of us who have had to adjust to this difficult reality have had a hard time in one way or another, and most of us will continue to be challenged by the adjustments we need to make in moving forward, but it is truly amazing to see how adaptive we are as human beings. And as we say in the recovery world, "This too shall pass."

For those of us who are struggling through any sort of mental health challenge, whether it be addiction, anxiety, depression, or any other form, there is absolutely no shame in surrendering to a program of recovery. Accepting help can be the very hardest part of the process, because it seems that no one will understand what pains us. I'm not going to suggest that my recovery is directly applicable to anyone else's, because every person is unique. I can say, however, that when you finally ask for help, finally make a commitment to let go of the things you cannot control, and finally start to change the things you can, significant growth and change do begin. It's not easy, and it requires a lot of patience and hard work, but these things do start to improve in time. For me, it didn't even take the five years that were prescribed for me. I went back to school and started my future in psychology before my third sobriety birthday, and here I am now at six, working as a mental health professional and publishing my first book. Change is possible. And it can lead to some wonderful things.

It has become clichéd in popular culture to make statements like "We need to start a dialogue about mental health" or "There's no shame in asking for help." These words sound like platitudes without substance much of the time. So my intent in writing this book has been to offer an example of how accepting help can actually change (and possibly save) a life. This stuff is not easy. And there are no shortcuts. The only way through it . . . is through it. However, the rewards on the other side are so worth it. And while it still may be cliché, it is also true that we cannot do it alone. So, rather than saying, "There's no shame in asking for help," allow me to say it in a slightly more positive way:

> *We have nothing*
> *to lose and everything*
> *to gain from asking for help.*
> *There is peace and freedom*
> *and purpose and connectedness*
> *and love and joy*
> *and serenity waiting for us*
> *on the other side of that journey.*
> *May you find peace and comfort*
> *in the hope of recovery.*
> *You deserve it.*

acknowledgments

I want to thank my family, in particular my parents, Kenny and Gina, and my brother, Josh, for providing me with unconditional love and support throughout my life, and for encouraging me to follow my passions wherever they lead. Pursuing my careers as a musician, as a therapist, and now as an author would not have been possible without your support and encouragement.

Thank you, David Fisher, for offering great advice to me when I was a child and for later advising me in my path toward publishing this book. I also want to thank my Uncle Fred and Aunt Michele for introducing me to David and suggesting I send him some of my writing.

This book would not have developed into its current form without the help and guidance of my first editor, Stephen S. Power at Kevin Anderson and Associates. Stephen gave me invaluable feedback that led to a second draft worthy of taking to publishers and was extremely helpful in finding an agent to do just that.

Thank you to Frank Weimann at Folio Literary Management for believing in me and helping me find an outstanding publishing house for this project. Everyone at BenBella Books has been an absolute pleasure to work with. My editors Scott Calamar and Leah Wilson gave me wonderful support and feedback in shaping this final product, and the entire staff at

BenBella has contributed greatly to making this a book of which I am very proud. Thank you all.

So much of what this project has become would not have been possible without the support of Maroon 5 and their management team, in particular my former bandmates Adam Levine, Jesse Carmichael, Mickey Madden, and James Valentine, as well as their day-to-day manager Chris Maguire at Full Stop Management. Thank you for everything you have done in getting this project off the ground. You truly have helped in bringing this message of hope to an audience that needs it.

I want to thank all of my inspiring friends from my time at UCLA, including Sara Bareilles for her support of this project. Similarly, I want to thank all my sober friends from the Matrix Institute and the Spirit of Matrix meetings for supporting me in my recovery and inspiring me to tell my story.

Last but certainly not least, thank you, Shan, for loving me unconditionally and for staying by my side through everything. Your belief in me, your capacity for empathy, and your ability to see the good in people have inspired me to be a better person and to pursue the life I am now living.

about the author

Ryan Dusick is an Associate Marriage and Family Therapist, the founding drummer of the world's most popular band Maroon 5, a mental health advocate, and an author. His life has been a long and winding road from aspiring pop star with anxiety, to heartbroken alcoholic, to thriving mental health survivor, and messenger of hope in recovery.

Ryan grew up right in the middle of Los Angeles, California, at the intersection of Hollywood and real life, and his journey of inspiration, devastation, and redemption has been a series of crossroads. As a boy, he dreamt of pitching for the Dodgers and writing novels, but arm injuries sidelined his burgeoning baseball career just as rock music became his new passion and purpose. Founding the group Kara's Flowers in 1994 with fellow Brentwood High School students Adam Levine, Jesse Carmichael, and Mickey Madden, Ryan and his bandmates worked tirelessly for a decade before the group changed its name to Maroon 5 and finally had its first hit album *Songs About Jane*. Multiple hit songs, two Grammy Awards, and 20 million albums sold later, Ryan found himself suffering and without direction when his career as a performer came to an end just as it was taking off.

After years of struggling with physical and mental health challenges, Ryan finally overcame in 2016, when he began his journey of recovery, culminating in a new life path full of meaning, purpose, and fulfillment. While earning his master's degree in clinical psychology at Pepperdine University's Graduate School of Education and Psychology, he decided it was time to write his story, in hopes of helping others who might see themselves in his personal struggles. Now working as a mental health professional at the Missing Peace Center for Anxiety in Agoura Hills, California, and beginning his new journey as an author and advocate, Ryan is spreading the message that recovery is possible, and some astounding things can come with it.